MONTE HUMMEL GENERAL EDITOR

Endangered Spaces

THE FUTURE FOR CANADA'S WILDERNESS

KEY PORTER BOOKS

Copyright © 1989 by Monte Hummel

Canadian Cataloguing in Publication Data

    Main entry under title:
    Endangered spaces
    ISBN 1-55013-101-X
    1. Wilderness areas — Canada. 2. National parks and reserves — Canada. I. Hummel, Monte, 1947–
    QH77.C3E58 1989   333.78′2′0971   C89-094088-6

Design and Illustration: Marie Bartholomew
Cartography: James Loates
Typesetting: Q Composition Inc.
Printed and bound in Canada

Key Porter Books Limited
70 The Esplanade
Toronto, Ontario
Canada M5E 1R2

89 90 91 92 93 5 4 3 2 1

Henderson Book Series No. 11

Henderson Book Series honours the kind and generous donation of Mrs. Arthur T. Henderson which made this series possible. The Canadian Parks and Wilderness Society gratefully acknowledges Mrs. Henderson's support of the Society's efforts to promote public awareness of the value of Canada's park and wilderness areas.

Above: Sunlight, soil and green life — all part of our "homesphere." CREDIT: FREEMAN PATTERSON.

Pages 6–7: The Great Sandhills of Saskatchewan provide unique dune habitats for plants and animals found nowhere else in the world.
CREDIT: LORI LABATT.

CONTENTS

PART FOUR
STRATEGIES FOR THE FUTURE

TO THE MEMORY AND CONTINUED WORK OF DOUGLAS H. PIMLOTT

ACKNOWLEDGEMENTS

This book was originally inspired by Douglas H. Pimlott, who died altogether too early in 1978, leaving Bruce Litteljohn and me a rough manuscript called *Canada's Wild Places*. "Doug's book" went on hold for ten years until Glen Davis, a conservation philanthropist, independently proposed a similar idea over lunch. To both Doug and Glen we are deeply indebted.

To the twenty co-authors, I extend my sincere thanks for being on time with every submission and most accepting of editorial changes. The book's excellent photographs were largely donated by some of Canada's best wildlands photographers, a much appreciated measure of their concern to save what they capture through their lenses. The photo by the late Bill Mason appears as a special tribute to his outstanding wilderness contribution.

Pegi Dover and Arlin Hackman at World Wildlife Fund handled many of the details regarding the production of the book, and Kevin McNamee from the Canadian Parks and Wilderness Society attended to the maps. Our editors, Laurie Coulter and Beverley Beetham Endersby and the whole team at Key Porter have been a delight to work with, leaving me with virtually no great tales of woe about "how difficult the whole project has been."

Endangered Spaces kicks off a ten-year campaign to complete a network of protected areas in Canada; therefore, its final acknowledgement will be in whether or not we succeed.

Monte Hummel
General Editor

FOREWORD

BUCKINGHAM PALACE.

The sorry story of the almost absent-minded degradation and destruction of so much of the world's biosphere is becoming only too well known to millions of people. Every other day there are disturbing stories about the burning of tropical forests, reclaimed wetlands, polluted rivers, lakes and oceans and the growing list of species of animals and plants becoming extinct.

Canada has an almost unique opportunity to ensure that future generations will be able to see examples of the state their land was in before the rush for development and exploitation began. The task is to conserve a whole range of viable ecosystems and habitats covering all the country's natural regions. It is also necessary to ensure that those human activities that impinge directly on the natural environment, such as forestry, farming and commercial fishing, adopt sound conservation practices.

I hope this book will help people to understand the importance of these tasks. They will have to be tackled in the very near future, or it will be too late. Canada's very rich natural heritage can only be saved for posterity if the people of Canada alive today really want it to be saved.

INTRODUCTION

This book places a fundamental question before all Canadians: How important is wilderness to the future of our country?

The contributing authors have no difficulty in answering this question; nor did the person to whom our book is dedicated, Doug Pimlott. All of us have quite firmly allied ourselves with the group of people whom conservationist Aldo Leopold called "those who cannot live without wild things."

But what do Canadians as a whole want? Do we envision for our country a future without wilderness? Will this future come about by design or default? Do we see wilderness as obsolete, a part of Canadian society that we have outgrown? Are we ignoring the inevitable, daily limiting our options through inaction and facing the prospect of meekly explaining to our children what we *should* have done? Or, are we deliberately planning to maintain part of Canada in a wild, natural state because many Canadians want it that way, and will value it even more in the future as wilderness disappears elsewhere? These important questions must be answered by Canadians now. We are the last generation, in one of the last countries on the planet, that still has any choice in the matter.

Endangered Spaces is much more than a loose collection of pieces written by conservation experts. In four sections, the book discusses what *has* happened, what *is* happening and *where*, and what *must* happen with respect to protecting wildlands and wildwaters in Canada. You will find coolly reasoned arguments supported by irrefutable data. You'll find the previously untold story-behind-the-story recounted by those who were in the trenches when such issues as South Moresby made the headlines. You'll find unembarrassed pleas from the heart, expressions of outright frustration, and an overwhelming sense of urgency. And, you'll find constructive blueprints for what can be done if you share our concern.

The authors are deeply rooted in the different regions and cultures of Canada. Some are veterans of the struggle and speak with the wisdom of experience; others, recruited early, will no doubt become tomorrow's mentors. But, most important, all share a concern about Canada's wilderness as something endangered, something that, *if* lost, would not only diminish our future but make it unlivable.

How important is it to *you* that wilderness plays a role in the future of our country?

Monte Hummel
General Editor

PART ONE

LEARNING FROM THE PAST

BRUCE LITTELJOHN

Wilderness and the Canadian Psyche

When the French built Fort Rouillé on Toronto Bay in 1750, they worked in a wilderness. To the south lay the huge, clean expanse of Lake Ontario. North, east, and west were great forests of maple, elm, beech, and pine, essentially unaltered by human activity. This was wild country.

Today, the huge geometric grid of Toronto obliterates the trails native people followed to the French post. Together with its nearby communities, the city forms a megalopolis as far removed from wilderness as any location in Canada. Our notions of civilization and culture have triumphed: Toronto, and other large urban centres, reflect what Northrop Frye has called "the conquest of nature by an intelligence that does not love it."[1]

The vast majority of Canadians are urban dwellers. In fact, a larger percentage of Canadians than Americans live in cities. Therefore our immediate concerns and daily realities, even our assumptions about what constitutes progress, are primarily generated by and contained by the ethos and patterns of the metropolis. The social structures and technologies that order our lives alienate us from wilderness, which, in large degree, may be defined as "the absence of social structure."[2] Where the natural order, best exemplified by wilderness, is concerned we appear to have become an exotic species or, as Neil Evernden, a member of the Faculty of Environmental Studies at York University, has put it, "natural aliens."[3]

We no longer comply with the ecological order of nature, and seem to have little interest in so doing except when environmental problems threaten us directly. Could it be that, whereas our bodies evolved in accordance with natural imperatives, our technology has made us enormously powerful mutants that cannot fit harmoniously within natural systems? Have Canadians lost sight of the ultimate power of nature, and of the role of wilderness in our own history? Can we now see it only as a playground or recreational resource to be enjoyed occasionally, or in strict utilitarian terms — as a storehouse of natural resources that exists solely for our material benefit? What is the relationship of wilderness to the Canadian psyche? Is it any longer a factor in our sense of who we are?

There is some evidence that wilderness continues to inform our sense of self, even on the level of popular culture. Walking our city streets, one sees sweatshirts emblazoned with loons and pine trees and bearing words such as "Beaver Canoe" or "Northern Reflections." Newsstands carry a few magazines that deal with wilderness pursuits: *Paddler, Seasons, Explore, Outdoor Canada*. Our coins and paper currency bear images of wilderness landscapes and creatures. Wildlife art galleries proliferate, as do the sales of wildlife prints. Ministries of tourism laud the natural glories of the country, and "adventure travel," whether by raft, canoe, sea kayak, or on foot, grows in popularity. The weekend and holiday exodus from cities continues, as Canadians seek out lakes, cottages, and parks where they can find at least some vestiges of wilderness. Camps for girls and boys, some of them featuring extended trips through wild country, remain active. Public-opinion polls consistently tell us that Canadians are concerned about "the environment."

For a variety of reasons, then, it seems wilderness continues to figure in our perception of ourselves as Canadians. The nature of our geography and our history (even though much of the latter deals with the conquest of nature) makes this so. "To Canadians," writes George Woodcock, "the wilderness has always been present as a physical immediacy and a state of mind."[4]

It is not surprising that wilderness has shaped our outlook and influenced our identity. Our native people, the Inuit and Indians, were a wilderness population, and in many cases continue to be. Given their small populations, their limited technology, and their belief that all things, animate and inanimate, contained spirits demanding respect, it seems that they complied with the natural order and existed as an integral part of wilderness ecosystems. They had no choice.

But what of the European latecomers? It was long after the rise and fall of great Asian, African, and European civilizations that Champlain, in 1608, began the first serious attempt at European colonization in northern North America. By the end of the French Regime in 1763, despite heroic explorations deep into the North American wilderness, the frontier of agricultural settlement had moved no farther west than the valley of the St. Lawrence. In the process, Frenchmen had become Canadiens — a new breed, deeply influenced by the imperatives of the wilderness environment.

Following the Conquest of New France, while fur-trade explorers, adept at the ways of the native peoples, travelled deeper into the wilds of Canada, agricultural settlement grew very slowly and towns even more so. By 1791 (less than two centuries ago) there were only about 15,000 non-native people in what is now Southern Ontario.

Settlement west of Lake Superior had barely begun by the time of Confederation in 1867. A few years later, when William Francis Butler travelled the western interior plains, he wrote of an ocean of grass and solitude: "One sees here the world as it had taken shape and form from the hands of the Creator. Nor did the scene look less beautiful because nature alone tilled the earth, and the unaided

Above: Northern Ontario, the land that inspired the Group of Seven, who called Canada "a painter's country."   CREDIT: KARL SOMMERER.

Opposite: These Georgian Bay, Ontario, pines illustrate the origins of an Indian saying, "The west wind shapes the pine."   CREDIT: PETER VAN RHIJN.

sun brought forth flowers."[5] This was wilderness, and except for modest development in the southern portions of the prairies, it would remain so well into the twentieth century. Northward development would come considerably later.

Our cities and towns, therefore, have only recently grown from tiny settlements in the bush, and the lonely log cabins of our pioneer forefathers can still be seen in many places. It is true, too, that many of our most colourful figures have been those deeply influenced by the wilderness: Etienne Brûlé, Samuel de Champlain, Sieur de La Salle, Louis Joseph de La Vérendrye, Sir Alexander Mackenzie, Sir George Simpson, Louis Riel's lieutenant Gabriel Dumont, Grey Owl, and the like.

At the same time, many of the best-known events of our historical development have occurred in a wilderness context: the Seven Years War, the expansion of the fur trade, the construction of the Canadian Pacific Railway, the drawing together of small provinces into a confederation — provinces separated by vast tracts of mountain, plain, and forest. The imminence of wildlands has imprinted these and many additional events with a special character that is distinctly Canadian. It is not surprising that the opportunity to experience wilderness — an opportunity that is rapidly diminishing for urban Canadians — aids us in understanding our historical roots and our national identity. Writing, in 1944, of a wilderness canoe voyage, Pierre Elliott Trudeau observed: "I know a man whose school could never teach him patriotism, but who acquired that virtue when he felt in his bones the vastness of his land, and the greatness of those who founded it."[6]

Just as students of our culture benefit from immersion in wilderness, so historians must consider, understand, and, ideally, experience wilderness if they are to write comprehensively of the explorer/fur trader, of frontier settlement, of traversing the country with pipelines, of northern development, of Canadians seeking recreation, of native peoples, or indeed, of the general Canadian milieu.

While visiting the citadel at Quebec in 1850, Henry David Thoreau looked out across the St. Lawrence and considered the forces that continued to shape Canada and Canadians. Recalling his thoughts of that moment, he later wrote, in *A Yankee in Canada*, of "an influence from the wilds and from nature . . . an influence which, like the Great River itself, flowed from the Arctic fastness and western forests with irresistible tide over all." More recently, W.L. Morton, one of Canada's gifted historians, has written persuasively:

> In Canadian history the St. Lawrence valley, the Ontario peninsula, and the western prairies have been the regions of settlement which have furnished and fed the men, the fur traders, the lumberjacks, the prospectors, and the miners who have traversed the Shield and wrested from it the staples by which Canada has lived. And this alternate penetration of the wilderness and return to civilisation is the basic rhythm of Canadian life, and forms the basic elements of Canadian character whether French or English: the violence necessary to contend with the wilderness, the restraint necessary to preserve civilisation from the wilderness violence, and the puritanism which is the offspring of the wedding of violence to restraint. Even in an industrial and urban society, the old rhythm continues, for the typical Canadian holiday is a wilderness holiday, whether among the lakes of the Shield or the peaks of the Rockies.[7]

Morton also notes that this wilderness heritage is distinctively Canadian, that our heartland is the wild and rugged Precambrian Shield, whereas that of the United States is the hospitable and relatively tame Mississippi Valley — one of Earth's most fertile regions.

A second distinguished historian, A.R.M. Lower, writing in *My First Seventy-Five Years* of summers spent on Lake-of-the-Woods during the 1940s, has reminisced: "I have never since been back. . . . And how far away now it seems. But, oh, those eleven thousand islands, that myriad of channels, that mixture of the primitive — I come back to that point — that mixture of the primitive and the advanced, how they grip me! They are Canada."[8]

In another of his books, *Canadians in the Making*, Lower comments on the heritage of Canadians:

> Four million square miles of the earth's surface for them to tend and move about in. Much of it might not appear valuable, but it was God's earth: rightly used, it was not only "valuable", in the sense that even the dull English Canadian can grasp, but *freedom*. Think for a moment, while the endless lines of cars

sent their carbon monoxide fumes into the city streets, of what stretched on and on into the silent North! In Canada there was space, and there always would be space, and the qualities and privileges that come from space.[9]

Lower wrote these lines about three decades ago. Today, having seen oil tankers in the Northwest Passage and drilling rigs in the Beaufort Sea, we might well question his optimism. Our knowledge of such developments and of concentrations of pesticide residues and radioactive toxins in northern mammals underlines the fact that wilderness is nowhere safe from our appetites and activities. It is a finite and rapidly dwindling phenomenon, both in Canada and in the world. Wild areas are, indeed, "endangered spaces."

The prospects for wilderness in a world of exploding population, consumerism, and technology, directed primarily towards goals antithetical to the preservation of that which is wild, are bleak. None the less, the wilderness — with all its diversity, mystery, space, freedom, challenge, and beauty — remains a vital component of our heritage as Canadians. It has marked our history and helped to form our national identity.

The impact of our wildland can be clearly seen in our arts and letters. From the works of amateur colonial artists, through later professionals such as Paul Kane and the Group of Seven, Jack Shadbolt, Jacques de Tonnancour, and the "Woodland School" of native artists, including Norval Morrisseau and Carl Ray, untamed nature has inspired fine painting in this country. How scant our artistic legacy would be without Tom Thomson's *Moose at Night*, or *Jack Pine*. What a loss to be without Emily Carr's great canvases of the western rain forest, J.E.H. Macdonald's *The Solemn Land*, or Lawren Harris's Lake Superior and Arctic paintings. Today, Ivan Wheale, Robert Bateman, Ed Bartram, and many others continue to interpret the wilderness in graphic forms of their own. Canada is, as A.Y. Jackson has noted, "a painter's country," and our painting has been nourished by wild nature.

Music, too, has been coloured by Canada's land and seascapes. Think of some of the lyrics of Joni Mitchell or Gordon Lightfoot, or of Harry Somers's *North Country Suite*, Murray Adaskin's *Algonquin Symphony*, and Phil Nimmon's *Atlantic Suite*. Filmmaking in Canada also reflects the influence of wild country. Bill Mason, Dan Gibson, and Christopher Chapman have provided striking examples in films such as *Waterwalker, Paddle to the Sea, Quetico*, and *White Throat*. Television and still photography have similarly been influenced, as can be seen in the work of artists such as Freeman Patterson, Paul von Baich, and John and Janet Foster.

The wilderness has also left its imprint on Canadian writing. From the early journals of fur-trade explorers, through the fields of poetry, nature writing, the short story, and the novel, this influence is obvious and profound. While there has been much indirect use of the wilderness in our literature, a substantial body of it confronts wild nature directly. One thinks of E.J. Pratt's poem "The Dying Eagle" or Archibald Lampman's "Temagami":

Far in the grim Northwest beyond the lines
That turn the rivers eastward to the sea,
Set with a thousand islands, crowned with pines,
Lies the deep water, wild Temagami:
....
All day with steady paddles toward the west
Our heavy-laden long canoe we pressed:
All day we saw the thunder-travelled sky
Purpled with storm in many a trailing tress,
And saw at eve the broken sunset die
In crimson on the silent wilderness.[10]

For Alfred DesRochers, in "I Am the Dwindled Son," the *pays d'en haut* of his *voyageur* ancestors remains a strong presence:

I am the dwindled son of a race of supermen,
The violent strong, adventurous; from this strain
I take the northland homesickness which comes
With the grey days that autumn brings again.
....
My joy or sorrow sings the landscape still.[11]

Finally, much of what both writers and painters have found in wilderness is well conveyed in "The Lonely Land" by poet A.J.M. Smith:

....
This is a beauty
of dissonance,
this resonance
of stony strand,
this smoky cry
curled over a black pine
like a broken
and wind-battered branch
when the wind
bends the tops of the pines
and curdles the sky
from the north.

This is the beauty
of strength
broken by strength
and still strong.[12]

In addition to producing fine literature, these and other poets strike an authentic Canadian note, for their work is rooted in the experience of our wilderness.

Not surprisingly, naturalists with strong literary inclinations have produced a large and sometimes distinguished body of wilderness literature. The short stories of Charles G.D. Roberts and Grey Owl's autobiography, *Pilgrims of the Wild*, are examples. More recent are Roderick Haig-Brown's books, and those of Franklin Russell, Harold Horwood, and Fred Bodsworth.

Wilderness is as well part of the imaginative dynamic of novelists and short-story writers who are not in the naturalist tradition. Even those who write primarily of the city, or of universal themes with no specific sense of place, frequently resort to the imagery of the wild, enriching their works with metaphors from nature. So it is that the novels and stories of W.O. Mitchell, Morley Callaghan, Jack Hodgins, Margaret Laurence, and many others are in greater or lesser degree marked by the wild.

George Woodcock, himself a prolific writer and astute observer of Canadian culture, goes farther, maintaining that "the literature of direct experience of the wilderness has continued in an unbroken tradition since Cartier" and that such experience "has given a special shape to our literature."

Some of our poets and novelists have regarded wilderness as an enemy. Others, aware of how quickly we are losing our natural areas, have taken a different view. For example, in Wayland Drew's recent trilogy, *The Erthring Cycle*, wilderness is a large and positive presence. Love, health, and laughter mark the lives of the hunting and gathering people who co-exist with and respect wild places. Others who live in futuristic, high-technology societies tend towards anxiety, competition, and destruction. They fear the wilderness. For one of Drew's major characters, caught between such societies and longing for the saner hunting-and-gathering life, there are "images of long and timeless days, of far rivers and forests forever green, of the warmth of the fire, the joy of the hunt, the hiss of northern lights. Only the sounds and the solace of the wild were in those images."[13]

Another of Drew's characters, in *The Gaian Expedient*, goes farther, using words highly appropriate to our times: "To go softly upon the Earth is to respect her, to love her. To violate the Earth is to violate Gaia [the Earth goddess]. She is patient. She endures. She is slow to anger. For a time she may acquiesce in this violation, but in the end she will turn upon her tormentors and destroy them."[14]

Our history, our painting, our literature, along with our music and film, are all fundamental elements of Canadian culture and identity. All have been deeply influenced and distinguished by the wilderness. Behind the weekend exodus to lakes and mountains, behind the loons on sweatshirts and adventure-travel brochures, are profound influences rooted in spacious, mysterious, and sometimes dangerous wilderness. Therefore, as we surrender our wild heritage, we surrender much of what distinguishes us as Canadians.

While this might be seen as reason enough to protect more of our endangered spaces, the cultural values of wilderness are but one small consideration. Indeed, we almost denigrate wilderness if we value and appreciate it only as an influence on arts and letters. For many Canadians there are ecological, recreational, and spiritual values in wilderness. If there is enough of it, we know that wilderness provides ecological stability and genetic diversity, as well as playing a vital role in the biological cycles that sustain life on Earth. We know that many people find psychic health and spiritual solace in wild places, along with aesthetic pleasure and inspiration. Others simply feel we have a responsibility for the health of the biosphere and that good stewardship involves the restraint required to let wilderness be.

Some of these reasons for preserving wild spaces are too people-centred to please proponents of the deep-ecology movement. Nature, after all, is much more than a stage for human concerns. It's more than stock or inventory for our manipulation and use. It has its own meaning and order. To this *we* must adapt, or suffer the consequences.

Part of that adaptation will involve a radical shift in our perceptions and the adoption of what leading conservationist Aldo Leopold called a "land ethic" — an ethic that recognizes the inherent values of wilderness without regard for societal concerns. Time is short if we are to achieve such wisdom. A new humility will have to be part of it, for, as poet Walter Bauer has written in "Canada":

> ....
> This earth says:
> I was here long before you and the likes of you came;
> Unmolested I conversed with wind and rivers,
> Don't forget that, my friend.
> The wind blows cold from Labrador:
> I have a message for you from the ice age,
> But I shall not decode it for you.
> The forests of the north surge like waves:
> We shall last longer than you.
> The Yukon and the Mackenzie flow with quiet patience:
> Son, don't make things too hard for yourself;
> Different times will come when you are gone, stranger.
> The Arctic expresses the sum total of all wisdom:
> Silence. Nothing but silence. The end of time.[15]

Canadians are rapidly approaching the end of the time available for setting aside wild country. We have a window of opportunity, but it is a framed window, a chance that has limits and must be taken while it is offered. We may have about a decade left in which to act. If we do not, and if we allow the erosion of existing wilderness places, we will do violence to an important part of our heritage and identity. We will do violence to ourselves, and to much more besides.

YORKE EDWARDS

Wilderness Parks:
A Concept with Conflicts

Whatever other convictions Canadians have held about wilderness over the past century, the face of Canada today proclaims that in the main we have regarded it as something to be destroyed. But, from the beginning there were other views, and through the years they have become more widely held than the old ones based on pioneer fears and robber-baron precepts.

When Canada was still very young, national parks created to preserve wilderness were proof of at least some public interest in its value. Through a century of our history, we have created even more such parks. Today their numbers give testimony that the public recognizes their importance. And the increasing awareness of the need for more of them is an indication of the alarming rate at which our unprotected wilderness is vanishing.

This picture of a century of accelerating wilderness destruction as well as preservation results from a kind of national schizophrenia. Not just the landscape has changed; Canadians have changed, and these transformations have been part of a world trend.

A WORLD VIEW

Now that Earth supports five billion people (a figure that grows by a million more every four or five days), there is probably no absolute wilderness anywhere.

Wilderness is land not altered by people, its plant and animal life affected only by natural processes. Manhandled lands may still be wild, to varying degrees, but they are not absolute wilderness, even though we call them such.

By definition, the wild's only enemy is people. When the first human looked about in wonder at the wilderness world, unaware that it was possibly the most improbable miracle in the universe, it soon began to disappear. To a degree, that first *Homo sapiens* began almost at once to destroy the wilderness. Today, perhaps 300,000 years later, the destruction is nearing completion.

The change was hardly noticeable through most of the long human journey through time. But about 5000 years ago the pace accelerated when we began making tools from iron. This destruction remained localized around camps and villages for thousands of years. Only a hundred years ago, perhaps in your parents' lifetime, wilderness still graced most of the Earth. However, the industrial revolution changed all that. After a slow start, its technologies, world trade, and exploding human populations set a new pace for wilderness destruction — "constant acceleration." If it continues, there will be no wilderness worth exploiting; Earth as a living planet will have been largely transformed into an artifact by a species of its own making.

The needs of our daily lives are fed by resources taken from the land. Yet, in the past fifty years we have indulged in a spree of consuming Earth's material products, which has resulted in more extensive destruction of Earth's live surface than that accomplished by our ancestors in all of the previous 300,000 years. At the present rate of change, little of the original green miracle that once enfolded the planet will survive into the twenty-first century.

The lands nearest to their original condition will be those saved in our national parks and other protected areas. Too few of these areas are preserved, however, and most of those that are, are changing despite their being "protected," as quietly destructive invasions debase their long-term heritage values. These places are absolutely priceless. They contain Earth's secrets of life and survival, manifested by natural lifeforms perfected over millions of years of countless trial-and-error evolutionary experiments. Their like will never be seen again should they vanish. We easily erase legions of living masterpieces, but we cannot make a blade of grass. We destroy a barely tapped databank that holds the only accumulation of information and knowledge about Earth and ourselves.

That original mantle of life was the environment that produced us — the womb of our species. Therefore, the last few centuries of our human time on Earth have seen us consume our own roots and foundations. It is in this sense that we are truly destroying our "heritage."

PEOPLE AND WILDERNESS

The first people in North America probably came about 15,000 years ago, after the last great glaciers began to retreat from what is now southern Canada. They encountered wilderness, then dwelt for thousands of years more or less in harmony with the environment that they occupied. In Canada, at least, these human invaders were not numerous enough to do much damage. Their small villages sat lightly on the land. The pollution they created did not overwhelm natural disposal systems. Fire was their only potentially destructive tool, yet the effect of it on their landscape was probably less extensive than that caused by lightning.

They were skilled hunters, but their weapons of wood, bone, and stone had limited efficiency for killing animals. In most cases, modest harvests of prey populations were easily replaced by high reproduction rates. Even when herds were vulnerable at river crossings or could be stampeded over cliffs, slaughter was local and infrequent and had no long-term effect on the abundance of the hunted species.

The First People were children of the wilderness and regarded it as their home. It provided their food and the materials they needed for dwellings, clothes, containers, ornaments, boats, and tools. Whether they dwelt in a burning desert, on a stormy coast, or in a forest with long subarctic winters, the First People were adapted culturally to their environment. As a result, they survived. They did not view wilderness as a possession, but as a part of themselves. "Ownership" in the Western sense was unknown and is often still meaningless to them today. They regarded land much as Europeans still regard air: as it is always there, there is no need to attempt to own it.

Wilderness also held other values for the First People. It was home to many spirits who guided and gave meaning to their daily lives. People went into wild places alone to fast and to endure other trials to appease the spirits. Sometimes they stayed there until the spirits gave them identity, abilities, or privileges. Wilderness had spiritual significance.

Now much of this has changed. And it did so tragically for the First People within the time of one long human life. Today, like the rest of us, the First People find themselves in a world of headlong change.

The harmony of the First People in the wilderness landscapes of the Americas was irreparably shattered beginning in the seventeenth century. Most of the new people came from European lands dominated by agricultural technologies. The newcomers saw the Canadian forest as an enemy to be feared, hated, and fought. Cleared fields were the measure of successfully "civilizing" the new land. Christianizing it consisted of piling and burning thousands of trees, then fencing, ploughing, seeding, and harvesting in order to produce food and fibre.

By any standards the European occupation of the Americas was ruthless. Greed, arrogance, and cruelty were the norm, and their booty was the natural wealth accumulated through Earth's long history. In North America the first treasures pillaged were marine mammals (the whales), then land mammals (the buffalo and beaver), and then fertile soils, minerals, forests, and grazing lands. This process of destroying wild landscapes continues today, much accelerated by mass production, mass consumption, and world rather than local markets.

Initially, the second invasion changed the First People even more than it did landscapes, Europeanizing them with goods and diseases. Colonization was, in fact, vigorously opposed by the fur trade as a threat to its huge profits. The adventuresome fur traders guarded their monopoly in high places for two centuries, and in so doing protected most of the Canadian wilderness and its people as well. Then a flood of European humanity, lured by free land and gold, weakened their hold.

Today the most complete destruction of wilderness in Canada is in the south. Settlers seeking agricultural climates and soils concentrated in fertile pockets in the Maritime southeast and on old flood plains in the valley of the St. Lawrence. Agricultural settlement expanded westward only as far as the Great Lakes for a century, then spread rapidly throughout fertile Southern Ontario into the rich soils of the hardwood forest, taking species such as the passenger pigeon with it.

It paused again at the barriers of the upper Great Lakes to the west and at the rock of the Canadian Shield to the north, but rich soils still lay ahead on the prairies. Here was a fertile region quite free of the burden of endless trees and stumps faced by the Ontario pioneer. The plains filled rapidly with agricultural people vigorously encouraged by the new Canadian railway, the world's longest, which now needed profitable business to justify its high cost. The lure for immigrants was free land, advertised throughout much of Europe and the United States.

The Rocky Mountains stopped the westward flood of European farmers. By any standard the mountainous west of Canada is not agricultural. Most surrounding lands are alpine or otherwise have forest soils and climates worthless to the farmer. Today, for instance, British Columbia has a population about the size of Toronto's, yet it would be hard-pressed to feed itself on home-grown produce.

When the flow of farmers stopped at the mountains, the population pattern of Canada was fixed. In the second-largest country on Earth, nearly all people were huddled in the warm and partly agricultural south, and in this area all its major cities were built. From sea to sea, perhaps 90 per cent of Canada has remained largely uninhabited, except for scattered small communities and temporary excursions into the uncomfortable North to greet tourists or to bring oil, metals, wood, and other products south. For most, the North is not for living in. Our desire to live like Europeans or Americans is best satisfied by locating near our southern border, there to receive northern resources to help finance our southern comforts. Such a population pattern is predictable for any northern nation wishing to be more southern, a condition not confined to Canada but also seen in Sweden, for example.

Southern settlement did not preserve the northern wilderness. The great virgin spruce forest that once covered all of Canada between the people-dominated south and the treeless Far North has been cleared where accessible and merchantable. World demand and improved transportation has pushed the cutting steadily northward. Overall, Canada's rampage of forest destruction has almost completely denuded the landscape of old forests of marketable trees. This timber was the accumulated wealth of ages, and yielded logs in sizes we will never see again in our polewood forests of the future. However, the loss is not confined to the old trees now gone. Everywhere huge portions of clearcut lands have not been returned to forest or have been slowly and poorly. This has been an officially recognized concern for more than seventy years.

While these transformations of Canada took place at the hands of the Second People, there was a small but important counterforce at work, especially among the urbanized and affluent. Canadians were influenced by a romantic view of wilderness prevalent in Europe and the United States. So, when the United States established the world's first national park at Yellowstone in 1872, the idea impressed some influential Canadians.

The arguments used to get government approval for the first Canadian park at Banff, Alberta, in 1885 centred on the attractions of bathing in hot springs. Originally, therefore, large wild parks in Canada were intended to generate tourist revenue by catering to the romantic and rich, most of them American and European, and were not established out of concern for wilderness preservation, although that cause eventually became a worthy end in itself.

In practice, people and wilderness were to mix. In fact, however, the former often destroys the latter and the formula for a benign mixture has never been usefully defined. This uncomfortable marriage of contradictory purposes has always plagued our parks and is an adjunct of conflicting Canadian attitudes to wilderness.

CANADA'S WILDERNESS TODAY

Few modern Canadians have even a general understanding of their country's land and life. Most live a short highway's drive from the United States and know much more about what is to the south than to the north. The narrowest large country in the world is Chile; most Canadians live physically and mentally in a similarly thin strip of country across the extreme south. The rest of Canada is too cold, too rocky, and too much scoured by glaciers to be suited to soft and luxurious living.

At first glance, Canada seems thinly populated in a world overstuffed with five billion people. But people cannot live on space alone. Although Canada has productive lands and seas in many limited areas, on average most Canadian land has a very small capability to sustain human life in European style. That huge areas have such limited capacity is the harsh reality of an essentially granite-hard and polar-cold nation.

Most Canadian forests are among the slowest growing in the world, which means the first cut removing virgin growth will be the only really lucrative one. Minerals supply boom-and-bust bonanzas, and tourism in northern latitudes is still strictly a summer ritual. The picture that emerges shows that nearly half of Canada's wilderness is well on its way to radical change. Its living wealth of natural resources, accumulated over 10,000 years, largely flows south, with little cash returning to repair the northern damage.

The far half of Canada's wilderness is the treeless Arctic, a frozen desert that few Canadians know and most consider as remote and foreboding as the surface of the moon. Yet it constitutes nearly half the land surface of our country, inhabited by many forms of life using ingenious strategies for survival and reproduction.

A friend once told me that a large map of Canada on his office wall had the most southern bit of the nation, Pelee Island, at the floor and Ellesmere Island at the ceiling. He used it for a private survey, asking visitors to point out the farthest north they had been. Most were on their knees at once, with most of Canada above them.

PARKS AS ARKS

The park is an idea at least as old as European history and much older in Asia. Originally kept as the hunting reserves of kings and landowners, these natural areas preserved the quality of life for the privileged few, not unlike bathing in hot springs.

A park is usually common land, maintained to a degree in a state of wildness. Some preserve patches of the world that made prehistoric people possible; others save the built artifacts of man's past; still others reserve suitable space in which to hike or walk, to kick a ball, or to roll happily on the grass.

The largest parks are those that can preserve wilderness. In Canada at least, the best-administered of these are the national parks. Provinces across the nation have designated large and outstanding parks, too, but generally these spaces are much more prone to commercial and related invasions and are not as reliably protected.

As mentioned earlier, the first Canadian national park centred on a natural hot spring reserved for "sanitary" use by the public. Soon, however, it was enlarged, then enlarged again, this time to be named Rocky Mountain National Park. Its purpose was to create a world-class attraction for tourists, an idea inspired by the successful tourist industry in the European Alps. This highly scenic and attractive park thus had a commercial purpose from the outset, including a monopoly on access and accommodation, with luxurious train and hotel service commanding high prices. Consequently, already bisected by a railway line, the park soon was invaded by roads, a large hotel, a golf course, and a growing town. To those who could afford them, the train and hotel offered a fashionable, pampering experience. Often there were more servants on the hotel staff than there were guests!

While commercial interests saw the mountain scenery through the mists of revenue, most of the hotel guests came for both aesthetic and romantic reasons. The success of the place was essentially a result of its geological and biological view. Soon that view became more focused. Where once park visitors were content to observe the landscape from the hotel's fashionable porch, later they were moved by it to take walks in it and to go canoeing, trail riding, camping, and even mountain climbing, finding the scenery more enjoyable when experienced at close range. This trend has persisted, except the hotel is no longer just for the railway-borne rich. The automobile and, later, the airplane changed all that. Now Banff's central valleys are crowded with people and cars all summer, most, again, enjoying the view, the car window having replaced the old hotel porch.

Nevertheless, the new popularity of the park includes off-road uses as well. Hiking and cross-country skiing are popular, ensuring that the wild park is appreciated and enjoyed. Furthermore, a huge percentage of Canadians and other visitors show an interest in the wildlife that animates the magnificent scenery. In fact, to most people these live elements in the view are its most significant feature.

Still with us today is the aggressive commercial perspective: the park is a tourist gold mine and should be mined even harder. Fortunately, those who see only the economic vistas are vastly outnumbered by the naturalists, scientists, and romantics who appreciate the park's wild landscapes. This group, like the money-makers, is more intense and diverse than previously. To them the park is not just scenic wallpaper to be enjoyed at a distance. Most enter the park on foot to enjoy it at a personal distance, rubbing elbows with trees, lying in alpine meadows to photograph dwarf flowers, stalking birds that sing unfamiliar songs. The best-selling books in the region are informative pocket-sized guides to the park's trails, geology, animals, trees, and wildflowers. This new breed of visitor can also be fiercely protective of the park's wildness, while being openly critical of the town, the hotel and motels, the golf course, the ski runs, and the other destructive human invasions.

In the early 1970s, when the Canadian Parks Service proposed Village Lake Louise, and several other instant tourist and ski villages centrally located in the park, urbanizing ideas once again stalked the mountain valleys. The flood of concerned public opposition from across Canada was startling. After public hearings the proposal was dropped. The public message remaining for future planners was loud and very clear: put townsites serving park visitors outside park boundaries, not inside.

Close on the heels of this debate came two more clashes of opinion over park issues, first the federal government's proposal to twin the Trans-Canada Highway through the park, and later, outside pressure put on the same government to hold the winter Olympics in the park. The road was twinned in spite of protests, but the Olympics was kept out.

Through all of this Canadians found strengths and skills previously unknown to them in defending their wild parks; from coast to coast they emerged with sharpened visions of the value of parks and the forces capable of destroying them. Parks were no longer valued only for their impressive scenery but also as priceless cultural and scientific treasures. In the process, many Canadians discovered their parks for the first time. Preserving the original face of Canada in parks had become a widely recognized national need.

Attitudes of people towards parks are not easily labelled since these attitudes are often a blend of many factors. However, in general, two enthusiasms prevail: attracting tourist dollars and preserving natural history. The history of Banff nicely exemplifies this difference.

People working in park organizations reflect these same public attitudes. The diggers are there, bulldozers ready, eager to create "another park" by punching roads through wild country to make parking lots, buildings, camp grounds with showers, picnic grounds — a long list. In opposition are those wanting such "improvements" kept out of wild areas. More balanced attitudes lie between these extremes, and some people appear to have taken no position at all.

The range of Canadian attitudes towards large wild parks has not changed much in a hundred years. Some people still view parks only as opportunities for personal gain. Those who live near parks are prone to regard them as regional and not as national assets. Pressures on our parks by people who would degrade or destroy them are constant and determined, a battle fought daily in every park office, and at local, regional, and federal levels.

On the other hand, the number of people enthusiastic about saving and creating more parks has increased dramatically. The environmental awakening of the 1960s changed forever the Canadian view of things natural. In those years, environment, wildness, and wildlife became major socio-political issues that are still changing Canada's way of thinking. Wilderness parks entered a new era of recognition nationally as irreplaceable treasures to be saved at all costs.

CANADIAN PARKS AND PUBLIC ATTITUDES

Through most of the past century, not many people had the opportunity to experience a wilderness park. Most Canadians were farmers or townspeople living sedentary and rather frugal lives. Travel was slow and inconvenient; roads were few. Many still lived near wild and unprotected lands that offered wilderness experiences close to home.

Now most Canadians live in cities where wildness is extinct except for an occasional bird or butterfly sailing overhead. The automobile and good roads have made us restless travellers. We go to wilderness parks annually by the millions. We are, in fact, crowding many parks to the extent that wildness is being destroyed. As favoured places become scenes of destruction, we are in danger of loving our parks to death.

Two social revolutions have recently changed Canadian attitudes towards wilderness and the use of parks. The 1950s saw a postwar explosion of high-density camping sites in parks, partly urbanized areas beside major roads. The car, the trailer, and the camper spawned the rush, and in the beginning such areas were constructed "to keep all their fires in one place so we can watch them." This enabled many Canadians to experience their parks at low cost for accommodation, but at significant expense to the quality of the landscape and the visitors' experience of it.

The 1960s' counterculture influenced the nation's regard for the land. As the sixties generation moves through time, taking charge of the nation, sympathy for wildness and wilderness grows at an unprecedented rate. This flame of conviction is not about to go out. Although the media have reported it as primarily an emotional response, it is based on the solid foundation of science and its quest for truth.

While many of us still enjoy our natural vistas from cars, determined to venture no closer to wilderness than smooth and dustless roads will take us, many others enter wild places quietly as would a wild creature, and find freedom, peace, and memorable experiences that enrich their lives.

Binoculars and cameras are now standard equipment for visitors and have turned birdwatching into the nation's fastest growing sport. Cameras have made it possible for everyone to capture wild experiences on film. Many photographers have gone far beyond just "point and click" to capture the very essence of wild places. Their superb pictures grace a growing record, in books and magazines, of the wild beauty of Canada. Less dramatic, but still substantial, has been the growing interest in botany, especially in the wildflowers found in almost every corner of Canada where native vegetation has been spared. Sky gardens above the treeline in the mountains are famous, as are the spring flowers in the hard-wood forests. Prairie, north woods, tundra, even the seas, have their colourful displays for those inspired by Earth's green and animated life.

The largest user group of all, however, may still be those who call themselves simply "hikers" or "paddlers," and seek the freedom and peace of a hidden lake or the silence of a narrow and winding trail. Such visitors are content to enjoy distant landscapes. Nearer details are part of the experience, too, but are valued more as part of a whole than as things to be named, classified, and understood in the way of the amateur scientist.

All of these interests can be passionately held and energetically indulged in parks, adding inspiration to otherwise colourless and increasingly predictable urbanized lives. Dull places offer dull living. Wild places offer inspiration, variety, and the unexpected — in short, adventure.

We can observe and appreciate others' enthusiasms, but can understand them best in ourselves. I often walked the streets of Toronto as a youth in the dawns of May, bound for wild bits of ravine where new leaves turning the trees green were alive with the migrating birds of spring. The silent streets of the sleeping city were all mine, and through a dozen years of doing this I always had a feeling of privilege as I marvelled at the dawn and thought of the colourful warblers and other birds that I seemed to have discovered. Close friends considered my interest eccentric at least, "weird" at most, and periodically my unusual behaviour even attracted the watchful police. However, a few friends joined the joyful pursuit; some with equal zeal.

Through a life of continued interest in wild places, I have never lost that feeling of privilege. At times, it was accompanied by guilt as I compared the apparently uninspired lives of others around me, and I often wondered how we could travel in such different directions. I also wondered why I was so lucky. Working in wild places, doing the "jobs" that could have been my hobbies, I have often paused after some especially memorable experience in amazement over being able to "work" at what I love. I have collected experiences enough to enrich several lives while seeking wild dwellers in wild country whose scenery stopped me still in my tracks.

For me, two attributes make such natural artscapes especially meaningful. First is the "spirit of place," with rock and wild lives the paint, their histories the brush, and the resulting creation a distinctive one that celebrates an instant in the geological and biological history of Earth. Second is the "promise of to-morrow," when an inspiring place is not just a pleasure of the moment but is safe from drastic change by man. Generations will be enriched by both.

HAROLD EIDSVIK

Canada in a Global Context

Parks of many kinds are now an accepted part of the global fabric. How, why, or when they were created is of little importance to the park visitor. However, if we as a society are going to influence the future, it is essential that we understand the past. (The terms "parks" and "protected areas" are used interchangeably throughout this chapter to refer to lands officially reserved for the conservation of nature.)

IN THE BEGINNING

Today we look upon parks as special places that provide a sanctuary for both man and nature, places where some relief from everyday stress can be found. Special places serving contemplative or spiritual needs have existed in eastern cultures since 500 B.C. The eastern religions of Shintoism, Taoism, and Buddhism held a reverence for nature not reflected in Christianity. Thus shrines such as the Bo Tree in Sri Lanka have protected nature and provided places for contemplation for more than 2000 years. In contrast, Christian theology often casts wilderness as the antithesis of paradise. St. Francis of Assisi is noted by author and lecturer Roderick Nash to be the exception that proves the rule: "He stood alone in a posture of humility and respect before the natural world."

Skipping a few centuries, we find new benchmarks in the royal forests and game preserves of England and France. The *Doomsday Book* of 1086 was perhaps the first inventory of lands, forests, and hunting preserves. Formal gardens such as Hyde Park (1536) and Richmond Park (established by Charles I in 1637) were some of the earliest lands to be called "parks." In the new world, Boston Common (1603) is often acknowledged as the first formal public open space in North America. The next major landmark was the establishment of Yosemite as a twenty-square-kilometre state park in California in 1864. This was followed by "the world's first instance of large-scale wilderness preservation in the public interest." On March 1, 1872, President Ulysses S. Grant signed an act designating over 800,000 hectares of northwestern Wyoming as Yellowstone National Park.

North American society as we know it today began with a frontier mentality. With forests and wildlands pressing society on all sides, the need to carve out a sanctuary for man was focused on human spaces rather than wilderness places. In the United States, this phenomena continued until late in the nineteenth century: in 1890, the U.S. Bureau of the Census signalled the end of the frontier. At that time, with a population in the United States of sixty-three million, the recognition of wilderness as an asset, rather than a liability, was underway. As wilderness became scarce, it began to grow in value.

In southern Canada a parallel course of action was being undertaken. However, in spite of the gradual disappearance of our wilderness, a frontier mentality still prevails in much of Canada. The vastness of the country, the "emptiness" of the North, and the paucity of population continue to be cited as a rationale for continued exploitation. Fortunately, the past two decades have seen the first strong indications that the Canadian frontier mentality is dissipating. They can be seen in the establishment of Ellesmere National Park, in the public and political support for South Moresby, in the efforts to stop the proposed logging in the Stein Valley of British Columbia, and in the battle for the Temagami wilderness of Ontario.

In 1960, Alvin Hamilton, minister responsible for national parks, called for help from the Canadian public:

> It is my feeling, as minister in charge of parks, that it is about time all those millions of people in Canada who use the parks and love them should band together and form themselves into a national parks association. How can a minister stand up against the pressures of commercial interests who want to use the parks for mining, forestry, for every kind of honky-tonk recreational device known to man, unless the people who love these parks are prepared to band together and support the minister by getting the facts out across the country?

Hamilton's call was heeded. Today Canadians are recognizing their shrinking frontier and the value of wilderness. Following the 1962 Resources for Tomorrow Conference, the National and Provincial Parks Association of Canada (renamed the Canadian Parks and Wilderness Society) was created to be a voice of the people.

THE PARKS MOVEMENT

The 1872 establishment of Yellowstone National Park in the United States sparked a global interest in parks. In 1879 Royal National Park was established in New South Wales, Australia, and in 1894 Tongariro National Park was dedicated in New Zealand. Thus, by the turn of the century, the national-parks concept, as we know it today, was underway.

In Canada, Frederick Law Olmstead, the noted American landscape architect

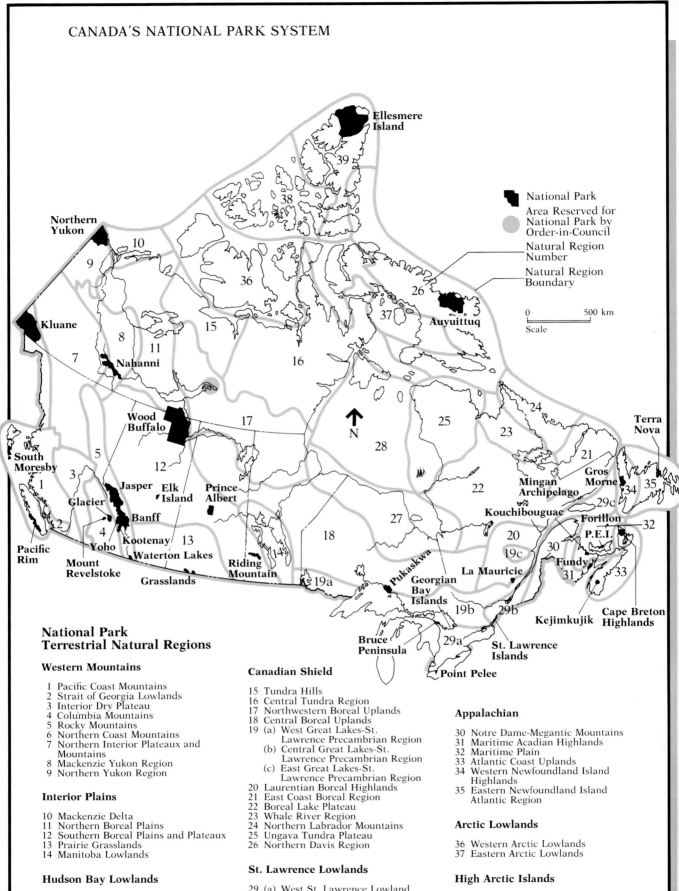

CANADA'S NATIONAL PARK SYSTEM

Ellesmere Island

39

Northern Yukon

38

10

9

36

Kluane

8

26

11

37

Auyuittuq

Nahanni

7

15

16

24

Terra Nova

Wood Buffalo

17

25

23

21

South Moresby

5

28

22

Gros Morne

12

35

3

18

27

20

Mingan Archipelago

29c

34

Jasper

Elk Island

Prince Albert

Kouchibouguac

Forillon

32

Glacier

Banff

30

P.E.I.

Pacific Rim

4

Kootenay

13

19c

La Mauricie

Fundy

33

Yoho

Waterton Lakes

14

31

Mount Revelstoke

Riding Mountain

19a

Pukaskwa

Georgian Bay Islands

19b

29b

Kejimkujik

Cape Breton Highlands

Grasslands

Bruce Peninsula

29a

St. Lawrence Islands

Point Pelee

N

Legend

■ National Park
● Area Reserved for National Park by Order-in-Council
Natural Region Number
Natural Region Boundary

Scale: 0 — 500 km

National Park
Terrestrial Natural Regions

Western Mountains

1 Pacific Coast Mountains
2 Strait of Georgia Lowlands
3 Interior Dry Plateau
4 Columbia Mountains
5 Rocky Mountains
6 Northern Coast Mountains
7 Northern Interior Plateaux and Mountains
8 Mackenzie Yukon Region
9 Northern Yukon Region

Interior Plains

10 Mackenzie Delta
11 Northern Boreal Plains
12 Southern Boreal Plains and Plateaux
13 Prairie Grasslands
14 Manitoba Lowlands

Hudson Bay Lowlands

27 Hudson-James Lowlands
28 Southampton Plain

Canadian Shield

15 Tundra Hills
16 Central Tundra Region
17 Northwestern Boreal Uplands
18 Central Boreal Uplands
19 (a) West Great Lakes-St. Lawrence Precambrian Region
   (b) Central Great Lakes-St. Lawrence Precambrian Region
   (c) East Great Lakes-St. Lawrence Precambrian Region
20 Laurentian Boreal Highlands
21 East Coast Boreal Region
22 Boreal Lake Plateau
23 Whale River Region
24 Northern Labrador Mountains
25 Ungava Tundra Plateau
26 Northern Davis Region

St. Lawrence Lowlands

29 (a) West St. Lawrence Lowland
   (b) Central St. Lawrence Lowland
   (c) East St. Lawrence Lowland

Appalachian

30 Notre Dame-Megantic Mountains
31 Maritime Acadian Highlands
32 Maritime Plain
33 Atlantic Coast Uplands
34 Western Newfoundland Island Highlands
35 Eastern Newfoundland Island Atlantic Region

Arctic Lowlands

36 Western Arctic Lowlands
37 Eastern Arctic Lowlands

High Arctic Islands

38 Western High Arctic Region
39 Eastern High Arctic Glacier Region

SOURCE: CANADIAN PARKS SERVICE

who was involved in the design of Central Park in New York in 1857, designed Mount Royal Park in Montreal in 1872. In Toronto, High Park was established in 1873, followed by Vancouver's Stanley Park in 1888. With the protection of Banff National Park in 1885, Niagara Falls in 1887, and Ontario's Algonquin Provincial Park in 1893, Canada, perhaps unwittingly, created "a system of parks."

The establishment of national parks at the turn of the century did not necessarily mean they were protected. For example while the U.S. Army managed Yellowstone from 1872 to 1916, resource utilization continued but in a more controlled manner. In Canada, a central administration for the four national parks established before the turn of the century was not created until 1911. When it was organized, however, Canada became the first country to have a national-parks service, today one of the most sophisticated in the world.

Between 1885 and 1929, Canada established fifteen national parks. But with the transfer of natural resources in western Canada to the provinces in 1930, the national-parks program ground to a halt. Only four parks were established in the next twenty years: Cape Breton Highlands in 1936, Prince Edward Island in 1937, Fundy in 1948, and Terra Nova in 1957. The next thirty years, though, saw the system double. The postwar boom, new cars, and new highways brought a new generation of visitors to North America's parks.

The first World Parks Congress in Seattle in 1962 stimulated professional growth in parks management. In Europe, the International Union for the Conservation of Nature and Natural Resources (IUCN) began its international conservation efforts. In Africa, recently decolonized nations used tourism, especially wildlife viewing in parks, to increase their foreign earnings. In Australia, a growing recognition of its recreational and tourism potential led to significant expansion of the park system.

Modest beginnings in the last quarter of the nineteenth century led to a profusion of parks in the twentieth century. Today the IUCN lists over 3500 protected areas encompassing 4,237,744 square kilometres in more than 125 countries. Of these protected areas, more than 1000 are national parks. The remainder include scientific reserves, landmarks, game reserves, and protected landscapes. In Canada, provincial parks that are free of resource extraction are incorporated in IUCN's national-parks category.

INTERNATIONAL PROGRAMS

The earliest attempts to create an organized international interest in conservation led to the Swiss League for the Protection of Nature. Dr. Paul Sarasin, one of Europe's leading conservationists, in 1913 described the Swiss National Park as a link in a global chain of protected areas. He said that nature did not understand political frontiers. He went on to say that each national protected area also contributed to an international network because the protection of species by one nation could not be limited in its benefits to only one nation; rather it produced benefits to all nations through a global chain.

Above: Although Canada has the world's largest remaining
healthy population of bald eagles, this magnificent bird
is already endangered in Ontario and New Brunswick.
CREDIT: STEPHEN J. KRASEMANN.

Right: The South Nahanni River, N.W.T., is a deserving
candidate for park protection.
CREDIT: PAT AND ROSEMARIE KEOUGH.

Pages 38–39: Wildlands and wildwaters that will stay that
way in Gros Morne National Park, Newfoundland.
CREDIT: J.A. KRAULIS.

The Swiss League fell into difficult times from 1914 to 1918, but many of its activists continued to press for an international conservation organization. In 1948, they, the French government, and Sir Julian Huxley helped create the IUCN or the International Union for Protection of Nature as it was then known. The organization celebrated its fortieth anniversary October 5, 1988. In those forty years, the IUCN has accomplished a great deal, including the drafting of the World Heritage Convention and the World Charter for Nature, and the development of biosphere reserves and a wetlands-protection program.

The World Heritage Convention was adopted by the United Nations Educational, Scientific and Cultural Organization (UNESCO) in 1972 and signed by Canada in 1976. This unique instrument protects areas of outstanding, universal value. It places obligations on nations to assist one another in protecting the sites as well as requiring them to assume a primary responsibility for their own heritage.

After almost one hundred years of conservation action, this was the first time Canada formalized an international obligation, to protect its own natural and cultural heritage as well as others. With more than a hundred countries as signatories, the World Heritage Convention is the most universal of the international conservation conventions. Canada has been exceptionally active in its implementation: Peter H. Bennett served as its rapporteur, this writer and Dr. J. Thorsell have served as technical advisers on natural areas, and J.D. Collinson, the head of the Canadian Parks Service, served as its chairman.

The ten World Heritage Sites in Canada demonstrate a commitment to the World Heritage Convention's mandate to protect areas of outstanding universal value. They include six natural areas — Nahanni National Park, Dinosaur Provincial Park, Kluane National Park, Canadian Rocky Mountain Parks, Wood Buffalo National Park, and Gros Morne National Park — and four cultural areas — L'Anse aux Meadows National Historic Park, Anthony Island Provincial Park (Ninstints), Head-Smashed-In Buffalo Jump, and Quebec City (historic area). These Canadian areas join other international sites and such "world wonders" as the Great Barrier Reef, the Ngorongoro Crater, Kilimanjaro, and the Grand Canyon, as well as the Pyramids of Giza and the Taj Mahal.

After the adoption of the World Heritage Convention, the World Charter for Nature was drafted by the IUCN and adopted by the U.N. General Assembly on October 28, 1982. The charter states that "special protection shall be given to unique areas, to representative samples of all the different types of ecosystems and to the habitats of rare or endangered species." The charter also gives clear direction to all nations, "to safeguard and conserve nature in areas beyond national jurisdiction." As director general of the IUCN, Dr. David Munro, a Canadian, pioneered the work on the World Charter for Nature. With the second largest land mass in the world, Canada has both a unique opportunity and responsibility to carry out the charter's mandates.

One way we could do this would be through the IUCN and UNESCO program "Man and the Biosphere," better known as "MAB." Within this program, "biosphere reserves" were identified as a mechanism for building a global network of protected areas, integrating conservation and development. In 1988, there were 269 biosphere reserves in the world, of which 4 are located in Canada.

A biosphere reserve is an internationally designated protected area managed to demonstrate the value of conservation. The concept involves a central or core protected area that functions within a buffer zone of mixed land use. Waterton Lakes and Riding Mountain national parks are biosphere reserves managed in co-operation with the Canadian Parks Service. Mont St-Hilaire Nature Conservation Centre in Quebec is managed by the University of Montreal, and Long Point Provincial Park in Ontario is managed by a number of agencies. MAB has yet to mature in Canada, but the experience to date has been extremely positive. The program needs a greater commitment on the part of UNESCO Canada, as well as the government, if it is to become a fully effective part of the global conservation effort.

Another international program has met with more success. The Ramsar Convention was set up to protect wetlands of international importance. With the co-operation of UNESCO, the International Waterfowl Research Center (IWRC), and IUCN, the convention now has 383 sites in 45 countries. The Canadian Wildlife Service has taken a leading role, and Canada now has the most extensive area in the world designated under this convention. These sites include Last Mountain Lake in Saskatchewan, North America's first migratory-bird sanctuary, and the 600,000-square-kilometre Queen Maud Gulf Sanctuary in the Northwest Territories.

The massive movement of migratory birds from the Canadian Arctic through the United States and on to South America, makes the Ramsar Convention on wetlands a potentially valuable vehicle for international co-operation. However, much work remains to be done to build the designation process into a management process with enforcement teeth, which will ensure that listed wetlands are not degraded.

There are, of course, many other international conventions related either to species or to regional habitat protection. The Migratory Birds Convention of 1917 between Canada and the United States was one of the first. In addition, there are other key international mechanisms for co-operation. Among non-government organizations, the World Wildlife Fund, in Canada and internationally, is among the most active and best known. The WWF and IUCN constitute a global complex of affiliated organizations with shared headquarters in Switzerland.

WHY ESTABLISH PROTECTED AREAS?

If we lived in a perfect world and managed our resources in a sustainable fashion, with future generations in mind, we probably wouldn't need protected areas. Unfortunately, we don't live in a perfect world. We drive species to extinction and eliminate irreplaceable ecosystems for short-term gain.

Parks are established in most cases for the benefit, education, and enjoyment of current and future generations—for the long term. How these values are perceived shifts with time, place, and personalities. Individuals may have different reasons for supporting a specific proposal. Their support may be for the

protection of a specific species, a landscape, or for profit. In essence societal goals are viewed as being environmentally oriented or economically oriented. In reality, most goals and motivations are both. The establishment of a protected area is a socio-political decision. Reasons for the decision may range from being idealistic to utilitarian, and parks have been established world-wide for reasons throughout this range. What follows are fifteen reasons for establishing parks.

Areas of a country can be protected for reasons stemming from ethics. These include:

- Intrinsic Reasons — All life has a right to exist for its own sake. The establishment of a park to protect wild species is one form of respecting this right.

- Heritage Reasons — As a people, North Americans, for example, are a reflection of their natural and cultural heritage. Losing our wilderness means losing our ability to understand the past and ourselves.

- Spiritual Reasons — Most frequently identified by aboriginal or native peoples, the protection of sacred places is a basic function of many parks. In Australia, Uluru (Ayers Rock) is an excellent example. In Canada, South Moresby, the Stein Valley, and Temagami demonstrate the concerns of our native people.

- Cultural Reasons — The wild world is cultural raw material for artists, musicians, poets, and writers. Without wilderness we would lose cultural enrichment.

- Aesthetic Reasons — Like great works of art, wilderness has a value worth preserving.

Reasons for establishing parks based on environmental concerns include:

- Research and Education Reasons — The biosphere reserve program illustrates two major objectives of protected areas. One is to establish monitoring stations that measure the pulse of the earth — water quality, air quality, biomass production, and so on. These fundamental scientific objectives require extensive protected areas, such as national parks, to serve as links in the Global Environmental Monitoring System (GEMS). Linked to research is education in the sense of outdoor classrooms and museums that serve to build the knowledge needed to link an ever-urbanizing population to its natural heritage. Thus nature interpretation plays a major role in most park programs. To paraphrase a famous interpreter, Freeman Tilden, "With knowledge comes understanding, with understanding comes appreciation, with appreciation comes conservation."

- Scientific Reasons — The single most important reason for protection of the biological diversity found in plant and animal systems represented by parks is that they are fundamental to the survival of species. Species are protected for their own sake or for their potential to provide the raw material for humankind's medicinal and food supply. Whether the rationale is social or economic is of little consequence. Either way, species must be protected. As wildlife biologist

Ian McTaggart-Cowan states: " . . . the maintenance of the best possible environment for future generations of men includes the maintenance of the entire gamut of variety in the living biota."

• Health and Recreation Reasons — There are two interlinked elements here, physical health and mental health. Outdoor recreation does not necessarily require pristine wildlands. Recreation can take place in second-growth forests and in modified landscapes, such as ski hills. On the other hand, the powers of wilderness in reducing stress and in offering a respite from the routine of daily life are invaluable.

Some environmentalists argue that economic reasons are not a sound rationale for the establishment of wilderness areas. However, this has not been consistently the case in Canada, where regional economic development and job creation through parks have provided major motivations for the preservation of a number of areas; for example, Louisbourg National Historic Park, and Gros Morne, Forillon, Kouchibouguac, and Kejimkujik national parks. The concern, of course, is that the following economic motivations not compromise the wilderness values of such areas:

• Agriculture and Medicine — Some data are now available on the agricultural and medicinal values of protected wild genetic resources. Included in an assessment of wildlife's "worth" are: meats, skins and ivory, fish for food and aquaria, vegetables, spices and chewing gum, fuelwoods, fibres and aftershave, herbs and medicinal wildlife, genes for crops and wildlife. Not all of these values are created through protection, but they are all closely linked to it. Yet the dollar values of these items are rarely available or taken into account in consideration of the economics of park establishment.

• Watershed Protection — The continued production of clear uncontaminated water for agriculture, hydro-electric development, and human consumption is a major by-product of many protected areas.

• Soil Protection — The lack of effective forest protection in high alpine areas is closely linked to the devastation of lowlands in, for example, India and Pakistan. The rapid siltation of hydro-electric dams from heavy upstream erosion can also be attributed to inadequate protection. In Canada, the soils of Riding Mountain National Park remain intact and provide a baseline against which soil loss on the adjacent prairie can be measured.

• Tourism and Job Creation — Linked closely to regional economic development is the provision of tourism and recreational facilities. The combination of government transfer payments, private-sector investment, and visitor expenditures is a prime motivator for park establishment in many countries.

• Public Ownership — Maintaining public ownership of unique natural resources is fundamental to protecting them for this and future generations.

Above: Altocumulus clouds float over the Spirit Sands in Manitoba's Spruce Woods Provincial Park.
CREDIT: LORI LABATT.

Right: The footprints of a bear signal the presence of wilderness.
CREDIT: GREG STOTT.

Opposite: These salt flats lend texture to the northern landscape of Wood Buffalo National Park, Alberta
CREDIT: GREG STOTT.

- Sovereignty — As a statement of supreme authority, the establishment of a national park demonstrates a clear social and economic position. Parks situated on international borders may serve as useful conduits or buffers for co-operation between nations. The Amistad National Park on the Panama/Costa Rica border is a good example, as is the world's first international peace park — Waterton/Glacier, on the border between Canada and the United States.

- Future Options — Industrial development frequently forecloses future options. As Chief Oren Lyons of the Onondaga Nation put it, "Conservation is a necessity, and development is a matter of choice." It is precisely because future options are kept open, however, that parks are never secure. This fact gives new meaning to the term "vigilance."

HOW MUCH IS ENOUGH?

In Europe, perhaps with the exception of northern Sweden, Norway, and Finland, wildlands have vanished. Wilderness opportunities simply do not exist. In the United States, excluding Alaska, 1.7 per cent of the country is legally designated wilderness and an additional 5.4 per cent is roadless. If Alaska is included, these numbers shift to 3.9 per cent and 11.7 per cent respectively.

In contrast, an unpublished review of the Canadian scene indicates that 72 per cent of the country remains roadless. These are land areas more than 16 kilometres from a public road. Applying these criteria, 2.4 per cent of Canada within national and provincial parks can be classified as wilderness. Therefore, the potential for converting unprotected wildlands to legally protected areas remains large in all of Canada except for Nova Scotia, New Brunswick, and Prince Edward Island. This represents a unique opportunity of world significance.

However, although Canada has vast wildlands, the competition for their use is intense. Native land claims will leave extensive areas wild, but there may be restraints on who may use these lands. Hydro-electric development is another continuing pressure, as are the forest and mining industries. Canada, therefore, has a deceptive wildness, since behind every square kilometre sits a lawyer and a plan. To ensure our future, an adequate number of these plans must be made for wilderness establishment.

But how much is enough? How much of our wilderness should be saved? The 1982 World Parks Congress in Bali called for 10 per cent as a target for protection. This guideline has since been endorsed by the United Nations Environment Program and more recently by the Brundtland Commission, which noted the call for a tripling of protected areas. Several small nations have exceeded this standard. For example, Botswana, Tanzania, Zimbabwe, and Bhutan, all have more than 11 per cent of their lands in protected areas.

Greenland has, by a factor of two, the largest amount of land dedicated to parks, including the world's largest park. It is followed by Canada, the United

States, and Australia. The U.S. federal government protects some 500,000 square kilometres and in Alaska, approximately 24 per cent of the state is protected. The U.S. Wilderness Society recommends that this figure should be raised to 50 per cent. It is generally recognized that Canada's national-park system is half complete. Thus, with 182,000 square kilometres (1.8 per cent) of Canada presently included in the national-park system, a completed national park system would incorporate 364,000 square kilometres (3.6 per cent) of Canada's land area.

PLANNING FOR THE FUTURE

From an international perspective, it is in the Arctic that Canada can make its major contribution to rounding out the global coverage of terrestrial protected areas. Marine conservation is another issue of major concern. The protection of marine regions is lagging far behind the work on terrestrial areas.

In the country's park system itself the concept of natural regions has been developed to provide criteria for the representativeness of the system. Of the thirty-nine natural regions in the country, twenty-two currently have one or more national parks. Of the regions with no national-park coverage, five have provincial-park coverage. Of the remaining twelve regions, four contain bird sanctuaries or game sanctuaries. And in the remaining eight regions, park studies have identified the following potential national parks: east arm of Great Slave Lake, Mealy Mountains, Torngat range, Bylot Island area, and Bjorne Peninsula. The situation in the remaining three regions in northern Quebec has been complicated by native land claims and at present they have no effective protection.

There is no doubt that wildlands suitable for completing a representative system of protected areas still exist. But they won't exist forever. One approach to improving the representation in the current national-park system would be to elevate the level of legal protection and management commitment in a number of sanctuaries and provincial parks. In the long term, order-in-council protection is inadequate legal protection to ensure conservation legally. This is the situation with most bird sanctuaries, game sanctuaries, and many provincial parks. As for management, many of these areas lack permanent or, for that matter, even seasonal staff.

Countries throughout the world have been turned into cultural landscapes with no scope for national parks as we know them. Canada is also being slowly transformed into just such a landscape. We should not lose by default the opportunity to enjoy the sublimity of wilderness. As Canadians, we need to focus on safeguarding our irreplaceable natural features, old-growth forests, free-flowing rivers, large blocks of virgin forest, waterfalls, coastlines, and lakeshores. We need to reinforce the protection of these heritage features. This should be our wilderness crusade.

Above: Glacier lilies scattered along Parker's Ridge in Jasper National Park, Alberta.

CREDIT: WILF SCHURIG.

Left: The western cougar must never suffer the fate of its eastern cousin, which is now endangered, if not extinct.

CREDIT: TOM W. HALL.

PART TWO

CURRENT ISSUES AND PERSPECTIVES

JOHN BROADHEAD

The All Alone Stone Manifesto

An isolated islet in a distant archipelago, All Alone Stone is small as islands go. On the largest maps it's just a speck near the bottom of Juan Perez Sound, in the centre of the place called South Moresby. Yet up close, when your hands are wet from jigging cod off its eastern shore, it's a substantial chunk of rock, skirted in seaweeds, clad in moss, and capped by wind-blown spruce trees. Crows with black beaks fly out on patrol. Oystercatchers with red beaks bleep about in the rocks. An eagle perches in a snag, the breeze ruffling its feathers, while another rides a thermal, watching.

An insignificant rock at first glance, yet magnificent to behold in detail — in this, All Alone Stone is a symbol. Gwaii Haanas (South Moresby) and Haida Gwaii (the Queen Charlotte Islands) were virtually unknown in 1974, not even shown on some national maps of the day. Yet, slowly but surely, the islands came to occupy, then consume, the nation's attention. As more people got closer for a better look or began to hear of them, an image formed in the dominion's mind of a place of such startling beauty and — well, differentness — that it could only be described in superlatives: isolated and biologically unique; an evolutionary showcase containing more endemic and disjunct kinds of plants, animals, and fish than anywhere else in Canada; the most earthquake-active; the oldest forests; the largest colonies of various seabirds and raptors; the highest energy coastline and the highest average wind speeds; the most peculiar mosses, not to mention people.

The conflict over whether to log or to save South Moresby also lent itself to superlatives. It was the hardest-fought wilderness-conservation issue in Canada's history. Thousands of people in government, industry, and public organizations participated in the debate. They came from labour unions, political parties of every stripe, native nations, logging companies, the media, churches, airline companies, and human-rights organizations. They came from international and grass-roots environmental organizations. Celebrities and even heads of foreign states spoke in support of saving South Moresby.

It was also the most expensive campaign in conservation history. Its participants spent millions of dollars on countless meetings, legal proceedings, and lobbying efforts. The final pricetag for settling with British Columbia was $106 million. Because it involved the largest withdrawal ever from a B.C. Tree Farm Licence, it included $31 million in compensation to logging interests and $1 million to their displaced employees.

Clearly, South Moresby had shaken the national tree. A profound moral dilemma had crystallized in the Canadian conscience, and it could no longer be ignored. It was this: which is more important — the integrity of the earth and the spiritual recreation of future generations, or short-term legal responsibilities to corporations and their shareholders? More to the point, what kind of system is this that renders the two mutually exclusive?

The South Moresby story holds many such questions, not all of them easy, some yet unanswered. It is told here because there are similar struggles over environmental issues taking place elsewhere in Canada — offered in the spirit of an object lesson to those faced with the political obstacle course that conservation advocates usually encounter. It is hoped that they will find in the South Moresby story a reminder that, ultimately, every obstacle holds within it the clue to its own undoing. What's more, while the answer may not be easy, at least it's usually very simple.

DARE TO DREAM

It began in the fall of 1974. A logging company had applied for permission to move part of its operations to the south end of the archipelago, from Talunkwan to Burnaby Island. The company couldn't have been leaving behind an area more ecologically devastated or moving to one more pristine.

Talunkwan Island, at least the half that had been logged, was suffering severely from the effects of gravity. Watersheds that had once been stabilized by an interlocking web of living tree roots and had regulated the flow of rain-water for millions of incubating salmon eggs, were now collapsing. Rain-water tumbled over bare soils and bedrock, collecting in torrents, carrying mud, boulders, branches, and stumps downhill and into the streams — scouring out spawning beds or burying them under an impenetrable layer of rubble. The streams of Talunkwan Island had joined dozens of others on the Islands whose salmon families had come to spawn no more.

On Burnaby Island, an important food-gathering area called the Narrows, wildly rich in intertidal life, was designated to become a log dump. And while black bears were retreating into hibernation and salmon eggs incubated beneath clean stream gravels, lines were being drawn on maps for logging plans. There was something fundamentally offensive about the prospect of repeating Talunkwan's fate on Burnaby Island. It was time to stop and reassess the plan.

The Haida of Skidegate Village, whose ancestral homelands are for the most part in Gwaii Haanas, met on the Islands with the premier of British Columbia. They objected to the plan because their culture was rooted in this wilderness and sustained by it, physically and spiritually. As they would say for the next thirteen years: the fate of the land parallels the fate of our culture. If you proceed with this logging, then you are signalling your intention to destroy that which makes us distinct as a people.

And so a different line was drawn on a map, this one by a Haida (Guujaaw) and an itinerant kayaker (Thom Henley). It was called the South Moresby Wilderness Proposal. It was conveyed to the provincial government along with a petition from five hundred Island residents, which stated that all logging should be deferred pending an environmental review. Scientists had only started to discover some amazing natural features, and a closer examination was called for before committing the area to logging.

Reluctant to disturb the status quo, the government settled on a non-decision: some studies would begin, but so also would the logging. Only instead of on Burnaby Island, logging would be moved to Lyell Island, still within the proposed wilderness area. And so the battle line was drawn, the issue the same at the outset as it would be thirteen years later.

On one side were "the industrialists" — corporations with shareholders and a provincial government obliged by its own legislation to allow the logging. They

Above: A drenched wilderness appears beyond the passage between Moresby and Graham islands of the Queen Charlottes.   CREDIT: J.A. KRAULIS.

Pages 56 and 57: Haida totem: endangered spaces mean endangered cultures.
CREDIT: VALERIE J. MAY.

asserted, in effect, that it was necessary that the area's unique ecological features be rendered into two-by-fours and cellulose fibres at the same time that they were being studied. They called it "Multiple Use" of the area's resources.

On the other side were "the preservationists" — at the outset a small ad hoc committee of Haida and other residents, who shared a different concept of responsibility. For them, "Multiple Use" meant singular abuse. They were motivated by a dream that, odd as it may sound, seemed to originate from the rocks, trees, and waters of the place itself. The dream was a good one. It was of a better world, of respectful relations and mutual benefits among two-leggeds, four-leggeds, no-leggeds, beaks, no beaks — the works.

Such a dream had a remarkable effect upon those who became its advocates. The Haida, having lived in the place for 10,000 years, had been the first to awaken to it. It was conveyed to a handful, and then to hundreds, then thousands of visitors who came to see for themselves, only to fall under its spell. It inspired the unshakable conviction that it was only a matter of time before the logging would end. Every time another tree fell, the dream and the conviction to achieve it only grew stronger.

THE HUNDREDTH MONKEY

In the annals of evolutionary biology, there's a fascinating (albeit controversial) story about a tribe of monkeys on the island of Koshima in the Japanese archipelago. Some researchers were feeding the monkeys with sweet potatoes, which they dumped on the ground before retreating to observe the monkeys' social interactions. The monkeys liked the potatoes well enough, but had an understandable distaste for the sand and dirt that coated them. Whether by accident or brainwave, one day a young female monkey was observed washing a potato in a stream before she ate it. Before long she was showing the technique to her mother, and then to her playmates, who in turn passed it on to their mothers.

It started with one, then two . . . a dozen, then fifty . . . until there were about a hundred monkeys washing their sweet potatoes — at which point something strange and fascinating happened. All of the monkeys over the whole island began to do it. They had adopted the behaviour as if by osmosis, regardless of whether they had seen it for themselves. Stranger still, all of the monkeys of the same genus on neighbouring islands, and even on the Chinese mainland, had also taken to washing their food.

The story is told here because something similar seems to have been at work in the movement to save South Moresby. It began with a place and a handful of people with a dream. A decade later, there were some three million people advocating the same idea. A ripple on a distant island had grown into a groundswell of international opinion.

As the monkey story illustrates, significant social change does not occur without a broadly shared experiential base. In the case of a wilderness proposal, a sufficient number of people must know the place and share a gut feeling for the values at stake, before the "critical mass" of opinion capable of precipitating political change can be attained. For the advocates of South Moresby then, the situation called for a simple, two-pronged strategy: start talking and start bringing people to the place.

At the outset, credible scientific analysis was identified as one of the key components for building an effective case for preserving the area. In South Moresby, various agencies were lobbied successfully to conduct field studies, which confirmed that the natural history of the place showed a number of remarkable features. Where more research was required but agencies refused to provide it, funding for independent study was assembled locally. Qualified scientists were enlisted to conduct research on topics such as eagle-nesting densities, intertidal communities, and the effects of logging on salmon habitat. Over time, a body of information was assembled that was sufficient to argue the case for preservation on scientific merit alone. Not that that was enough.

Another ingredient that featured prominently in the South Moresby campaign was the use of images. It's not a simple matter to describe the impacts of logging on fish habitat, nor the effects that ripple out through associated ecosystems. So, photographers were coaxed to go into the field (most of them simply volunteered) to acquire images equal to the place and the issue. They returned with superlative photographs of wildlife and ancient ecosystems, and devastating shots of landslides and debris-choked salmon streams. It's no exaggeration to say that at least 100,000 photos were examined over the years, and then winnowed down into ever-improving slide shows for public presentation. Over time, an accompanying narrative was perfected to bring to life the interrelations between and within ecosystems, to convey a sense of being there and what the place is all about.

The show was taken on the road at every opportunity, presented to small-town naturalists' groups; to politicians, singly and in groups, from the municipal to the federal level; to assemblies of thousands in conference halls; and to impromptu audiences in railway cars. It was told in corporate boardrooms, high-school classrooms, and private living rooms. No audience was too small and no request for a show was denied.

Although the slide shows were received positively, another, less transitory medium was needed to reach a much broader constituency, especially within those social circles that rarely attend slide shows in public auditoriums. The answer was *Islands at the Edge — Preserving the Queen Charlotte Islands Wilderness* (Douglas and McIntyre, 1984). In effect it was the slide show between covers, written by seven experts in the natural, cultural, and political history of the area. Careful attention was paid to assembling the most accurate information available, and to the highest design and production values possible. It had to be the kind of book that people would enjoy giving and receiving, that would linger on coffee tables in the living rooms and offices of opinion leaders in Canadian society. It had to invite the reader to browse for the sheer pleasure of looking at it, because once the intended audience got past the pictures and into the text, the message was surely a radical one. The book was released in time for Christmas 1984, and its promotional campaign resulted in nation-wide publicity for the issue, and a sellout of the first printing in three weeks.

The final ingredient in the Hundredth Monkey Syndrome was getting people into South Moresby to experience the place directly. It's one thing to sit comfortably in an auditorium or an armchair, but to go there is to arouse a sense of wonder that a hundred photographs can only hint at. Standing in the pitch-black forest while 30,000 seabirds return to their nesting colonies, crashing into the trees and tumbling to their burrows in the ground beneath your feet, you can begin to suspect the depths of your ignorance about the natural world. And cooking up a feed of abalone or halibut has a way of getting the place directly under your skin. Entering the bay at Ninstints Village — the intricately carved poles arrayed along the beach in front of the old Haida longhouses — is to be confronted with an idea of what it means to be human and in harmony with one of the earth's most dynamic and prolific places.

This not unpleasant task fell to a handful of adventure-tour operators. As wilderness explorers–turned–entrepreneurs, they delivered one of the more important elements in the South Moresby networking strategy. The tour experiences they offered were as special as the place. Haida and other experts in the area's natural and cultural history accompanied their tours as resource persons. Renowned artists and photographers led special workshop expeditions, resulting in many of the images that were later incorporated into slide shows and publications. The tour participants they sought were from a specialized market — writers, professionals, captains of industry, and senior politicians — and their intention to lobby their customers while providing a memorable holiday was explicit. Some operators even incorporated into their tour costs a surcharge, allotted to the environmental groups fighting to save the area. But the most effective lobby of all was the place itself, as illustrated by one commercial-tour operator's account.

He had taken a walk along a small salmon stream with one of his clients, a forester by profession, and had left him for a moment's peace in a mossy grove of sitka spruce. When the man failed to appear at the beach twenty minutes later, the tour operator retraced his steps, only to find him sitting on the same spot, deep in thought. All my life, the forester said, I've drawn lines on maps and consigned places like this to be logged . . . if I could have understood what I feel and see here now, I doubt that I could ever have done it.

Perhaps the forester was "the hundredth monkey," perhaps not. But while he sat there in the moss, something profound had been conveyed. Without his urban filters, without the alienating armour of glass and steel, concrete and technology — one man alone in an ancient ecosystem — he had encountered the archetype of wilderness, an overwhelming realization that we are a small part of a wondrous and formidable mystery.

It was an experience that has stirred the depths of man's religious imagination

for millennia. It was something of inestimable personal value, something that should be cherished and protected for others to come to know, something unthinkable to destroy. And so it was that, whether or not visitors to South Moresby arrived as skeptics, they returned home convinced that there was only one good thing to do about such a place.

THE ART OF WAR

In 1974, the first South Moresby Wilderness advocates had no idea of the magnitude of effort ahead of them. They thought it might take them a year, unaware that it takes an average of about fifteen years to create a park in North America. They had yet to reckon with the depth of the institutional forces that would align against them.

At the time, the major players in the B.C. logging industry were engaged in an unprecedented consolidation of their control over the province's forests. The provincial government was enacting legislation and regulations to suit the industry's objectives. Tree Farm Licences had acquired an "evergreen" clause: they were automatically renewable, without resort to public review unless the Minister of Forests deemed it necessary — which he emphatically did not. When the industry encountered difficult market conditions, the province responded with a policy called "sympathetic administration," which meant that more trees were being cut, more habitat damaged, more forest land left unreplanted, and more wood left to rot, or to be burned or buried as "waste," than ever before.

And on every occasion that the Haida asserted their ownership rights in South Moresby, the spectre of "Land Claims" arose to haunt the status quo. Always the same response: "This is a *federal* issue . . . it has to be dealt with in the proper forum at the proper time . . . meanwhile, we must get on with our business."

Thus it was that, when logging operations were established on Lyell Island, the Crown committed the equivalent of a military offensive. Its intention was clear. The wilderness proposal and the world-view that it represented were anathema to "the industrialists," and reducing a Tree Farm Licence for a park was unthinkable. Yet for those who wanted to protect South Moresby, the prospect of Multiple Use abuse was equally repugnant. The time had come to talk fundamentals. It was the moral equivalent of war.

War, of course, is an ancient undertaking. And as long as you find yourself inexorably drawn into one, you would do well to study its history. In the fourth century B.C., for example, there lived in China a legendary general by the name of Sun Tzu, who was famous for having never lost a battle in hundreds of encounters. As the story goes, he retired at a venerable old age and wrote a concise account of the principles of his strategy, called *The Art of War*, which is still considered a classic.

Although it's a long march from the Middle Kingdom to All Alone Stone, there are ideas in Sun Tzu's book that environmental advocates might wish to contemplate — ideas such as: never underestimate the importance of spies. It is essential that you understand your enemy — his plans, strengths, weaknesses, advantages, and limitations. Likewise, you must have an intimate knowledge of the terrain that you will operate in. As Sun Tzu is fond of repeating, "It will benefit you to meditate on this matter."

Another important principle is the unceasing cultivation of allies, which in many ways is how the lobby to end the logging grew to such proportions. The South Moresby Wilderness was endorsed by nearly a thousand agencies and organizations in Canada, the United States, and around the world, each of them more or less ready to respond at critical points in the campaign. Equally important, efforts to build personal networks of supporters paid off in the crucial final months of the campaign, with people in government and political-party machines prepared to advocate to their leaders that there was only one way to end the conflict.

The approach taken in seeking out supporters was single-minded: leave no stone unturned. Never presume that someone will be uninterested, because you never know where a new ally or opportunity is going to appear, and sometimes they appear where you least expect them. Often enough, the time and effort spent cultivating meaningful relations with one person will result in leads to new sources of support, whether financial, logistic, or political.

When the door to a new contact does open, make sure that you've done your homework, that you understand your audience and what their potential interest in your issue may be. When lobbying government or professional people, it's a rule of thumb that the higher up the ladder you go, the more valuable their time is and the more limited their attention span can be. So lay out your case concisely, remembering that a handful of explicit photos may save you hours of explanation. As a final preparation, rehearse the interview with a colleague or two, and reverse roles. It's a good way to examine your own assumptions and prepare yourself emotionally for those of your audience.

Above all, extend the courtesy of allowing your audience to arrive at their own moral judgments about the situation. They'll do that anyway, so the most valuable thing you can do is to listen and acknowledge their viewpoint. If you don't like what you hear, jumping to the defensive or otherwise reacting negatively will only make matters worse. Paying careful attention to what they say, on the other hand, will let them know that you respect them as people.

Then again, there are times when you are staring an adversary in the face, someone who seems dedicated to frustrating all efforts at reconciliation. Try as you may to keep to the high road, you can't help thinking that life would be better if that person simply wasn't around. In this case, you would do well to consider Sun Tzu's counsel that the act of attacking is the most risky business of all. Never engage the enemy in battle unless you are absolutely certain of the outcome. If you aren't, forget it. You will have conserved precious resources, risked nothing, and lost nothing.

But if you must attack, lead your adversary into his or her own weakness; and never forget that the wise course of action is to present no target until it's too late, or never at all. One of the more spectacular examples of this principle at work in South Moresby involved the resignations of two provincial cabinet ministers. It was January 1986, and the issue, featuring prominently in the media, had become a war of images. Some industry and government members had taken to attacking the credibility of park advocates. They were "wilderness fundamentalists," unwilling and unable to compromise their position. You might have thought that a band of Haida and quasi-religious confidence artists had perpetrated a grand sham on an unwitting public by exaggerating the values of South Moresby.

Credibility is a tenuous commodity, especially for politicians. Bearing Sun Tzu's counsel in mind, in this instance it was passed along to the media that an examination of the financial holdings of some government members might result in an interesting new angle on the issue. Reporters discovered that indeed, both the Minister of Forests and the Minister of Energy, Mines and Petroleum Resources held private investments in companies that stood to profit if logging continued. As members of the cabinet committee on land use, they were both making decisions to this effect.

The barrage of media criticism that led to their resignations caused irreparable damage to the credibility of the government and, by association, of other logging advocates. More important, when both ministers maintained that there was nothing morally wrong with holding such investments, they brought into focus the fundamental dilemma posed by South Moresby: their decisions would be the same regardless, because the government's legal obligations to permit the logging were paramount over the heritage values that the Haida and environmentalists sought to protect.

But for those less inclined to such a militaristic approach, there is a gentler strategy that is equally as important: you must cultivate an untiring sense of curiosity about those who are implicated in an issue with you. Until you understand the hopes and fears of your adversaries, they will remain your adversaries. For the art of successful negotiation requires that you understand what your adversaries value and need as people — and then give it to them — before you can get what you want. If what you are ultimately seeking is respect for your own values, and if what you value is a dream of respectful relations of mutual benefit, then the only way to achieve it is to grant it. Simple in theory, yet formidable in practice, but the biggest medicine of all.

PRIME TIME CRIME

The final act in the South Moresby story belongs to the Haida. In October 1985, the issue had reached a pivotal point. Provincial politicians had balked at Canada's proposal for a national park reserve, while pressure was mounting from the logging industry to issue new logging permits. The new cutting was planned for the south face of Lyell Island, which had been untouched by modern clearcuts.

B.C.'s Minister of Environment had travelled to the Islands, and in meetings with the Council of the Haida Nation and Hereditary Chiefs he pledged (on many handshakes) that no new logging would be permitted on South Lyell until the province had decided on Ottawa's proposal. Days later, the Minister of Forests issued the cutting permits.

In the face of such duplicity, the Haida Nation concluded that there was no other option for protecting their homeland but to blockade logging operations. The companies countered with a suit for damages against the Haida and asked for an interim injunction against the blockade. After four days of testimony by the Haida in B.C. Supreme Court chambers, the President of the Council of the Haida Nation concluded his argument against the injunction, saying:

> When our people speak to you, understand that we are a nation in every sense of the word; that we have for many years been trying to deal with our place in relation to Canadian society. We all feel somewhat insulted that people allege that we do not have a place in protecting our homelands, that land that our people love and feel deeply about.
>
> I ask you to hear what we say in a spirit of rightness and in a spirit of understanding. The Haida have worked to the best of our abilities to reconcile the differences between our people and yours . . . and to have people understand who we are as a self-respecting people and a people who are respectful of others. Our constitutional, legal, rightful place in our homeland is not being respected.

The judge, obviously struggling to overcome his personal inclination to grant that respect, ruled that the law he was sworn to uphold gave him no choice but to grant the injunction. Thus the blockaders would be liable for contempt-of-court charges if they continued — which they did.

The international media exposure that ensued propelled Haida Gwaii onto the world stage. Standing on a logging road, the Haida reminded us, in an uncommonly dignified way, that we all share responsibility for safeguarding our natural heritage. Ears across the nation heard the Haida speak of a higher law, of respect for the integrity of the environment for its own sake and for the sake of future generations. Eyes around the world watched them being arrested.

On national television, a seventy-two-year-old Haida woman, arrested with an eagle feather in one hand and a Bible in the other, looked into the camera and said "Forgive them, Lord, for they know not what they do." An RCMP officer, obviously at odds with supervising the arrests, offered: "If I was free to say what I thought of politicians and the courts, I would, but I'm not, so I won't."

Coincidentally, in Ottawa, the prime minister was initiating sanctions against the apartheid government of South Africa — whose prime minister retorted that Canada wasn't exactly treating its own native people in an exemplary fashion. The remark apparently struck home, because as a way to end the conflict, the Minister of Indian Affairs made an unprecedented offer to side-step federal Land-Claims policy and sit down with the province in negotiations with the Haida.

The province declined; the arrests continued. In the end, seventy-two Haida were arrested and charged with criminal contempt of court. During the trial that followed, the Chief Justice of the B.C. Supreme Court mused that he was considering issuing a court order forbidding any Haida to travel to Lyell Island. Long-distance telephone circuits in Ottawa and Victoria began to feel the heat, as human-rights groups and newspaper editorials across the country cried foul. The Canadian parliament responded with a rare accomplishment, a unanimous resolution to end the confrontation and to respect the interests of the Haida in their homeland. It was one of the few positive exchanges between the Crown and native nations in the country's history. It also marked a shift in public attitudes towards aboriginal rights: a B.C. opinion poll revealed that a solid majority supported resolution of the Haida title issue.

That the conflict was ended and the logging stopped on July 11, 1987, is history. With this, it can be said that Canada acknowledged its dilemma. Indeed, the federal government has agreed that the Islands will serve as a national model for "sustainable development," thus extending the symbolic role of this isolated archipelago in the evolution of Canada's environmental ethic.

Yet, a nagging question remains: Did the Crown really take its basic dilemma to heart? Or could the national park reserve actually be a political manoeuvre to avoid altogether the Haida and the aboriginal-rights issue that they represent?

The questions arise because, a year and a half later, the promises spoken by Canadian politicians to the Haida remain no more than words. On the contrary, government agencies are systematically deleting all acknowledgement of the Haida's aboriginal rights from official documents related to South Moresby. Also, negotiations to share responsibility for managing the proposed park reserve have been stalemated by a federal refusal to agree to anything more than a token role for the Haida.

The Haida have made it clear that until a framework for management that respects their interests and responsibilities is reached, there will be no South Moresby "park," and they will continue to manage Gwaii Haanas without Parks Canada. Much the same as the dispute over logging, this issue holds powerful ramifications for the task of completing parks systems in Canada. Many wilderness areas sought for preservation also involve aboriginal-title issues, so other native nations are watching with justifiable concern. If Canada cannot deliver on a unanimous resolution from its own parliament, then there is little hope for establishing the respect and goodwill required to negotiate protective regimes with native nations in other areas.

And so the South Moresby story ends, as it began, with a dilemma for Canada to ponder. The Haida have proposed a new model for parks in Canada — one that is inspired by the principle of respectful relations and mutual benefits between people of all origins and the natural world. The question is: Is Canada even capable of responding in kind, or will the Haida go on to show us how it's done on their own?

KEVIN A. McNAMEE

Fighting for the Wild in Wilderness

Extraordinary measures have been required to protect Canada's parks and wilderness reserves from exploitation. Citizens opposed to mining in Strathcona, British Columbia's oldest provincial park, were arrested while defending the park. A $7 million fence was constructed in Banff National Park to stop the wildlife carnage on the Trans-Canada Highway. Citizens in Ontario and Manitoba had to mount extended battles to scuttle plans to log Quetico and Atakaki provincial wilderness parks. These few examples symbolize the extent to which development has intruded into Canada's wilderness parks. They illustrate that not only must we fight to establish parks in the first place, but we must also engage in a continuing struggle to protect them once they are established.

Threats to protected areas emanate from various sources. Industry seeks new treasures through the extraction of resources. Tourism developers seek increased profits through expansion of facilities for visitors whose sheer numbers trample and stress resources. Politicians cut budgets for resource protection and parks management. And numerous external pressures, such as acid rain and water pollution, affect parks as much if not more than they do the rest of the landscape.

Conservation agencies and environmentalists are increasingly challenged to retain parklands as living, breathing ecosystems that foster wilderness. They must struggle with forces seeking to develop these areas as well as answer other more "natural" management questions. Should fires burn in national parks? Should pest infestations be left unsprayed? Should aboriginal people be allowed to hunt and trap?

Media headlines focus on battles to set aside the Stein Valley or Temagami for protection, but they pay scant attention to the frustrating issues that threaten to seriously degrade already protected wilderness areas. The struggle to retain the wild will be placed front and centre in this chapter. It may not move you to lie down in front of a bulldozer. But, perhaps the next time you visit a national or provincial park, you'll more fully appreciate the job of the park manager and the role the public can play in protecting some of Canada's endangered spaces.

MANAGING THE WILDERNESS RESERVE

Politicians usually strike the initial deal to establish a new park. As a result, some immediate threat to wilderness destruction is removed. A park agreement is ratified. Lines are drawn on a map. Conservationists breathe a sigh of relief. Now what?

Park authorities must now develop a management plan to guide the use and protection of the new wilderness reserve and to protect and buffer the wilderness park from development. This is a difficult task. Parks and wilderness reserves are afloat in a sea of development that may eventually degrade park resources. Their managers are subjected to strong pressure from political, commercial, and environmental interest groups either to allow or to prohibit various activities in the park.

Several fundamental principles have been developed over the years to guide the management of parks and wilderness reserves. First, protected areas must be large enough to sustain whole ecosystems. Second, the forces of nature must be allowed to act freely without human manipulation. Third, the use of technology, especially motorized travel, must be either prohibited or restricted to certain designated zones in certain parks. Fourth, the area must provide opportunities for solitude and some kind of primitive or unconfined recreation.

Various government agencies in charge of parks and wilderness reserves have attempted to reflect these principles in legislation or policy. The U.S. Wilderness Act, a model piece of wilderness legislation, defines wilderness in broader terms: "Wilderness, in contrast with those areas where man and his own works dominate the landscape, is . . . an area where the earth and community of life are untrammeled by man, where man himself is a visitor who does not remain."

Canada's national-parks policy states that natural resources in parks "will be protected and managed with minimal interference to natural processes to ensure the perpetuation of naturally evolving land and water environments and their associated species."

The application of these fundamental principles to real parks can be difficult. Park managers are challenged on a day-to-day basis to evaluate environmental impacts of specific proposed developments against the rather philosophical nature of these more general principles. Will the use of powered jetboats in Nahanni National Park Reserve really compromise the park's wilderness values? Will aircraft access to remote northern parks affect wildlife or destroy wilderness values? How can the environmental impact of political commitments to allow timber extraction in Wood Buffalo, Gros Morne, and Algonquin parks be minimized?

The answers provided by park managers to some of these questions do not necessarily coincide with the view of environmentalists. And on some occasions, the shared views of park managers and environmentalists are disputed or overridden by politicians, and decisions that are not in the best interest of the park are made.

MAKING WILDERNESS-MANAGEMENT PHILOSOPHY WORK

Some clear management guidelines for protected areas exist as a result of years of park-management experience, accumulated scientific knowledge, and evolving public attitudes and support for wilderness. For one, there is almost universal support for the prohibition of industrial resource-extraction activities in parks and wilderness areas. Excluded activities include logging, mining, oil and gas extraction, and construction of hydro-electric dams. Industrial activities are in definite contravention of the basic management principles because they inhibit the free functioning of natural forces, introduce technology, and severely compromise opportunities for solitude and unconfined recreation.

It's not just the activity itself that is of concern. It's all the structures and activities required to support industry, such as utility corridors, and work-crew camps, that cause environmental degradation. They remove park resources, pollute the air and water, alter wildlife migration and use patterns, turn wildlife into "problem animals," destroy habitat, create noise, and scar the landscape.

Resource extraction is prohibited from parks, much to the consternation of the forest and mining industries. The preservationists' philosophy strongly conflicts with industries' assertion that multiple use should predominate. The removal of decadent, overmature, insect-ridden, or wind-thrown trees is not allowed in parks. To industry, this is a waste. Parks philosophy recognizes that our forests are the product of centuries of growth and have managed to attain their majestic state without society's "help." Equal weight is given to undergrowth, detritus, moss, and nurse logs that maintain the forest as a vibrant, active, and diverse natural habitat. Parks policy attempts to allow ecosystems to produce more than just cubic metres of lumber.

Finally, the South Moresby, Nahanni, and Kluane national parks were established in response to threats to log, dam, and mine these unprotected treasures. It only follows that industrial activities must continue to be excluded.

A more complex issue is the recreational use of parklands and the development of tourism facilities. Canada's parks have a dual, sometimes conflicting, mandate: to protect park resources and to provide outstanding opportunities for use and enjoyment. The challenge in protected areas is to manage this tension between use and protection. It is accomplished primarily by allowing non-consumptive, wilderness-based recreational activities such as hiking, canoeing, camping, mountain climbing, nature walks, birdwatching, and photography. If controlled, these activities do not destroy ecosystems, allow for unconfined opportunities for solitude, and are based on non-mechanized forms of travel. This permits parklands and wilderness areas to maintain their unique non-urban character.

Zoning plans are now developed to indicate where certain activities such as mechanized travel are allowed or prohibited. Most national parks are primarily

zoned as wilderness. Recreational facilities (roads, roofed accommodation, camp grounds) are minimized within recreational zones.

The construction of tourism facilities in parks, such as hotels, ski areas, restaurants, and other amenities, is an even greater concern than the recreational use of parklands. Such facilities contribute to both a loss of wilderness and a taming of the wild. Opportunities for solitude and unconfined recreation are diminished as crowds gather to view various attractions. They pollute; visitors to Banff National Park, for example, are warned not to drink the water near several facilities. Support facilities such as utility corridors, employee dormitories, and parking lots contribute to further loss of parkland. Finally, such facilities become an attraction in themselves. Wilderness becomes "scenery," simply a backdrop for urban-based lifestyles.

However, the total elimination of recreational users from parklands is not an option, except for extremely sensitive areas. Nor is it desirable; contact between people and natural environments is more likely to increase public and political support for wilderness protection. For example, 96 per cent of Canadians who have visited a national or provincial park favour spending government funds to preserve our wilderness areas. But, in Alberta, where a very strict Wilderness Areas Act prohibits virtually every use of such areas, legislation has negatively affected support for the establishment of new wilderness areas. Stopping an Albertan from riding a horse in the mountains is akin to denying a Newfoundlander the right to fish. It just doesn't make horse sense!

HOW WELL HAVE WE DONE?
Canada is blessed with some of the most remarkable wilderness areas and parks in the world. But how well has our country done in keeping these places wild? Where do we stand after a century of managing and using national parks? The answer is simple and disappointing: we don't know, but there are some strong signals that all is not well.

Individual parks clearly communicate how society's activities are degrading park resources. Lakes in Ontario's Killarney Provincial Park are biologically dead, killed by acid rain. Quebec's Forillon National Park is on the International Union for the Conservation of Nature's (IUCN) endangered-wilderness list because of acid rain. A wilderness park in the Temagami region of Ontario is also on IUCN's list because of the potential impact of a proposed logging road.

There is virtually no comprehensive analysis of the ecological integrity of Canada's national parks and wilderness systems. An unpublished 1987 Canadian Parks Service report on natural resource-management problems in national parks concluded that visitor impacts and transboundary concerns were the issues most frequently identified by park staff. Visitor impacts included trampling and compaction of soils and vegetation, and deleterious effects on landforms. Transboundary concerns were related to impacts emanating from adjacent lands, such as pollution.

Perhaps one of the more extensive reviews of park-resource protection pro-grams was completed in the United States. A 1980 *State of the Parks* report examined threats to over 320 units of the U.S. national-park system. None of the parks examined was reported to be immune from external and internal threats. Large parks such as Yellowstone are experiencing significant and widespread impacts linked to the encroachment of development activities on the park. The report identified a total of 4345 specific threats to park resources, which were grouped into general threat categories, including aesthetic degradation (land development and logging); air pollution (acid rain and hydrocarbon pollutants); physical removal of resources (mineral extraction, poaching); visitor impacts (campfires and trampling); and water quality and quantity (oil spills and water diversions). There is no reason to conclude the situation is any better in Canada.

A 1987 survey of major mammal populations throughout western North Amer-ica's parks revealed how dramatically parks are failing to protect ecosystems. The study found that fourteen national parks have lost a total of forty-two mam-mal populations. This meant that 40 per cent of the original species had disap-peared since these parks were first established. Ecologist William Newmark concluded that national parks are simply too small to support the diversity of species originally found in the regions in which the parks were established. Only the largest aggregations of parkland in western North America — Banff, Jasper, Kootenay, and Yoho — had not experienced any appreciable loss of wildlife.

WILDERNESS STRUGGLES

Actions taken by citizens, environmental groups, and park agencies to preserve wilderness areas focus on the most prominent of these threats outlined above, namely extractive activities, visitor impacts, and facility development. Because some of these threats are sanctioned by politicians, or occur outside park-agency jurisdictions, it is mainly private citizens, non-government organizations, and independent scientists, who rise to the defence of Canada's parks and wilderness areas. The National and Provincial Parks Association of Canada (now known as the Canadian Parks and Wilderness Society) was formed in 1963 as a citizens' organization to promote the preservation and expansion of Canada's national- and provincial-parks system. In the years that followed, provincial groups such as the Alberta Wilderness Association, Algonquin Wildlands League, Newfound-land Wilderness Society, and Western Canada Wilderness Committee were formed to protect parks and wilderness areas within their regions. They and private citizens have actively worked to keep wilderness areas wild by writing letters, marching on legislatures, lobbying politicians, publishing books and articles, and delivering briefs to public hearings in order to bring the plight of parks to public attention. Their goal is unmistakable: to get politicians to exercise the political will to stop threats to protected areas.

Why do people fight to preserve a park? Why would someone get arrested trying to protect a wilderness area? The simple reason is that they care about

Above: A salt marsh
near Riverside, New
Brunswick, provides a
haven for waterfowl and
other wildlife.
CREDIT: FREEMAN
PATTERSON.

Centre: Sandstone cliffs
welcome the Atlantic
Ocean in P.E.I. National
Park.
CREDIT: MILDRED McPHEE.

Below: Temagami, the
"deep water country"
of Ontario, is listed
internationally as a
threatened area.
CREDIT: TEMAGAMI
WILDERNESS SOCIETY.

Opposite: One generation
provides nourishment
for the next.
CREDIT: MARIA ZORN.

Pages 66 and 67: A
black-tailed deer feeds
along the Bedwell
River of Clayoquot
Sound, slated for clear-
cut logging in B.C.
CREDIT: ADRIAN DORST.

the environment. Such people are motivated by an intense belief that there is a need for undisturbed wild places both within the world and within each individual's life.

Most reasons for action stem from the fact that decisions to develop parks and wilderness reserves violate the public trust. The public-trust notion holds that those areas are preserved by government on behalf of the current generation in a wilderness state, in perpetuity, for the benefit of future generations. Any activity approved by government that detracts from the wildness of an area, introduces technology, or affects the ecosystem is regarded as a breach of the public trust. In the absence of legislation or any definitive social contract that clearly upholds this trust, park supporters must take action in order to force government to maintain its side of the social contract.

Over the years, there have been many issues that have prompted outbursts of public opposition to government proposals to develop protected areas. Struggles to protect parks and wilderness areas focus on three basic parts of a park or reserve: the boundary, park resources contained within the park, and pressures from outside the park boundary that affect park resources.

Manipulating Park Boundaries

Boundary issues arise over political manipulation of the boundary or the ecological inadequacy of such boundaries. Very few park boundaries are defined by legislation; in fact, only national and some provincial park boundaries have any real degree of legal permanency. The Canadian parliament can change park boundaries only through legislation. And parliament has exercised that right. The boundaries of Banff National Park have changed ten times since 1885. A portion of Cape Breton Highlands National Park was deleted in 1958 for hydroelectric development. Provincial cabinets can, and have, changed park boundaries late on a Friday afternoon, with no public or parliamentary discussion.

Park boundaries are also the result of political compromise and therefore do not reflect ecological realities. Straight-line boundaries are a throwback to when parks were originally established to protect scenery and not ecosystems. As wilderness around parks disappears, and development impinges, the ecological inadequacies of park boundaries become most noticeable.

Due to a significant boundary change, Waterton Lakes National Park is Canada's most threatened national park. In 1921 the Canadian government reduced the park by over 50 per cent, resulting in a park that no longer preserved an entire ecosystem. Now, more than fifty commercial and industrial developments encircle the park, threatening the park's aesthetic value and its viability as a functioning ecosystem.

Grizzly bears and wolves that migrate out of the park, while still being within their ecosystem and habitat range, wander into hostile territory where they are killed by vehicles or shot. Ranchers are sometimes forced to take action to protect their livestock and crops. Unless quick action is taken to protect the grizzly on lands outside the park, in this area the grizzly is doomed.

The federal government is powerless to act, however. It has no legal jurisdiction over the provincial Crown lands outside the park. The Alberta government has committed much of these lands to industry for oil and gas development. The province rejected an initial request from the Alberta Wilderness Association to declare the lands adjacent to the park a provincial wilderness area. Furthermore, it angered conservationists when it issued a gas exploration permit in an area the government itself had zoned a prime protection zone.

Undaunted, conservationists are co-operating on a joint program to secure broader protection for the Waterton Lakes–U.S. Glacier National Park ecosystem. The Alberta Wilderness Association, Canadian Parks and Wilderness Society, Montana Wilderness Society, and U.S. Wilderness Society have launched the Crown of the Continent program. The goal is to develop a conservation regime that will ensure the protection of the area's wildlife and wilderness values through the co-operation of government, industry, and landowners.

On the Line for Strathcona

Eight decades of abuse of Strathcona Provincial Park culminated in 1988 with the arrest of sixty-four citizens protesting mining in the park. In 1987 the B.C. government deleted 30,000 hectares from the park and reclassified portions of the park to allow for industrial development, issuing a six-month mineral-exploration permit. There was no public consultation on the matter. A committee of public inquiry later concluded that, for many people, "these changes were cavalier erosions of the sanctity of the Park." In short, the B.C. government had committed a serious breach of the public trust.

The history of Strathcona is a sad one of abuse and neglect. Established in 1911 to protect an alpine and forest mountain-wilderness area in the centre of Vancouver Island, by 1988 the park was described as a "mess". Its current triangular boundaries do not reflect the ecological realities of the area, and the park itself is a confused tangle of industrial activities, recreation areas, and wilderness.

Resource industries have obtained permission over the decades to exploit the park. The staking and development of mineral claims was permitted until 1973. Logging operations continued over the years. Through various water-development projects, B.C. Hydro has raised water levels and diverted waterways. Westmin Resources Ltd. operates a mine in the south-central section of the park. Over the years, the government has negotiated land and timber trades of Strathcona parkland in exchange for parklands elsewhere in the province. In essence, the government has treated Strathcona's wilderness treasures as nothing more than baubles for trade or exchange.

The B.C. government responded to public outrage by establishing the Strathcona Park Advisory Committee. The committee concluded that government had lost credibility in its dealings with the public on the issues of Strathcona Park. The reasons for this loss of credibility were clear. The committee concluded it was widespread opinion that the government was "perennially giving up pieces of Strathcona Park to the benefit of industry" and appears "to have responded primarily to the needs of resource extraction activities on the periphery of the park rather than to park values."

It would appear that the Friends of Strathcona, the citizens' organization formed to protect the park, won their fight. The committee concluded that "there is no place for further development of mineral claims in Strathcona." The government accepted the recommendations of the advisory committee and agreed to prohibit further claim staking, deny further exploration permits, and work to reacquire all remaining mineral claims. Further timber harvesting will be prohibited and all remaining forest tenures will be reacquired. A permanent legal boundary, based on wilderness protection, recreational use, and wildlife and ecological values, is to be established.

However, the exact location of a permanent boundary continues to be the subject of considerable debate. Although logging and mining are no longer possible within Strathcona's current boundary (except for the Westmin mine), there

Above: An Arctic loon near Churchill, Manitoba, an area proposed for national park status.
CREDIT: R. BARRY RANFORD.

Centre: Late afternoon light catches two caribou bulls squaring off in the Ogilvie Mountains of the Yukon Territory.   CREDIT: GEORGE CALEF.

Below: Great gray owls, rarely sighted, are ghosts of the boreal forest.   CREDIT: GARY R. JONES.

Right: Caribou dig for lichens on Shaeffer Mountain, Yukon Territory.   CREDIT: GEORGE CALEF.

Pages 78 and 79: Aerial view of an arctic glacier on Ellesmere Island, where a national park was formally established in 1986.   CREDIT: STEPHEN J. KRASEMANN.

is an ongoing dispute over areas deleted from the park in 1987. While environmentalists want an immediate return to the 1987 boundary plus the additions recommended by the advisory committee, the government will subject boundary proposals to further public review. Thus, industrial development of former parkland and important lands that may soon be added to Strathcona is possible.

While Strathcona is indeed a victory, it is a sad commentary on what citizens have to do to force governments to protect parks and uphold the public trust. The Friends of Strathcona did not win through a court case or any other "reasonable" dispute-settling mechanism. They won only through picketing, civil disobedience, and widespread public sympathy for those tactics. Only then did politicians acquiesce to the public will. How many more Strathconas must there be before governments become stronger advocates for park values?

Strathcona also demonstrates that even in the face of rapidly depleting wilderness and a century of park philosophy that now precludes resource extraction, a park is not safe. Unless some strong institutional changes are made to protect such parks as Strathcona, park resources, like the proverbial cookie jar, will remain within the grasp of a hungry industry.

Assault on the Arctic

No issue better illustrates the problems behind transboundary issues than the Arctic Refuge issue. The U.S. administration's proposal to explore for oil and develop Alaska's Arctic National Wildlife Refuge, an area adjacent to Canada's Northern Yukon National Park, constitutes a critical transboundary threat to Canadian wilderness.

In 1987 the Reagan administration advocated oil development within the coastal plain area of the Arctic Refuge, a portion of undesignated and undeveloped de facto wilderness. The U.S. Congress must pass legislation to allow for oil exploration. To block this authorization, conservationists, native people, and the Canadian government are pressing Congress to pass legislation to include the coastal plain in the U.S. National Wilderness Preservation System.

Likened to Africa's Serengeti Plain, the coastal plain is the most biologically productive part of the Arctic Refuge. It is part of the principal calving ground for the Porcupine Caribou Herd, which migrates across the Alaska/Yukon border. In 1984, Canada established the Northern Yukon National Park primarily to preserve that critical portion of the herd's calving ground located in Canada.

The plan to develop the coastal plain is of immense concern to citizens of both countries. A shared international resource, the 180,000-head caribou herd is the source of food and basis of a subsistence lifestyle for 7000 aboriginal people in northern Canada and Alaska. It will also impact on the broader diversity of wildlife found in this area, such as snow geese, muskoxen, wolves, and grizzly and polar bears.

The U.S. Department of the Interior's draft environmental assessment of the proposal concluded that "a population decline and change of distribution of 20 per cent to 40 per cent of the caribou would occur"—a loss of up to 72,000 animals. In short, drilling in the "nursery" of the Porcupine Caribou Herd will have disastrous effects on the herd.

In the blizzard of statistics that has gathered around this issue, two are very critical. First, there is only a 20 per cent chance of discovering oil on the coastal plain. Second, if oil is discovered, the United States will only gain a two-hundred-day supply, based on the current rate of consumption. Risking the coastal plain, jeopardizing the future of the Porcupine Caribou Herd and the native people who depend on it, and the broader wildlife and wilderness values of this ecosystem, *for two hundred days' worth of oil*, is unconscionable. The chairman of the Porcupine Caribou Herd Management Board captured it best: "I'd say to the average American, 'on your 201st day you will have no oil, and we'll have no caribou'."

The Canadian government's position is clear. It has called on the U.S. government to legally protect the coastal plain by designating it wilderness. Unfortunately, the Canadian government has no legal jurisdiction in this issue and, thus, no direct control over the future of this critical area. Such is the nature of transboundary wilderness issues: one party is almost always powerless.

Canada must continue to convince U.S. legislators that decisions related to the coastal plain will have direct international consequences for both countries and for aboriginal people. If two countries fail to protect such a critical wilderness area because of the lobby of one industry for two hundred days' worth of oil, what hope does North America have of solving some of the globe's more pervasive environmental problems?

WHY ARE PROTECTED AREAS THREATENED?

In examining threats to protected areas, a number of institutional forces can be identified.

Most parks and wilderness areas suffer from a lack of legal protection. Park boundaries are rarely set in legislation. Rarely does legislation prohibit industrial resource-extraction activities, nor does it set legal limits on the use and development of parks for recreational purposes.

Park programs suffer from a lack of funding and personnel operating in the field to monitor and protect park resources. As in Africa, for example, our national parks have become a major focus for poaching activities. The efforts of dedicated field staff to protect park resources have been blocked, on occasion, by politically motivated decisions of politicians or senior civil servants. Over the last two decades, environmental programs have not been a real government priority. Rhetoric abounds, while actual budgets have been continually cut and reduced against inflation. For example, less than 6 per cent of the Canadian Parks Service's 1987 $300-million budget was directed to natural resource conservation work. And it never recovered from the cutting in 1984 of its Park Study Unit, which provided information on wildlife populations and behaviour.

Increasing resource developments adjacent to parks and wilderness areas are slowly destroying the ecological integrity of these reserves. Park agencies have

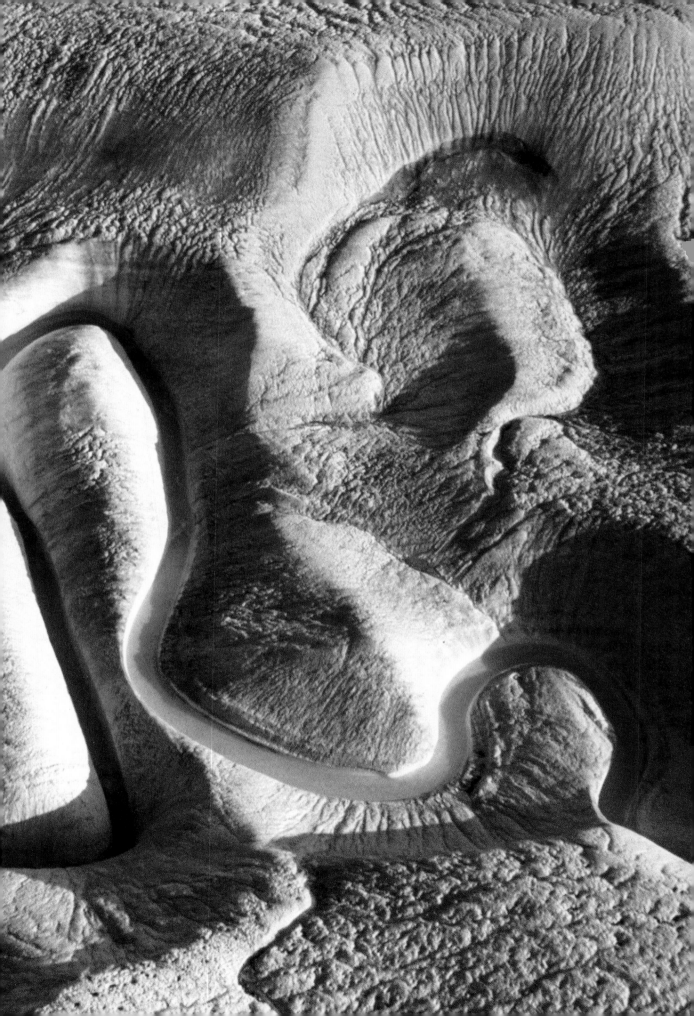

failed in many cases to secure co-operation from adjacent landowners, because the policy of letting nature take its course is seen as having a detrimental effect on land adjacent to parks — loss of livestock to bears or wolves, destruction of crops by wildlife, and so on. Landowners are demanding corrective actions within specific parks to protect their property, despite the fact it is they who have settled within a park ecosystem, and that many of them benefit economically in other ways from the park's existence.

Diminishing resources outside reserves is also a concern. Resource industries are slowly working up to the edge of park boundaries, and will begin to lobby for park access once resources are depleted on the outside. Ron Arnold, executive director for the U.S.-based Center for the Defense of Free Enterprise, is encouraging the Canadian forest industry to "initiate tactical programs . . . to change every non-timber land-use designation in Canada to multiple use within 50 years." One can safely assume that parks will be first on such a hit-list.

Parks are already under heavy pressure to serve economic goals. Most major park developments, such as roads, accommodation, and recreational facilities, are meant to increase tourism revenues and economic gains to local communities. This is understandable, given that 70 per cent of Canada's national parks are located in economically depressed regions. Governments, however, do little to encourage development outside parks that may be of more benefit to such communities.

Finally, it is clear that politicians and park agencies have failed to act as strong, vocal advocates for park values and the preservation of wilderness. Instead of rejecting proposed park developments out of hand, politicians and park agencies agree to "review" them, sending out a signal that perhaps our parks are open for business. And rarely do politicians lobby for increased parks-program budgets.

For its part, the public and environmental organizations, while mounting a strong defence of park values, have failed to sufficiently influence politicians on questions of wilderness protection and park funding through the ballot box or in the halls of government. The fact that Canada has as many parks and wilderness reserves as it does is testimony to the commitment of those who have refused to give up the fight.

A FUTURE AGENDA

All is not doom and gloom. Some positive steps have been taken. The National Parks Act was strengthened in 1988. Legislative limits to townsites and ski areas will prevent future expansion of these areas. Wilderness zones will be defined and protected by order-in-council. Fines for poaching have increased from $500 to $150,000. Park-management plans mandating protection of ecological integrity through protection of natural resources are now legally required. New oil and gas pipelines and railway corridors cannot be constructed in a national park except by a separate act of parliament.

In Ontario, the provincial government reaffirmed park values by prohibiting mining, hunting, and constructing dams within wilderness and nature reserve parks. Unfortunately, logging continues in Ontario's, and Canada's, first provincial park, Algonquin.

Several Canadian national parks have been declared biosphere reserves under the UNESCO program. The purpose is to integrate park-management practices and surrounding land management to maintain the integrity of the regional ecosystems. Biosphere reserves exist at Waterton Lakes and Riding Mountain national parks. This should go a long way to working out better relations with adjacent landowners.

As promising as these actions are, governments will simply have to give the protection of park resources a higher priority. Programs and attitudes must recognize that wilderness is one end of the land-use spectrum and that urbanized areas are at the other end. Legislation, policy, and management programs must entrench this fact. The goal of all actions and decisions must be to retain the wild end of the spectrum rather than push it towards the other end.

Future national and provincial parks and wilderness reserves must be established on an ecosystem basis. Actions to protect lands adjacent to new parks must be defined within federal/provincial park-establishment agreements. Governments could also support programs being developed by conservationists aimed at integrating the management of parklands and adjacent territory that are critical to an ecosystem. Such projects are now underway to protect the newly established Grasslands National Park and its surrounding environment. More use of the "Man and Biosphere Reserve" program would assist in this regard.

Provincial governments could alleviate recreational pressures on national parklands and their own wilderness areas through the provision of more diversified and geographically distributed recreational opportunities. In addition, marketing messages and advertisements could play an important role in directing recreational users to appropriate sites. Commercials for national parks too often communicate that these wilderness areas are nothing more than large playgrounds.

Biosphere reserves, park boundaries that are ecologically defensible, and location of recreational facilities outside parks, all speak to the need to integrate parks into regional economies and environments. Too often parks are established as separate from the social and economic fabric of the region in which they exist. With external threats to parks increasing, governments and conservationists must search out and use various mechanisms to protect parks on a regional basis.

More legal protection for parks and wilderness areas is required. For example, a revision of Ontario's Provincial Parks Act for the centennial of the province's parks in 1993 could be an excellent model for other jurisdictions. The Act should be revised to incorporate the boundaries of major wilderness parks and to prohibit logging, mining, and other extractive activities.

Park agencies must undertake, and politicians should support, a comprehensive park-resource inventory to assess the health of Canada's parks and wilderness reserves. *State of the Parks* reports are critical in identifying threats, and corrective action required. Such reports could identify external threats to areas and pinpoint jurisdictions that could help in developing park buffer zones. A recent amendment to the National Parks Act requires a *State of the National Parks Report* to be submitted to parliament every two years. The first one is to be completed in 1990 and will mark a critical time in Canada's fight to keep wilderness wild.

OH, TO SEE A GRIZZLY IN 2001!

Ellesmere Island was established as Canada's thirty-second national park on September 20, 1986. Close to the North Pole, it is Canada's most northern and most remote national park. The park protects a biologically unique and highly productive High Arctic ecosystem.

The ceremony creating the park was held in chilling sub-zero temperatures within the park. It was a special event for me. I was a signatory to the park agreement on behalf of the people of Canada. Only a month before, I had criticized the federal government in the media for not fulfilling its commitment to establish the park. To his credit, federal parks minister Tom McMillan moved quickly to establish Ellesmere Island National Park Reserve.

I left Ellesmere with mixed emotions. By speaking out on behalf of a national conservation organization, I had ensured that final act of political will required to establish the park. I had played a small but important role in ensuring the work of committed civil servants and the vision of people such as Hugh Faulkner and Thomas Berger were not in vain. It was reassuring to know that, on occasion, the "system" can work.

But as our plane left this magnificent wilderness, I knew Ellesmere was not secured. This wilderness reserve is not beyond the grasp of society, despite its remoteness. Too many tourists can cause irreparable harm to an area where footprints remain for decades and the flora is the product of centuries of nurturing. In its first two years of operation, park visitation to Ellesmere has exceeded predictions. Airborne pollutants from urban areas are gathering over this area in an "Arctic haze." Ellesmere will not be immune to the greenhouse effect or ozone depletion.

The message is clear: even remote parks such as Ellesmere Island are not inviolate. Park status is not an end in itself, only the beginning of a constant vigil over an area whose health mirrors our natural destiny. As benchmarks, parks are living testimony both to what our planet was before it was civilized and to how our actions are degrading the world's natural ecosystems.

In future, wilderness areas will signal society much like the dove carrying the olive branch to Noah's ark indicated the threat was passed. If in 2001 we see a grizzly bear or migrating herds of Arctic caribou, it will be a signal we may yet survive. But for now, the flood waters are rising. To keep the wilderness wild, we have a long fight ahead.

ELIZABETH MAY

Political Realities

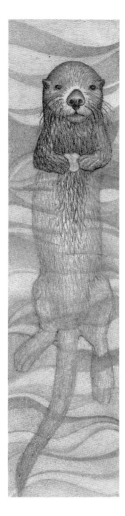

My life and work in the environmental movement changed dramatically in the spring of 1986 when the Minister of the Environment, the Honourable Tom McMillan, asked me to work for him. This was a highly unlikely proposition for several reasons. I'd been an environmental activist and lawyer fighting budworm spraying, uranium mining, nuclear power, and herbicides in Nova Scotia for over ten years.

No previous Environment minister had ever sought out an environmentalist to join his political staff. It was an offer with obvious risks. I knew that if I accepted many people would assume I'd sold out. Moreover, I knew I'd have to be constantly vigilant with myself to make sure I hadn't. These things are subtle; they sneak up on you.

I laid down tough conditions: that I'd be party to all decisions affecting environmental issues and that I'd have a meaningful role and not be used as window-dressing. McMillan accepted my conditions.

As senior policy adviser to the minister, I had an invaluable experience. I was schooled in the ways of power and politics. First I'll outline what I've learned about power. Then I'll explain political realities and how South Moresby, one of Canada's endangered spaces, was saved.

SOME REFLECTIONS ON POWER

Power is not real. It is an illusion maintained by the belief of the powerless that others hold it. For instance, Ottawa and Toronto believe that they are at the centre of things. Toronto is surer of this than Ottawa. In reality, every community believes *it* is the centre of the universe, but the rest of Canada does not support Cape Bretoners or Westerners in this delusion. However, people in Toronto have thousands of people elsewhere in Canada who willingly support them in their delusions. Because of this, we all give up a little of our power to Toronto and Ottawa. Places where money is accumulated or where decisions are made become powerful. These two elements — money and decision-making — help to define power.

I quickly discovered that from the vantage point of the Minister's office, I had a lot of power. Phone calls were returned. Doors were opened. Bureaucrats seemed nervous, even frightened, of my phone messages. A call from THE MINISTER'S OFFICE was ominous. I watched how others around me created the illusion of their power. Other assistants in ministers' offices didn't return phone calls. They created obstacles to the supplicant who wished an audience with the minister. They would, they assured a caller, do their best to arrange a meeting, but the minister was very busy. Perhaps, if the caller would phone again next week, the powerful assistant would have been able to approach the minister and place the petition for an audience before him. Perhaps not. This game could be played out over months. The obstacle created by those in gate-keeper positions could be removed only by themselves. In fact, the gate-keepers were the obstacle. And yet supplicants who might vaguely suspect this to be the case could do nothing but continue to phone from week to week, thanking the brick wall for its valiant efforts.

These games were not restricted to political staff; there are powerful gate-keepers throughout the bureaucracy. People near money — Treasury Board and Finance. People near decision-making — the Department of Justice and the Privy Council Office. All those nameless, faceless bureaucrats who advise the chairmen of cabinet committees about which departmental memoranda have achieved sufficient consensus in "the system" to be placed on a cabinet agenda.

I was fascinated to realize how little the political masters really do. Cabinet committees were carefully managed and choreographed by the "central agencies." An original idea would be as out of place at a cabinet meeting as a ouija board.

It's not that ministers can't think or that they can't conceive an original idea. It's just that the business of government is to squelch ideas. The good idea must first be ground down fine within a department. Then the department in question must conduct "bilaterals" — in other words, go from one department to another, convincing other bureaucrats that the proposal is not a threat. If another department is not convinced, chances are the good idea will never make it to a cabinet committee meeting. The gate-keepers at the Privy Council Office will see to that. If through some miracle of tenacity and political pressure an idea does make it to cabinet committee for a decision, the ministers around the table will respond, based on the script of criticisms advanced by the Minister's own senior bureaucrats — revenue implications . . . negative impacts on the departmental constituency. . . .

Bureaucrats, contrary to their reputation, are anything but unimaginative. They can invent original and compelling reasons to kill a good idea.

Despite hundreds of creative, caring, committed bureaucrats within the system, bureaucracy as a whole in Ottawa functions like a gelatinous single-celled amoeba. Its one overriding response to any stimulus is "resist change." It's an amoral, controlling fossil. Everyone lets it play these perfectly predictable power games: people in Ottawa know the rules.

However, people who can break the code can be powerful too. I figured out how to break the rules, to do a lot of good things and not get corrupted in the process. The trick was not to take power seriously. The trick was to share it. I created direct access to the Minister for as many people — inside and outside the department — as I possibly could. And if it wasn't direct, at least the committed civil servants and outsiders could circumvent the obstacles between them and the deputy minister by getting an idea directly to me — and thereby to the Minister. We short-circuited the system.

I also started identifying the kindred spirits in the bureaucracy with whom I could network. Sharing the power, unclogging access — all this created more power, more activity, and more positive energy than someone expending energy being an aggressive gate-keeper could possibly have managed.

SOUTH MORESBY

The principle of sharing power worked best with the saving of South Moresby. The major reason for this was the nature of the activists on that issue — the core of people who maintained the conviction throughout that the logging of these precious islands would be stopped. The activists on that issue saw politicians for just what they are — not institutions, not symbols, just other people. They tend to be people with big egos. They tend to be men. They tend to want reassurance, stroking, love. Who doesn't?

The people working on South Moresby never depersonalized their approach, never polarized the question into "us" versus "them." Of course, the gulf between B.C. politicians, who wanted logging and attacked the environmentalists as being draft-dodgers and hippies, and the South Moresby supporters was huge. But it didn't poison the well of conviction from which the South Moresby crew drew their nourishment.

Establishing themselves as reasonable people with federal politicians, finding more and more converts, even in unlikely places, they understood that almost everyone wants to be an environmentalist at heart. You just have to work harder with some than with others to find their soft spot. Maybe it's a cottage on the lake. Maybe it's a favourite fishing spot or a hunting trip with a father who passed on years ago. But somewhere in the heart's memory is a special love of the natural world. Once you find that love and identify it with larger issues, the polarization vanishes. You may not have made a convert to the immediate cause, but you have made contact. No matter what preconceived notions may be held by that single politician or industrialist about "environmentalists," there will always be an exception in his or her mind. You have become a real person, with honest concerns, family, home. You are no longer a caricature; neither is the other person.

Of course, environmental issues are too urgent to wait for slow education of the least enlightened. We must always act *now*. The environmental movement must attack, criticize, hold politicians accountable. We have a role in shaking society and government awake, by its shoulders. But that waking must be done with love. You can't change someone you alienate.

The difference between a successful, effective environmental group and one that seems to spin, and spurt and gargle in its own rhetoric, is the choice of energy used. The same goal can be reached using a number of different attitudes, emotions — energies. The medium can be anger, hostility, or cynicism (arguably the worst). Or there's positive energy that I think of simply as love. Choose that, and balance comes more easily to your own life, while change comes more easily to those you seek to change.

The choice of energy manifested itself in the South Moresby crew in a number of ways. In my experience, no other group did as much personal lobbying of Ottawa MPs as the South Moresby crew. Thom Henley was the inspiration for many — able to transfer to others his deep love of the islands and the unshakable knowledge that they would be saved. He met with politicians, spoke at rallies, rode the national train caravan from Newfoundland to British Columbia, and somehow kept the home fires burning. John Broadhead served as creative wizard — writing, designing, strategizing, and fund-raising. Colleen McCrory lit up the airwaves, sitting on the doorsteps of editorial boards in Toronto until they were forced to contend with her and her suitcases of posters and files. Paul George, gruff and undiplomatic, provided strokes of genius through full-colour posters, postcards, and the message in caption form — "Supernatural Windy Bay . . . let it be." Vicky Husband did much of the Victoria and Ottawa lobbying. Among a thousand other unsung and unknown services, she held the family together, those in the close-knit B.C. group and those in its colonies of committed supporters outside the province — notably Kevin McNamee, from the Canadian Parks and Wilderness Society, Gregg Sheehy from the Canadian Nature Federation, who co-ordinated the great Save South Moresby Caravan cross-country train in the winter of 1986, and the World Wildlife Fund's own Monte Hummel, who pulled many a miraculous rabbit out of his hat (who else can request and obtain telegrams from royalty?)

MP after MP was visited by earnest and persuasive members of the South Moresby crusade. And converts were won over — Charles Caccia, then Opposition Environment critic; John Fraser, Speaker of the House; and of course, Jim Fulton, NDP member from B.C. Tom McMillan was also quickly recruited within days of becoming Environment minister through the skillful efforts of the South Moresby group at a major parks conference at Banff. They hijacked the conference. By the time the new minister arrived to speak, there was a palpable ground-swell that South Moresby must be saved. And so Tom McMillan (Progressive Conservative) joined Charles Caccia (Liberal) and Jim Fulton (New Democrat) in the fight to save South Moresby.

This was another unique aspect of the issue. It was totally non-partisan. John

Fraser, an early convert to the movement, called it "the conspiracy." In the moments of crisis, when the premier of British Columbia, Bill Vander Zalm, broke off negotiations, when all appeared to be lost, what saved it again and again was a little network of conspirators — Jim Fulton, Charles Caccia, John Fraser (perilously balancing his role as Speaker with a fierce determination to stop the logging), and Dalton Camp — the Conservative power-broker. And then there was me — the environmental lunatic Nova Scotia Tories had warned Tom not to hire. Each of us had our own pressure points and contacts. Among Fraser's was Brian Smith, then attorney general of B.C., who at one point was the only member of Vander Zalm's cabinet other than Vander Zalm prepared to reopen the negotiations.

Jim Fulton, the same Jim Fulton who threw a dead fish on Brian Mulroney's desk in the House of Commons, was now looking to that same Brian Mulroney for leadership. When the negotiations were at their most sensitive, Fulton would call the prime minister's office to find out if a well-placed question in that day's Question Period would be strategically helpful. He wanted Mulroney to do the right thing. And what's more, he believed that the prime minister would. In fact, Mulroney did seem to understand what was at stake. From the first time McMillan called him for help, Mulroney was on-side.

The conspiracy had fine moments; for example, the May 14 unanimous resolution in the House of Commons that the area be saved. It was a triumph of political telepathy as a brilliant idea formed a complete circuit from Jim Fulton to Bill Blaikie to Tom McMillan, who said that the government party certainly had no objection to the "inspired suggestion" from the Honourable Member for Winnipeg–Birds Hill that Fulton's motion be deemed to have been passed unanimously. Brian Tobin rose to throw the support of the Liberal party behind the idea. The circuit was complete with Fraser, who looked out over the empty benches of the House in morning session and ruled judiciously. The House can do anything where the will is unanimous to do so. He gave it the "going . . . going . . . gone" approach of an auction while we held our breath that those who would vehemently object to such parliamentary sleight of hand were asleep elsewhere.

And so it came to pass that a non-votable Opposition motion from a member of the New Democratic Party was unanimously adopted by the Canadian House of Commons. For nearly the full day of House business those vaulted ceilings and stained-glass windows were transformed into towering sitka spruce, cedars, totem poles, and green, green forest, moss, and ferns. Members spoke of the eagles' cry, and of the powerful beauty and pride of the Haida Nation. And it spoke with one voice. Miles Richardson, President of the Council of the Haida Nation, said that the Great Spirit had hovered over Parliament Hill that day. He was right.

You want political realities? You get what you expect. Expect Tories to be a bunch of environment-abusing, corporate leeches and you'll get that back. Try expecting people to be people, expect people to care about their children, to want a healthy planet, and you get *that* back. If South Moresby taught me anything, it was to leave no stone unturned. Constantly try to expand your network by adding new contacts. Find the hundredth monkey.

However, expecting is not enough in itself. An issue needs public awareness and public pressure as surely as a seedling needs water and light. Letter-writing campaigns *are* effective. It didn't hurt that the Minister received more letters on South Moresby than on any other single issue — more than on acid rain, the Great Lakes, or PCBs.

The letters were largely generated by David Suzuki's CBC program about South Moresby on "The Nature of Things." Although the potential of the media is tremendous, as a segment of society, they are sound asleep. The public is worried. Many want to help solve our environmental problems, but they need tools. And information is the most empowering tool there is. We desperately need more television, radio, magazine, and newspaper coverage of the in-depth variety. For the most part, however, that type of coverage is reserved for political or economic issues. Meech Lake. Free Trade. Brian's shoes. Turner's kitchen cabinets. The day's headlines are a competition of body counts from sudden deaths as a result of accidents, battles, or natural disasters. The only body counts that don't count are from starvation, sickness, and chronic misery. Those events are only "news" if the enormity of it staggers the imagination. The growing deserts, the poisoned seas, the extinction of species, the stripping of the planet's forests, all go on from day to day, threatening our future, diminishing our present, but it's just not "news."

The news media didn't make South Moresby a national issue. The activists did, by cultivating media contacts through personal visits, providing background material, educating and giving advance notice of events that could be covered.

The pivotal event — the single news story that made South Moresby a national issue — was the Haida blockade of the logging road on Lyell Island in November 1985 and the arrests of seventy-two Haida men and women. Of course, the Haida Nation had been central to the fight to save South Moresby since its inception. Guujaaw, then known as Gary Edenshaw, was a co-founder with Thom Henley of the Islands Protection Society in 1974. And it was the opposition of the Skidegate Band Council in that same year that was largely responsible for the decision of the provincial government to deny logging permits on Burnaby Island — south of Lyell — absolutely critical if the wilderness proposal was to succeed. The alliance of the Haida and non-native environmentalists always provided a source of derision to their opponents. People would try to tell Tom McMillan that these dumb environmentalists were just being used by the Haida, who would log the area anyway. When that failed, they'd try it the other way around. The Haida were the dupes of environmentalists who were using them to get press coverage. Of course, the truth was emphatically to the contrary.

So it was a natural progression of commitment that led the Haida to their base camp at Sedgewick Bay on Lyell Island. They were prepared for a long blockade. Bunkhouses had been built, food stored. The young men and women were ready to be arrested if it came to that. They would block the road and stop the logging trucks from moving on to cut any more of Lyell's trees. But the first three to be arrested weren't young. They were the Haida elders, respected and loved by the younger generation. They insisted on being the first to face arrest. Long into the night, open discussion and debate went on, as young people tearfully pleaded with their elders not to risk jail. But the elders prevailed. The first three to be led away by the RCMP were Ethel Jones, Ada Yovanovitch, and Watson Price, Chief of his clan and in his eighties when he blocked the logging road.

How do you get your message to politicians? The media, sure. But better yet, and at the same time, try to meet the politician in person. Try to be a friend. And if you can't see politicians, try to be a friend of the people around him.

Of course, there are different styles. We need both the friendly persuasion type and the two-by-four threat. When Vander Zalm had broken off negotiations, public pressure at the provincial level was critically needed. John Broadhead and others managed to raise $15,000 overnight to purchase a full-page ad in the *Vancouver Sun*, urging the premier to go back to the bargaining table. The ad, with a beautiful photo of Windy Bay and the heading "For Our Children's Children," provided the phone and telex numbers for the premier's office. And in case anyone missed the phone number in the paper, Tara Cullis, David Suzuki's wife, had managed to raise the money to hire a small plane to fly over Vancouver's crowded Sunday-afternoon beaches with a banner, "Save S. Moresby — Ph. VdZalm" with the number. It was estimated that 30,000 people responded and jammed the government lines. However, the ad hadn't painted Vander Zalm into a corner. Broadhead had written it carefully, crediting the premier with good, effective bargaining, with having succeeded in getting a very favourable offer out of the federal government. "It will be to your everlasting credit," he wrote, "to accept the federal offer and save South Moresby for our children." Colleen McCrory was equally right in saying on "As It Happens," "Vander Zalm is holding a gun to the heads of the people of Canada." But Colleen is a straight shooter. John is a strategist. We needed both.

People have asked what influenced the federal government to put $106 million forward to save South Moresby. Did we pay too much? In fact, money was the easiest part of putting together the South Moresby National Park Agreement. What was difficult was getting Lyell Island included in the park. And for that, we will always owe Tom McMillan a great debt.

I watched the Minister's own senior bureaucrats exert every pressure within their power to get the Minister to cave in and accept a park agreement with B.C. on the basis of inadequate boundaries. A deal with B.C. with those reduced boundaries could have been concluded in the fall of 1986. The bureaucrats tried everything — even guilt trips:

"Mr. Minister, if you keep insisting on including Lyell Island (which by the way, Sir, does not add a thing from the viewpoint of national park values) — if you keep insisting, we could lose the whole thing. It will be your fault when Burnaby Island and the rest of the area we could save gets logged."

And sometimes, McMillan would look as if it was more than he could bear. Sometimes it was more than I could bear, and I'd start to think that it *was* acceptable to log some, not all of it. However, the certainty and support of the South Moresby activists kept McMillan's resolve firm. So we just held on tight, not capitulating, and waiting for a miracle. When that miracle happened, when Vander Zalm agreed to a park with the same boundary that Thom and Guujaaw had drawn, well, the money just wasn't a problem. Governments are used to bargaining over money. Bargaining over principle, bargaining to save Windy Bay, the heart of the proposal and the spiritual heart of the movement, *that* was fraught with risks.

That's another lesson South Moresby has taught me: hang on and wait for the miracle. Once you sell out or cave in, the miracle won't come. The chain of events that led to saving Lyell Island would have been impossible to predict. And no rational person would have postulated that such a chain of events was possible. If we had counted on what was possible, we would have given up.

After months of stalemate — the feds holding out for more of Lyell, the province standing firm on the reduced boundaries — British Columbia came up with a new proposal. Although Bruce Strachan was the Minister of the Environment at the time, the proposal had all the earmarks of B.C.'s former Environment minister, Stephen Rogers. At the April 8 negotiating session in Victoria, Bruce Strachan unveiled to Tom McMillan B.C.'s new proposal on boundaries. McMillan thought he had jet-lag, or maybe that Strachan had brought the wrong maps. B.C.'s map had coloured in for the park with bright fluorescent highlighter, *all* of Lyell. *All* of it!

Then Strachan moved on to describe the rest of the deal — $200 million in trust for B.C., and the federal government would maintain logging operations within the park at current levels for ten years. Furthermore, the federal government would compensate the logging companies, plus a few other conditions, all adding up to more money than anyone had ever contemplated. The killer was that idea of logging in a national park, managed by the federal government.

For a month, we stalled, trying to figure out how to respond to their offer. It was a trap. B.C. wanted to be able to say, "Well, we offered the federal government all of the area. But they turned us down. They wouldn't pay for it."

In the meantime, there was a moratorium on logging, and B.C. was saying that unless the federal government gave its blessing to logging one of three possible cutting blocks on Lyell Island, they'd end the moratorium and log anyway. The threat was that they would start logging, unless logging was authorized!

After a month of back and forth, we were prepared to admit publicly that negotiations had broken down. On May 12, Tom went to Senator Lowell Murray and Deputy Prime Minister Don Mazankowski to get their approval for a press release that would lay out the federal and provincial positions and ask B.C. to keep negotiating. It was the only tactic we could think of to spring B.C.'s trap. These were not ordinary times in Ottawa, though. Usually, a minister doesn't check press releases with senior cabinet members, but the word was out: Don't rock the boat with the provinces in the critical lead-up to the constitutional talks planned for early June — what's now known as Meech Lake. Mazankowski and Murray said there was no way we could issue a press release that would infuriate a province at a time like this. Instead, Mazankowski agreed to help by making a direct appeal to Vander Zalm.

Late that evening, McMillan and the deputy prime minister phoned B.C.'s premier. McMillan convinced Vander Zalm of the tremendous appeal of the area to tourists — using all the stock phrases he'd learned as Tourism minister. Vander Zalm suddenly became the only person on his cabinet who liked the idea of a park. And then he asked, "Well, do we agree on *anything*?" Tom whispered to Mazankowski, who then told Vander Zalm, "Yes, we like your boundaries from the April 8 offer."

That was the miracle. After that, although nothing was easy, and we nearly lost it half a dozen times, the hard part was over. Public pressure mounted. B.C. announced negotiations had broken down, and Knowlton Nash dutifully reported on the "CBC National News" that there would be no park at South Moresby. The stage was set for the prime minister to save the day, which he did.

In the time it took to save South Moresby, representing less than 0.1 per cent of British Columbia's forests, 25 per cent of the world's forests were logged. We have a long way to go and many hard fights ahead of us, if we are to have any future at all.

Saving wilderness, stopping the flow of toxic chemicals into our food, our bodies, our children; healing the scars of planetary abuse; reversing the trends of climate change, ozone destruction, the despoiling of our oceans and ourselves — it won't be easy. But we must have a vision. Each of us has one, deep inside, somewhere — of a healthy planet. A safe world. For purposes of political shorthand we have the report of the World Commission on Environment and Development, *Our Common Future*. An unprecedented level of consensus is beginning to emerge in Canada, a gelling of agreement among environmentalists, industry, and governments, that there is something to all this "sustainable development" stuff, even if we're not quite sure what it is.

Our generation has to accomplish all this. The first step is to believe we can. The rest will be a miracle.

GEORGES ERASMUS

A Native Viewpoint

To understand the native or indigenous point of view on conservation or environmental matters, one must understand our history, our cultures, and the way we see our relationship with nature.

Can I, as a Dene, a citizen of an indigenous nation, express it any better than one of our forefathers, Chief Seattle, did in 1852 in a response to the U.S. government, which wanted to buy his nation's land? He said:

Every part of this earth is sacred to my people. Every shining pine needle, every sandy shore, every mist in the dark woods, every meadow, every humming insect. . . . We know the sap which courses through the trees as we know the blood that courses through our veins. We are part of the earth and it is part of us. The perfumed flowers are our sisters. The bear, the deer, the great eagle, these are our brothers. The rocky crests, the juices in the meadow, the body heat of the pony, and man, all belong to the same family.

The shining water that moves in the streams and rivers is not just water, but the blood of our ancestors. . . . Each ghostly reflection in the clear waters of the lakes tells of events and memories in the life of my people. The water's murmur is the voice of my father's father.

The rivers are our brothers. They quench our thirst. They carry our canoes and feed our children. So you must give to the rivers the kindness you would give my brother.

. . . So if we sell you our land, you must keep it apart and sacred as a place where man can go to taste the wind that is sweetened by the meadow flowers.

We love this earth as a newborn loves its mother's heartbeat. So, if we sell you our land, love it as we have loved it. Care for it as we have cared for it. Hold in your mind the memory of the land as it is when you receive it. Preserve the land for all children and love it, as God loves us all.

Chief Seattle captured in those words the reverence that we have for nature and the earth. To us, on these continents now known as the Americas, all the land was virtually a conservation area — one large "park" if you can imagine it that way — and that was how our ancestors wanted it maintained.

In Chief Seattle's day, the colonial governments in the Americas still correctly dealt with the indigenous peoples on a nation-to-nation basis. This was consistent with the Royal Proclamation of 1763, which had laid down the broad guidelines under which the Europeans could acquire land from us by treaties. As far as we are concerned, we were self-governing peoples or nations; we were the caretakers of our lands, which were never meant to be "sold" in the way the Europeans understood the term. The treaties are agreements between us and the Europeans to share the land and the responsibilities that go with taking care of it. The treaties are evidence of our nationhood and a faculty of our self-determination; they were never meant to yield our nationhood to any other nation, nor to yield our original stewardship or "title" to our lands to any other nation.

Today, the whole matter of environmental preservation or conservation of lands and waters in several areas of Canada is bound up with the thorny issues of treaty rights, aboriginal title and land claims. In addition, there is the difference in cultural points of view between indigenous and non-indigenous peoples: the former regard the "wilderness" as an integral component of our Mother Earth with which we must live in harmony, while the latter see the wilderness as a recreational and, perhaps, luxurious aspect of their lives.

In general, the non-native environmental movement has been relatively sympathetic to our major concerns regarding the protection of natural areas and "wilderness." Nevertheless, one must also accept that reserving lands for legal designations, such as a national park, may compromise our aspirations. This is not to say that the aboriginal peoples are against the conservation or environmental movement, or the creation of national parks, but there must be some minimum conditions if conservation lands and waters are to appeal to us.

It is unnecessary for me to stress that the indigenous peoples have a keen interest in preserving areas as close as possible to their original state. Accordingly, we would frequently want to support the creation of conservation lands or waters to achieve that purpose. Conservation has always been integral to the survival of indigenous peoples. Without renewable resources to harvest, we lose both our livelihood and our way of life. Aboriginal communities have everything to gain from conservation — and much to offer: a profound and detailed knowledge of species and ecosystems, ways of sharing and managing resources that have stood the test of time, and ethics that reconcile subsistence and co-existence. We recognize that people are an integral part of nature, and express spiritual bonds with other species, including those we harvest.

Conservation and development-policy-making and -planning often seem to assume that we, the aboriginal peoples, have only two options for the future: to return to our ancient way of life or to abandon subsistence altogether and become assimilated into the dominant society. Neither option is reasonable. We should have a third option: to modify our subsistence way of life, combining the old and the new in ways that maintain and enhance our identity while allowing our society and economy to evolve. As original conservationists, we now aim to combine development and conservation, and to put into practice the concept of equitable, culturally appropriate, sustainable development. As such, the goal of the World Conservation Strategy is our goal too.

There could be situations where a modern land-claim treaty is being negotiated and it is agreed that a certain percentage of land area is to be retained under native ownership. For example, under the agreement-in-principle signed by the prime minister and the Dene in September 1988, the Dene will preserve about 16 per cent of their traditional homeland under their direct ownership. In such situations, the native people concerned might well wish to create conservation lands or parks outside of their lands in order to expand their area of influence to protect the lands and waters under their immediate control.

Unfortunately, our experience with conservation lands and waters, or parks, has been discouraging. So far, in many cases when parks have been created, the federal government has made solemn promises that our lifestyles and cultures would be allowed to continue without restriction. Yet, once regulations come into effect, we find ourselves relegated to the level of other users who do not possess aboriginal or treaty rights. Rules and regulations are brought into being that not only jeopardize our traditional ways of life but also restrict or purport to eliminate our legal rights.

All of a sudden we are told that we may no longer take certain plants for medicines or foods. We are told we may no longer pitch tents in certain places in which we had gathered for generations. Or, we may no longer start fires. Or, we may no longer carry firearms . . .

Our aboriginal rights, and even our treaty rights expressed in writing, are either totally or partially ignored or overridden in the name of conservation or the public interest when we have every right, in terms of history, tradition, law, and interest, to practise our lifestyles and cultures while preserving nature and harmonizing with it. In the matter of conservation and environmental protection, the native peoples stand second to none. Environmentalists should recognize that we, the aboriginal peoples, are their best allies in the task of conservation.

As the World Commission on Environment and Development recognized in its 1987 report, *Our Common Future*, indigenous peoples "are the repositories of vast accumulations of traditional knowledge." Referring to isolated communities of indigenous peoples, the report said, "Their disappearance is a loss for the larger society, which could learn a great deal from their traditional skills in sustainably managing very complex ecological systems."

ACCEPTABLE GENERAL CONDITIONS

In my view as an indigenous leader, therefore, there are several ways in which conservation could "make sense" and be acceptable to Canada's aboriginal peoples.

First, in areas where land title has not been dealt with, the right of the indigenous title and self-government must be constitutionally recognized when conservation spaces or parks are being proposed.

Second, in areas where there are treaties, including harvesting rights and continuing rights to self-government, there must be joint management of conservation spaces by aboriginal peoples and non-natives.

Third, aboriginal and treaty rights of native peoples have to be respected in any conservation space or park. Laws and regulations that have an adverse effect on the legitimate exercise of an aboriginal or treaty right must be repealed. Policies and practices aimed at subverting aboriginal or treaty rights must be brought to an end.

Fourth, native people must have a large measure of control over decisions affecting the creation, design, and management of conservation spaces and parks.

Fifth, hiring practices in conservation areas must reflect a far greater acknowledgement of the native contribution, experience, and potential in contributing to conservation.

Let us examine the creation of parks. A factor of major importance would be the prior recognition by governments of legitimate control and management by the aboriginal peoples concerned if aboriginal title land is involved. Under the existing system, the federal government exercises total control. In some cases an "advisory" body may be established, but the native peoples are regarded as mere users of some of the wildlife. This view is inadequate. The parks authorities decide the extent of the use of the wildlife and the conditions under which hunting, trapping, or fishing will take place. The result is that we are in the situation of being virtual beggars in our own traditional lands and territories.

Look at the situation in Wood Buffalo Park, which straddles the Alberta/Northwest Territories border. There, the aboriginal peoples can never be certain that they will be granted annual hunting and fishing licences. A number of variables are involved, including the public interest, which makes an ancient way of life subject to the apparent modern-day whims of an alien culture, all in the name of conservation.

The firm view of the aboriginal leadership is that we would be much more inclined to support conservation policies and practices, including parks, if our basic rights were first legally recognized and respected.

PRINCIPLES AND ARRANGEMENTS

Why is it necessary for the federal government to eradicate aboriginal title in order to establish a park? Why, instead, should there not be a policy that included the recognition of aboriginal title and the settlement of outstanding claims in which conservation would be an integral component? Modern treaties with aboriginal peoples could contain a system for periodic review of conditions governing the conservation areas. On the other hand, what kind of stability can there be when the federal government seeks to create conservation lands and waters in unsettled areas that are still under native land claims?

Federal and provincial governments should seek joint-management schemes with us for conservation lands and waters. I lay emphasis on the word "joint" because the roles of the aboriginal peoples should be no less than those of the other two levels of government. Indeed, there are places in Canada where ours should be the senior role in conservation policies and management. These are areas over which the aboriginal first nations have never surrendered our aboriginal title in our traditional lands. At least three such major areas come to mind: British Columbia, the Yukon, and the Northwest Territories.

In the Queen Charlotte Islands of British Columbia the Haida people have not relinquished their aboriginal title. They are prepared to consider a conservation park under definite conditions, two of which are that their title to their own traditional territory as well as their right to self-government over that territory be legally recognized. The same situation obtains in the Yukon and the Northwest Territories. Had these principles been observed from the outset, conservation lands and waters would have enjoyed native support and co-operation.

As well as the underpinnings of title and self-government in traditional areas, there are other important principles that should govern conservation arrangements. Aboriginal peoples have to be assured of a continued ability to practise their traditional economies — to hunt, to trap, to fish. Problems like those of the Micmac Nation in Nova Scotia ought never to arise. There a treaty executed in 1752 recognizing the hunting rights of these aboriginal people was upheld by the Supreme Court of Canada. Yet they are denied the right to hunt by the provincial government in the name of conservation.

Management of conservation areas ought to be in the hands of the aboriginal peoples, with sufficient financial resources to enable them to undertake relevant research and studies to ensure that the habitat is always maintained and that the wildlife populations remain strong and productive. The more control and management there is in the hands of native people, the greater the likelihood that wildlife will remain strong and healthy.

NATIVE AND NON-NATIVE CO-OPERATION

Clearly then, as users of "wilderness" lands and waters, we have a high interest in the preservation of wildlife when our livelihood is at stake. But that is not to deny the substantial interest by the non-native elements of the population or the possibility of an alliance between native and non-native interests.

It must equally be acknowledged, however, that the native and non-native approaches are based on widely different concepts of the so-called wilderness. To non-natives generally, the human being or the human community is not a natural part of the ecosystem. The human species is elevated to a sophisticated level that is above wildlife. Therefore, "conservation" seems to mean "nature without humankind." To a native person that approach to the relationship between humankind and the "wilderness" and wildlife is inadequate. Traditional communities and early societies have demonstrated that it is possible for human societies to evolve with a detailed knowledge of their terrain, their geography, and the wildlife in their environment.

The non-native view of the "wilderness" is typified in their concept of game management. Whereas the native manages the game, the non-native manages human access to the game. And this seems to be a losing battle against the encroachments of mega-projects and corporations. On the other hand, while always attempting to manage the wildlife, aboriginal people are in the vanguard of those defending the "wilderness" as an integral part of our cultural milieu. Not only are we fighting the onslaughts of mega-projects and corporate-development aspirations, but also the urban expansions of non-native societies and their attendant pollutants.

It is interesting that there is probably no native language anywhere in the world that contains the term "wilderness." To the non-native, it connotes "a large desolate area"; to the native person it is an extension of his or her world and culture. The mountains of British Columbia, the plains of the Midwest, the "barren" lands of Denendeh or the High Arctic, the forests of the Maritime regions — these all are essential elements in the native habitat and part of our Mother Earth — certainly not a "wilderness."

The "wilderness" concept must surely have evolved as a contrast with urban settings. We are told that the whole "progress" of humankind stemmed from the discovery of farming contemporaneously with the development of cities. As early as 5500 years ago, the Sumerians in the Middle East became the first to build and live in cities. And gradually humankind began to divorce itself from what came to be known as the "wilderness."

Fortunately, people are becoming increasingly aware of the dangers posed by the appalling spectacles of sprawling metropolitan and industrial complexes, together with the disappearance of forests, lakes, and wildlife. That is gratifying to native peoples. What is at stake is much more than our native livelihood; it is the very survival of our indigenous cultures and societies, and the survival of the planet.

There is, therefore, a need for an alliance between the First Nations and others who, for whatever reason, care enough for the "wilderness" to safeguard those areas for the benefit of all our succeeding generations on this planet, which we share.

A STEP IN THE RIGHT DIRECTION

The approach that has been adopted in South Moresby in the Queen Charlotte Islands seems to be a minor step in the right direction in the creation of a conservation park. That approach demonstrated some positive and some negative aspects.

On the positive side, it was gratifying for the Haida people that a park was, at last, going to be created. The Minister of the Environment did stress that the Haida would have a "major role," and not merely a "symbolic" one, in the management and planning of the park. In that way, that ancient nation would continue to protect the unique and fragile ecosystem of their traditional home-lands. Now it remains to be seen how "major" the Haida role will be.

On the negative side, the park was created in an atmosphere of tremendous hostility between the federal government and the provincial government of Brit-ish Columbia. There was no recognition of the title of the Haida Nation and, in fact, the Haida were excluded from the federal-provincial negotiations. To com-pound matters, the federal moneys went to the provincial government rather than to the Haida people.

SIGNPOSTS TOWARDS THE CREATION OF SPECIAL CONSERVATION LANDS AND WATERS

In view of what I have said earlier, there are certain definite guidelines that are worth repeating for the satisfactory establishment of conservation lands and waters in areas where native peoples have a legal as well as a cultural interest:

First, we must be involved, depending on the continuing rights that we have in the area. Although a proper land surrender may have occurred, certain ab-original or treaty rights may still be in existence. For example, there might be unhindered rights to fish, hunt, and trap, "as formerly" recognized in a valid existing treaty executed between the Crown and the First Nation concerned. Again, whether or not a proper land surrender occurred, undoubtedly our tra-ditional pursuits are rights that have been recognized by law. Also, if a change is envisaged in the land status, from unoccupied Crown land to a conservation parkland, our traditional rights for access to game must be preserved and respected.

Second, even in those situations where surrendered land is involved, native peoples must have, as a minimum, a direct partnership role in the management scheme. Unless we are directly involved from the beginning and throughout, we find that our rights are undermined over a period of time.

Third, care must be taken to ensure that the wildlife is not adversely affected by the roads and other facilities that are built to accommodate the public and their access to the conservation lands and waters. Overdevelopment can drive away the animal wildlife and may eventually endanger species. Accordingly, there is a necessity to involve those who best know the terrain and the wildlife — the native peoples. We must be involved in the design of the conservation areas and of public access and facilities.

There are abundant opportunities for native personnel to play key roles in preserving wildlife, roles ranging from managers through game wardens to park rangers. We have the experience, the skills, and the interest required.

With those major signposts in mind, native and non-native peoples alike should go a long way towards ensuring the security of Canada's open spaces and natural wildlife for all of us who share the riches of this vast land and wish to preserve it for future generations.

STEWART HILTS

Private Stewardship

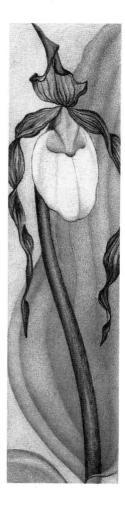

The development of national parks has been one of the great gifts of the conservation movement to the world. This book is a statement of the importance of continuing this work in the most innovative ways imaginable, as we struggle to protect the world's great wild places before they are lost forever. But it is also time to supplement the traditional theme of parks and wilderness protection with a new idea — that of private stewardship.

There are numerous reasons for broadening our perspectives to include the private landowner and other members of the private sector. These range from the lack of financial resources to protect all natural areas as parks, through the need to protect not only regionally and locally significant ecological sites, but the entire rural landscape — most of which is owned privately.

We need to move beyond the success of government-established parks, with their unique features and definite boundaries, to recognize the role that private organizations can play in conserving small sites in partnership with landowners practising sustainable development in the countryside as a whole. In other words, we need to use the symbol and example of our national parks as a catalyst to promote good stewardship of the rest of our landscape, and the development of what Aldo Leopold called a "land ethic" in society.

WHY PRIVATE STEWARDSHIP?

Traditionally, provincial and national parks have protected unique and beautiful landscapes, or popular recreation resources. They have also been owned and managed directly by public agencies, i.e., the government. However, as an approach to protecting the world's natural heritage, they are like icing on the cake — the most spectacular highlights and bright spots. We also need to pay attention to the cake itself — the rest of the landscape.

Basic scientific knowledge has advanced immeasurably over the past two decades, as we have come to understand the species diversity that makes up our natural heritage. One of the three basic principles of the World Conservation

Strategy is the preservation of genetic diversity. Even within species we now recognize that there is a range of genetic variation, which means that saving one population of each rare species will not usually be enough. In fact, we do not even have accurate estimates of the number of species in the world, especially in groups such as insects, where new species are routinely discovered in such developed areas as Southern Ontario. And it has been forecast that between 15 and 20 per cent of all species will march into extinction in the next twenty years, whether or not they are known.

The point is that our parks only capture a fraction of the globe's biological diversity. To use an analogy from the World Conservation Strategy, they are like the tip of a conservation iceberg. Beneath the well-known provincial and national parks are innumerable local and regional ecological sites protected as conservation areas, municipal and regional parks, private nature reserves, and so on. Beneath these is the rural landscape itself, most of it in private ownership. It is here that the bulk of our natural heritage must be conserved.

Phil Hoose put the concept another way in the title of his book, *Building an Ark*. Addressing U.S. nature-conservancy programs, which have traditionally relied on acquisition of natural areas, he pointed out that for several reasons we need a more varied tool-kit. Many landowners have no wish to sell. There is rarely enough money to match priorities. And in some areas, there is growing opposition to further public land acquisition. "The government" is not always welcome. We need, therefore, "a whole system of tools to protect land" — many of which leave the land in private ownership.

In a cynical mood, one could easily predict that our best parks will ultimately be left as "islands of green" in the midst of a human-dominated, largely degraded landscape. By then they will be subject to such overwhelming pressure that the parks themselves will be largely degraded as well. The alternative is to employ our parks as the symbol, the positive inspiration, for better management of the 95 per cent of our land that is outside parks. The careful management into which we put so much effort *inside* our parks can provide an example for good private stewardship by landowners *outside* parks.

In various practical ways, this vision has already been recognized. It is apparent in the concept of the biosphere reserve, which reaches out beyond the protected core area (usually in a national park or equivalent), to link the lands of surrounding landowners and agencies in a "zone of co-operation." It is also apparent in the multitude of provincial programs to protect ecological areas, environmentally sensitive areas, special places, areas of natural and scientific interest, wetlands, and other sites. The terminology may vary, but there is now extensive recognition that we need a wide variety of measures to conserve our natural heritage.

CHANGING PARADIGMS
In my view, this growing recognition of the need for a "landscape," or "private-stewardship" approach to conservation reflects a fundamental shift in our thinking — a new paradigm for conservation. It is a broader, expanded view.

One change in this paradigm is simply recognition that government finances, critical as they are, will never be enough. Although the term "privatization" does not always ring well in our ears, neither does the idea that big government can take care of every problem by simply spending more of our tax dollars. Financial constraints are real and will likely continue.

In the face of this, we have already succeeded in stretching available financial resources in many innovative ways. The private sector has contributed immense resources and energy to conservation projects. In fact, I would venture that the private, non-profit sector is now driving the conservation movement in Canada.

For at least a decade or two, ideas for achieving conservation objectives without resorting to public acquisition have been discussed. In recent years, these have become official policy in many jurisdictions. But old ways die hard in agencies that have successfully built their programs on public ownership and management of land. There is a real need today to go beyond thinking about innovative private-stewardship tools such as easements, management agreements, and incentives, to actually *implementing* such alternatives — not to replace government acquisition, but to complement it.

Even more fundamental is the need to change our view of the role of private landowners. Unfortunately, there has been a tendency to see landowners as unsympathetic to environmental concerns. Legislation has often been justified by the need to balance private greed with the public good. The controls needed to guard against extreme examples of land abuse have tended to paint all landowners with the same brush.

They do not deserve it.

I well remember one incident that drove this home for me. It occurred in a university graduate class, which I teach, where students were debating what type of legislation was needed to "force" farmers to practise good land stewardship. The discussion was painting the average landowner in a pretty negative light. Finally, one quiet student, herself from a farm, leapt out of her chair, thumped her fist on the table, and said, "No! Farmers are just not like that!"

I agreed with her intuitively then. And now, after five years of directing a landowner-contact program that has involved visits with nearly a thousand rural landowners, I am convinced more than ever that she was right.

We err in the wrong direction if we design our systems to control a few individuals who are at the extreme, for in so doing we destroy the motivation of the great majority. Most landowners in rural areas have a very real and personal attachment to their land. This is a positive starting-point that can be used to build a broader acceptance of conservation goals, if we recognize the immense contribution that thousands of such individuals can make.

NON-GOVERNMENT ORGANIZATIONS AND STEWARDSHIP

One of the most direct and obvious forms of private-sector stewardship that has developed in Canada during the past two decades is the purchase of land as nature reserves by private, non-government organizations. It is a very tangible contribution to conserving our natural heritage, with the potential for tremendous expansion.

In Ontario, the Federation of Ontario Naturalists and the Bruce Trail Association are notable leaders in this field. The federation acquired its first nature reserve in the early 1960s. A fund-raising campaign entitled the "Battle of the Bulldozer" saved the well-known Dorcas Bay Nature Reserve on the Bruce Peninsula, one of the best places in the world to see the rare dwarf lake iris and the ram's head lady-slipper, both indigenous to the Great Lakes region. Other sites were purchased and donated. Now the federation owns and manages a system of ten nature reserves, scattered across the province from Sault Ste. Marie to Lake Erie, from Ottawa to Pelee Island.

The driving force behind this work, as is typical in many non-government organizations, has been a small group of dedicated volunteers who have served on the federation's Nature Reserves Committee. These individuals have inspected properties, negotiated purchases, raised funds, and volunteered their weekends to work on management projects — private stewardship in action!

Not only has the federation purchased its own nature reserves, it has actively encouraged agencies to protect other sites, and in several cases donated the funds to catalyze such purchases. The Bruce Trail Association has similarly donated funds to assist agencies, usually conservation authorities, with the acquisition of natural areas. It has directly purchased several hundred hectares of land through which the volunteer-built trail passes, largely on the basis of unwritten "handshake" agreements with landowners.

Spring wildflowers grace this gentle New Brunswick landscape, a section of the Saint John River valley that is being protected by the photographer through an endowment to the Nature Conservancy of Canada.   CREDIT: FREEMAN PATTERSON.

The same story can be repeated in varying ways across Canada. In Prince Edward Island, the Island Nature Trust has developed an active natural-areas program, and now owns five properties. At the opposite end of the country, the Nature Trust of British Columbia has acquired more than 7100 hectares of land to protect natural heritage values and wildlife habitat.

Perhaps most successful has been the Saskatchewan Wildlife Federation, which administers programs protecting over 9300 hectares of wildlife habitat through its Saskatchewan Habitat Trust. In this province, a unique level of co-operation has been reached between anglers, hunters, and naturalists to enable this success. In fact, they claim to have the largest per-capita participation of any sportsmen's organization in the world, and exert considerable influence over the protection of an additional 28,700 hectares through their landowner-agreement programs. The Manitoba Wildlife Federation operates a parallel Manitoba Habitat Trust, protecting some 8000 hectares through various programs.

In addition to these major provincial groups are many smaller, local ones. Several local naturalists' clubs in Ontario have raised money and purchased nature reserves. Local sportsmen's groups have done so as well. In New Brunswick and Alberta new organizations are currently being formed to expand this effort.

Operating at the national level are several other key non-government organizations that contribute immensely to the success of the provincial groups. Notable are the Nature Conservancy of Canada and the more recently established Wildlife Habitat Canada. In hundreds of cases, funds provided by the Nature Conservancy have been critical to land purchases. Wildlife Habitat Canada is now playing a similar role, though it emphasizes direct private-stewardship programs rather than acquisition projects.

Much has been accomplished. But if we consider the success of similar groups operating in the British Isles and the United States, it appears that we have only begun to tap the potential. Groups such as the National Trust in Britain and the U.S. Nature Conservancy have for decades been buying land as nature reserves, as have many other organizations in these countries. If we can achieve a higher level of involvement by the average citizen, we might vastly expand such stewardship programs in Canada.

PRIVATE STEWARDSHIP AND INDIVIDUAL LANDOWNERS

The most innovative story of private stewardship in Canada today is the success several groups are having in negotiating directly with private landowners. As the Wildlife Habitat Canada report *Wildlife Conservation on Private Lands* documents, there are at least eight such private-stewardship programs now underway, with more being negotiated annually.

Some of these projects have copied the work of the U.S. Nature Conservancy in actively negotiating stewardship agreements, either written or oral, with individual landowners of identified natural-heritage sites. Others have built on past projects in the wildlife area, particularly in the midwestern states and in the innovative Red Deer County project in Alberta undertaken in 1978–80. These projects use leases as a prime tool.

The object in all of these is to arrange some form of protective conservation agreement with landowners, and to leave the natural habitat itself in private ownership. What is most surprising about these projects is the success they are having in achieving such landowner agreements. With only preliminary results in from three of these programs, over 11,000 hectares are now covered by some form of voluntary private stewardship agreement with nearly 500 landowners. Continuing results from these projects, and from others ranging from the WWF's Operation Burrowing Owl project on the prairies through Manitoba's HELP (Habitat Enhancement Land-Use Program), to Prince Edward Island's Co-operative Watershed Management Project, will reveal the potential that private stewardship can play in conserving Canada's rural landscape.

Take a look at two examples:

In Ontario, the Nature Heritage Stewardship Program has been running for five years. It started cautiously in 1983–84, with approaches to about 150 owners of natural areas between Windsor and Ottawa. Staff hired during the summer visited and interviewed landowners to ascertain their attitude towards protecting the natural values of the land they owned. While much nervousness was expressed over such a direct approach, the results were very positive. Only a few landowners refused such a visit, while the majority were clearly interested and supportive.

Over the following two summers, 29 sites identified under the Carolinian Canada project of the Nature Conservancy and World Wildlife Fund were targeted. During the same time, a Natural Heritage Stewardship Award plaque was designed and approved by the province, which would require an explicit oral conservation agreement with landowners before it was awarded. Asked directly about making such a stewardship agreement, more than 300 of 539 landowners contacted expressed interest.

In 1987, the real test finally came as these 300 landowners were revisited in an attempt to reach handshake agreements. Over 275 said yes! As a result, 3400 hectares came under this kind of private stewardship — representing 40 per cent of all private landowners and 40 per cent of the privately owned land within all the targeted sites. This total has now climbed to over 4000 hectares as landowner contact continues.

A second project was undertaken in the spring of 1988 in 11 sites along the Niagara Escarpment. Here results were even more positive: 57 per cent of landowners contacted (85) agreed to the terms of an oral stewardship agreement, and another 24 per cent (35) expressed clear positive personal commitment to conservation.

These results are for landowner-contact programs that offer no direct financial incentive, and are based on establishing a relationship of trust between the contact person and the landowner.

A critical complementary incentive has recently been introduced by the Ontario government, a Natural Heritage Tax Rebate for landowners of identified provincially significant areas of natural and scientific interest, wetlands, and some other sites. Parallel to existing rebates on privately managed forest land and agricultural land, this tax rebate will further encourage landowners to conserve natural areas. A written agreement to do so will be required for eligibility.

The Prairie Pot-hole Project in Saskatchewan provides another example of private-stewardship projects. Based in the municipality of Antler in southeastern Saskatchewan, it lies in the heart of pot-hole country — the landscape dotted with small wetlands that produce the majority of North America's duck population every year. Here the objective is specifically to protect waterfowl habitat. A series of options has been designed based on the ecological requirements of waterfowl and the realistic preferences of local farmers. These range from simply providing artificial nesting structures in small wetlands, to leasing good agricultural land for dense-nesting cover plots. The most successful of the alternatives has been the lease (technically a licence) of natural habitats, including pot-holes themselves, at an average annual cost of $10.50 per hectare.

The prairie project, similar to those in Alberta and Manitoba, differs from Ontario's Natural Heritage Stewardship Program in several ways. It primarily employs written agreements of five to ten years' duration, although they have a friendly ninety-day cancellation clause. The prairie program actually makes payment to farmers to achieve the agreements, whereas Ontario's program is voluntary and oral. These different approaches perhaps reflect the varying landownership patterns. The prairie projects entail virtually 100 per cent direct farmer ownership. In Ontario, more than half the landowners involved are rural non-farm residents.

Certain common themes are apparent in both programs, however. Stewardship agreements and landowner involvement are, in both cases, strictly voluntary. Emphasis is placed on flexibility and direct personal contact. Both programs recognize the educational value of contact as probably the greatest long-term benefit. Both strive for a program that is fair, equitable, easy to operate, and efficient, but above all acceptable to landowners.

Other questions remain unanswered. For example, are the handshake agreements used in Ontario strong enough to provide long-term protection? Are the leases used in the prairies going to become a long-term financial burden, and condition landowners to expect payment for conservation of natural habitats? Can such programs be designed to appeal to all types of landowners? And how can involvement with the agricultural sector be improved? Is there an opportunity to bring an integrated conservation message to farmers; for example, pulling together the principles of soil and water conservation with natural-heritage values? And, most important, will there be the commitment to carry on funding of such programs beyond the "pilot project" stage?

PRIVATE-STEWARDSHIP ENHANCEMENT TECHNIQUES
Just as we have ecological techniques for habitat enhancement and management,

we must devise the institutional mechanisms to assist individual landowners with their stewardship efforts. In recent years, numerous reports have been issued examining some of the alternatives, which number in the dozens. Options can range from oral stewardship agreements; through written agreement, management agreements, leases, conservation easements; to purchase and sale-back techniques.

On the one hand it can be argued that the stronger legal techniques are better, giving more permanent protection. On the other hand, simpler techniques appeal to far more owners, and even with a small failure rate may serve to protect more hectares. In fact, U.S. experience has suggested that failure rates are very low, even for oral agreements.

It also should not be forgotten that fundamental structural changes in the rules and regulations governing private landowners and the incentives available to them can have an immense effect on their stewardship decisions. The best example is the U.S. Farm Bill. Under the bill, many farmers must now commit themselves to certain conservation practices in order to keep receiving government agricultural subsidies. Such an approach has been termed "cross-compliance."

In total, though, the evidence from both the United States and Britain, as well as the promising pilot projects now underway in Canada, suggests that we have only begun to open the door on the potential of private-stewardship programs. We need to continue to experiment and innovate until we come up with the appropriate mix of "carrots and sticks" that will make good stewardship the normal way of doing business in the countryside.

CO-OPERATION — A BASIC PREREQUISITE

If private-stewardship programs are to succeed, perhaps the most fundamental need is for mutual respect and co-operation. Most obvious is co-operation with landowners. But behind this lies the difficult challenge of co-operation within the conservation community itself — between naturalists and sportsmen, for example. Protecting natural habitat is, after all, a shared underlying value. If conservationists approach the coming years split among themselves, their effectiveness will be drastically reduced.

We also need co-operation among the various conservation sectors represented by government departments — Parks, Wildlife, Forestry, Water, and Agriculture. Landowners deal with a unified whole — the piece of land they own and love. It is only bureaucrats who divide these concerns up and approach them in a piece-meal manner.

Thus, overall co-operation is perhaps the greatest challenge we face. But again there are promising examples. Perhaps Ontario's Natural Heritage League is one of the best — a loose coalition of government and non-government groups that has succeeded in bringing together partners who would not have otherwise worked together. We need many more such attempts in the fight to protect our natural heritage.

JON LIEN

Eau Canada! A New Marine-Parks System

Canada has the longest ocean coastline of any country in the world. Coastal boundaries touch ten of our twelve provinces and territories. Our motto "A Mari usque ad Mare" — "from sea to sea" — reflects a national awareness of the maritime roots of our cultural, social, and economic history.

Many Canadians look to our oceans for jobs. Some view them as an interesting, ecologically important part of our world. For others they are a peaceful and satisfying place for recreation. Whatever the basic viewpoint, our oceans are endangered spaces in need of protection.

To aid in conserving our ocean environment and to teach Canadians about the sea, Canada has just begun a marine-parks program that will establish a system of protected ocean reserves and encourage visitor activities. A quarter of a century has been spent trying to formulate this marine-parks policy. Now all we need are the parks!

THE NEED FOR OCEAN CONSERVATION

When the first explorers and settlers came to Canada's east coast, stories of unbelievable ocean riches were common. Our seabird colonies provided sea-weary sailors with North America's first "fast-food take-outs." Such hearty exploitation of eggs and nesting birds had an important impact on some populations of seabirds; for example, it resulted in the extinction of the great auk.

Few species were completely immune to the impact of such early human activity. Basque whalers, in small boats, came to the shores of Labrador to kill large whales with hand-held harpoons. Even this primitive technology was able to seriously deplete numbers of some species of whales.

Many still have faith in the oceans' ability to provide. It is frequently claimed that the ocean is an untapped reservoir of bountiful resources on which future wealth and progress will be based. The image frequently created is that the ocean is the last frontier, a wilderness area on Earth that has yet to fully serve mankind's needs. The basis for such claims rests on the fact that while oceans cover nearly

80 per cent of the surface of the planet, only 15 per cent of the world's protein and only 25 per cent of our energy are derived from marine sources.

But do such figures warrant the view of the ocean as a yet unexploited wilderness? Such optimism has proved unfounded before. After the Second World War, people were enthusiastic about the ocean's potential for economic activities. Between 1950 and 1970 the amount of fish caught by the world's fishermen tripled. Modern fishing vessels and "factory ships" multiplied, equipped with the latest technologies. However, this increased demand on the ocean ecosystem was having an impact. By the late 1960s and early 1970s there were ominous warnings that something was seriously wrong. Yields from the "ocean wilderness" levelled off, then began to fall. Fish stock after stock, in ocean after ocean, showed signs of depletion. As overexploited stocks collapsed, the modern fishing fleet simply moved to new ocean areas with new, previously unexploited stocks. By the 1970s, there were few fish stocks that had not been exploited. Catches continued to fall. Modern fishing technology in two short decades overexploited the capacity of the ocean wilderness to provide protein. Today, world fish extraction from the oceans appears to have stabilized at about 18 kilograms per capita per year, not 50 as experts had predicted.

In the early part of this century, whaling of fin, blue, and humpback whales was highly successful, and has continued for most of this century. Like fish catches, whale catches have generally declined. In 1946 the International Whaling Commission (IWC) was established and began the first efforts at international control and management of oceans. However, areas of the ocean that supported large whale populations were treated as a "common resource." Because national and company self-interest encouraged short-term exploitation, participating members voted for quotas based on these interests. As a result, world-wide whale numbers continued to decrease until exploitation of whales became impractical. Finally, in 1987, the IWC declared a ten-year, world-wide moratorium on commercial whaling.

Our impact on the ocean ecosystem has been clear in additional ways. In the 1950s, ocean travellers noticed that they encountered garbage in all areas of the ocean. With the increased use of plastics and disposable products, the problem is worse today. Hospital wastes, syringes, and "technical garbage" are returned to recreational beaches. Endangered marine turtles frequently mistake plastic garbage bags for jellyfish; ingestion is commonly fatal, as it is for seabirds and marine mammals entangled in discarded monofilament lines or nets.

Yet pollutants need not be seen to be dangerous. Heavy metals and organic compounds from central Canada find their way to rivers, lakes, and finally to the sea, thousands of kilometres away. In ocean waters off eastern Canada, some species of sharks are still not safe for human consumption because of high levels of metals accumulated in their bodies. That's a level of accumulated metals probably unsafe for the sharks as well. Beluga whales in the Gulf of St. Lawrence have tumours and die prematurely because of pollutants in their ocean home. Even animals such as seals and polar bears found in Canada's Arctic Ocean contain toxins that can be traced to our industries and consumer lifestyles in southern Canada.

As the value of the ocean environment has become more evident, nations have moved to establish some control over exploitation and abuse. For the last several decades, marine conservation therefore has been one of the most important global environmental concerns. National controls of continental shelf and slope waters offshore to 322 kilometres are now recognized. What was formerly a "common resource" has been divided into national enclosures.

It is difficult to predict whether this restructuring of the ocean commons will work to protect the marine environment. Establishment of national jurisdictions over a 322-kilometre limit could represent a new awareness of the need for ocean conservation. But how will they cope with fish, whales, and seabirds unaware of national boundaries? What will they do with ocean currents that daily carry water from one national area into another, along with the trillions of bits of life that live in them?

THE NEED FOR AN OCEAN-AWARE PUBLIC

The goal of ocean education is not to produce marine biologists and oceanographers, but to help the average Canadian understand and care about our ocean heritage. Without a concerned public, marine conservation will be difficult. The paradox is that the opportunity to learn about the ocean probably requires protected reserves where it can occur in the first place. In a recent survey, our national parks were identified by Canadians as the number-one national agency providing knowledge about Canada to adult audiences. National marine parks therefore must become one of the major means of marine education in Canada.

There is a great lack of educational ocean experiences for Canadians. The U.S. government established the Sea Grant Program as a means of teaching Americans about the sea. But Canada has no similar ocean-education program, marine curricula are scarce in Canadian schools, and, for most Canadians, opportunity for direct contact with oceans is extremely limited.

At present, most teaching in our national parks with a marine component is limited to the intertidal zone. Only a few parks offer boat trips to see marine birds or mammals. To be successful, ocean conservation must be understood by those who ultimately support it — the general public. How will it be taught? A recent survey of Canadian school children found that knowledge and commitment to oceans developed most successfully if the student had guided, direct contact with the marine environment.

THE UNIQUENESS OF MARINE ECOSYSTEMS

Ocean ecosystems are not just wet and salty land ecosystems. They tend to be different in several ways that have important implications for ocean-conservation efforts. Some people have argued that we should not even call protected ocean areas "parks" to avoid confusing people about the nature of such areas.

Marine ecosystems tend to be larger than terrestrial ones — much larger. For

Above: West coast sea lions.
CREDIT: R. BARRY RANFORD.

Centre: Two walrus.
CREDIT: FRED BRUEMMER.

Below: Sea anemones and starfish in Pacific Rim National Park.
CREDIT: MILDRED McPHEE.

Opposite, above left: Beluga whales congregate in arctic estuaries.
CREDIT: FRED BRUEMMER.

Opposite, below left: The sea otter, an endangered species.
CREDIT: STEPHEN J. KRASEMANN.

Opposite right: A seabird sanctuary at Cape St. Mary's Bird Sanctuary in Newfoundland.
CREDIT: J.A. KRAULIS.

instance, we talk of the "Grand Banks ecosystem"—an area of tens of thousands of square kilometres. Within such a vast area, a habitat may be either fixed or moving. A good example of a fixed habitat would be a coral reef. The Great Barrier Reef Marine Park off Australia, several thousand kilometres long, contains fixed habitat. However, such opportunities in ocean ecosystems are rare.

Most marine habitat tends to be moving or transient. Water critical for open-water spawning and survival of eggs and larvae that drift over banks is an example of transient habitat. It is not possible to describe such areas accurately by reference to fixed boundaries. Water masses do not follow boundaries, but move through vast ocean areas, carrying their dependent life. Although an important component of marine life is the flora and fauna that hold to the bottom, even many of these plants and animals depend on transient water habitat for different stages of their life cycles.

Terrestrial parks are impacted by air that flows over them—acid rain, for instance. But the air column that flows over terrestrial parks does not carry all the essential nutrients necessary for life. In contrast, the water column is *the* principal factor in most marine ecosystems. Because of the size and transient nature of this critical marine habitat and the use of the entire water column by most marine species, the problem of delineating a park area in the terrestrial sense is very different.

Furthermore, many of the species found in one part of the ocean spend a great deal of their lives elsewhere, as eggs, larvae, or adults. Therefore, efforts to protect isolated habitats within fixed boundaries would likely be relatively insignificant in many cases. A quick description of animals I usually see in July while puttering along in a boat off my home in Newfoundland will illustrate this point: the humpback whales wintered in the Caribbean but spent the early summer off Labrador, the arctic terns spent the winter south of the Equator, the Manx shear-waters on islands near England — all eat zooplankton and small fish carried by the Labrador Current from the Canadian Arctic.

For the majority of our ocean species found within a designated marine park area, protection there will make little difference if conditions *outside* park boundaries are harming them. Marine ecosystems are extremely susceptible to "down-stream effects." Because water accumulates and carries materials and life from one ocean to another, ocean areas may be affected by toxins, nutrients, and so on, that can originate thousands of kilometres away. For example, improper disposal of waste in Montreal critically affects water quality in the Gulf of St. Lawrence. Most designated-boundary areas will be continuously violated by the waters that move through them.

Another characteristic of marine ecosystems is the variability within them. Entire populations and communities can vary from year to year. The implication of this for marine parks is that conserving wildlife there will be quite different than in terrestrial parks. Where particularly critical habitats, such as breeding or nursery areas, can be identified, marine-park protection can be significant for some species. But these will be small. In Lancaster Sound, for example, such areas constitute less than 5 per cent of the total area. To protect many species will mean monitoring very large, mobile water masses.

Given the differences in species protection for marine as compared to terrestrial areas, concerns about resource utilization will vary. Most user activities are prohibited in terrestrial parks. In a marine ecosystem, for many resources it wouldn't matter if user activities occurred within or outside a park area. Thus, in many circumstances, it may be reasonable to allow commercial fishing within marine parks. If parks are defined by prohibition of user activities, their size and usefulness in promoting ocean conservation will be limited.

Finally, Canadian parks have always had a dual role: preservation as well as catering to visitor activities, including research and education. However, using marine parks as "benchmarks" for research will be difficult given the transient nature of their resources. And our educational activities will still be largely limited to the surface of the water — only a small percentage of Canadians will be willing to try scuba or submarines. This means that marine-park educators will have to be extremely creative in bringing the great unseen marine environment to life for visitors.

THE IDEA OF MARINE PARKS IN CANADA

Marine parks did not become an internationally recognized concept until 1962, when the First World Conference on National Parks concluded that countries should begin to establish marine reserves to defend the ocean ecosystem. Between 1969 and 1972 Canada established four national parks with marine boundaries: Forillon, Auyuittuq, Kouchibouguac, and Pacific Rim. Many existing national parks, such as Terra Nova, Cape Breton Highlands, and Prince Edward Island national parks, were already bordered by the sea, but such terrestrial parks by design and management practice offered little substantial protection for Canada's ocean environment. Even if their boundaries were extended for some distance out into the surrounding seas today, it is unlikely they would provide significant conservation impact except for a few tidal habitats or bays. Nevertheless, it was a start, a step in the right direction.

In 1970, Canada's National and Historic Sites Branch initiated our first substantial effort to examine the role of marine parks in conservation and education. Their submission to the federal cabinet, supported by the Minister for National Parks and the Minister of Fisheries, gained approval to establish, in principle, a marine-parks system in Canada and a marine park in the Strait of Georgia off the British Columbia coast.

A working group, representing several government departments, was established to consider other marine parks, to examine the problems of defining boundaries, and to tackle such management programs as deciding which activities would be permitted and how they would be managed co-operatively by various agencies with overlapping jurisdictions. In 1971 this group recommended five additional sites for marine parks. It looked as though things were moving well!

However, this early effort was slowed down by practical difficulties in achieving co-ordinated government action among the array of agencies required to properly manage and protect the marine ecosystem. After a brief flurry of activity, this early positive momentum was lost. There was not an informed and interested public to encourage renewed efforts, or to protest, and the movement floated to a standstill.

Despite these difficulties, by 1972 the concept of marine parks was acknowledged and accepted by Canada's park managers. Three marine regions were identified in each of the Pacific, the Arctic, and the Atlantic oceans. In each of these nine marine regions, sites were identified by their representativeness, recreational or conservation values, and exceptional natural features. The actual field-work associated with identifying these sites involved our national-park agency in the realities of marine ecosystems and the maze of interested users.

Progress was slow, but it was progress. Next, co-operative efforts were made with several provincial governments. British Columbia and federal park managers investigated establishing a marine park surrounding the Race Rocks near Victoria on Vancouver Island. A survey of the Bay of Fundy on Canada's east coast was conducted to find areas of significance. In 1979, our Canadian park managers began to study basic issues, such as the activities of fishermen and their inclusion or exclusion from a marine park. In co-operation with the government of New Brunswick, they began a feasibility study of West Isles in the Bay of Fundy to test the usefulness of the evolving marine-parks policy.

Finally! In 1983, a draft policy for our national marine parks was completed. Marine parks were special areas in our three oceans, set aside and managed to protect and conserve their natural and cultural resources for the benefit, education, and enjoyment of this and future generations. The policy reflected the long, careful work of park managers. The key ideas in the policy were based on the awareness that terrestrial-park management programs did not apply to marine ecosystems. This new awareness of the ocean environment was quickly seen in the recognition of twenty-nine marine areas — twenty more unique ocean regions than identified in previous work.

Park managers then consulted the public to solicit reaction to the policy. In general, from meetings held across the country, there was excellent public support for the concept. The public was concerned about allowing commercial fishing within marine-park boundaries, and the co-operative approach of multi-agency management of the areas. Both of these concerns have their roots in "land-lubber ecology" and "hiking boot" park experiences. It took park managers two decades to overcome their terrestrial-ecosystem biases, and public consultation showed that now the general public needed to deal with the same problem.

Nearly a quarter of a century after the endorsement of the concept of marine parks, Canada's marine-park policy was approved by the Government of Canada, and the official announcement was made by the Minister of the Environment to the annual meeting of the Canadian Parks and Wilderness Society in 1986.

For the time being, the policy will be implemented through existing national parks legislation. The announcement came during a period of severely restricted budgets, and even now there are only three individuals in the Canadian Parks Service who devote their time to the implementation of our new marine parks policy. While Canada has begun an exciting new adventure, the effort is small and threatened by limited human and financial resources, a lack of understanding of the marine ecosystem by terrestrial park managers, and the absence of organized popular support. But it *is* underway.

PRESENT EFFORTS

We already have our first marine park — Fathom Five on the Great Lakes. Marine parks are under consideration in other areas, including West Isles in the Bay of Fundy, Saguenay Fjord/St. Lawrence River Estuary, at North Baffin Island/Lancaster Sound in Canada's Arctic, and in South Moresby/Gwaii Haanas in the Queen Charlotte Islands off British Columbia.

Fathom Five/Bruce Marine Park

Perhaps it is a bit surprising that our first marine park was established in the fresh water of Lake Huron, off the Bruce Peninsula. The Great Lakes are, of course, included as one of the marine regions of Canada, with each individual lake, in turn, represented as a subregion. The Bruce became the first marine park in Canada largely because it was small, simple — in that there were already water-based parks in the area — and provided park managers with a relatively unthreatening start for the great adventure.

Fathom Five was a small Ontario provincial park begun in 1973. The major attraction of the area was archeological — there were nineteen major shipwrecks in the park. Georgian Bay Islands National Park bordered Fathom Five, and was composed of a large number of small islands, underwater shipwrecks, and interesting geological features. These units were simply combined to produce Canada's first marine park.

It is a good example of a particular kind of marine park, one that functions primarily as a recreational area. There are certainly conservation aspects to management of the area. The archeological treasures — the shipwrecks — are protected. Scuba diving and recreational boating are the main visitor activities. One hopes that interpretation programs will inform Canadians about the broader conservation problems of the Great Lakes.

West Isles

During 1975–76 the New Brunswick government conducted a study to identify tourism opportunities in the Bay of Fundy. The result of this investigation was a fairly vague idea that a marine park would be a good tourism project. West Isles was designated as a likely location.

West Isles is a beautiful, productive area in the Bay of Fundy, with resources that attracted settlers and fishermen several centuries before tourism and park managers discovered it. Park managers from federal and provincial agencies examined the possibility of a marine park for West Isles between 1978 and 1982. Study after study was done, without direct public involvement or consultation. Local concerns about a large-scale government project that could alter traditional use of the area were aroused. Because the national marine-parks policy was still in the development stage, it was not communicated to local residents what traditional uses would be allowed. And by the time public comments were solicited in 1983, local opposition to any marine-park activity in the area was well organized and vocal. The park was opposed because residents, particularly fishermen, feared bothersome government regulation and interference from tourist activities. Although our marine-park policy permits many human activities, even commercial fishing in marine parks, this was not clearly communicated, and the first public-planning exercise for a marine park in Canada resulted in a full retreat by marine-park advocates.

No amount of openness later could rectify the suspicions aroused by early exclusion of local people from the park-planning process. Therefore the take-home lesson from our West Isles experience is simply that local residents must be allowed to participate in such a process. The nature of marine parks must vary, depending, in part, on local residents' requirements.

MARINE REGIONS OF CANADA

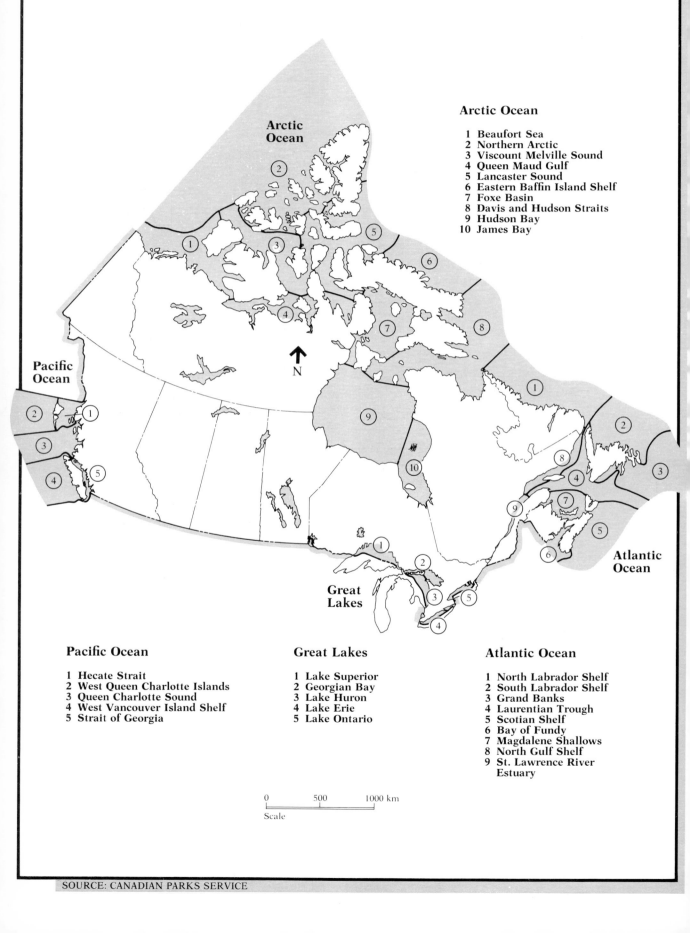

Arctic Ocean

1 Beaufort Sea
2 Northern Arctic
3 Viscount Melville Sound
4 Queen Maud Gulf
5 Lancaster Sound
6 Eastern Baffin Island Shelf
7 Foxe Basin
8 Davis and Hudson Straits
9 Hudson Bay
10 James Bay

Arctic Ocean

Pacific Ocean

N

Atlantic Ocean

Great Lakes

Pacific Ocean

1 Hecate Strait
2 West Queen Charlotte Islands
3 Queen Charlotte Sound
4 West Vancouver Island Shelf
5 Strait of Georgia

Great Lakes

1 Lake Superior
2 Georgian Bay
3 Lake Huron
4 Lake Erie
5 Lake Ontario

Atlantic Ocean

1 North Labrador Shelf
2 South Labrador Shelf
3 Grand Banks
4 Laurentian Trough
5 Scotian Shelf
6 Bay of Fundy
7 Magdalene Shallows
8 North Gulf Shelf
9 St. Lawrence River
   Estuary

0   500   1000 km

Scale

SOURCE: CANADIAN PARKS SERVICE

It is not clear at present if the West Isles marine-park proposal is completely dead. A recently planned round of consultations with local people has been deferred to some undetermined future date.

Saguenay Fjord/St. Lawrence River Estuary

At the confluence of the St. Lawrence and Saguenay rivers, mixing of fresh- and salt-water masses creates a unique upwelling and dynamic ocean environment. A total of six distinct marine and estuarine ecosystems provides for an important diversity of invertebrate, vertebrate, and plant species.

The best-known wildlife is a relic endangered population of beluga whales that are year-round residents of the area. These animals have been the subject of much public interest. They are full of toxins flushed through the river system and exhibit a variety of pathologies and excessive mortality. Initially this population numbered some 5000 individuals, but now they are down to about 400.

Public consultations about the proposed marine park conducted in 1987 indicated that the major concern of residents was water quality. They perceived that the major goal of a marine park would be rehabilitation of waters within the area. With this goal in mind, when given a series of options on park size, residents naturally chose the largest marine park presented to them. However, even with the fairly large park of 750 square kilometres being considered, improvement of water quality will require co-operative management among a variety of agencies. Rehabilitation of environments that have suffered degradation from human activity is a proper goal of a marine park. However, such reclamation is typically more expensive than preventive measures.

In 1988 the governments of Canada and Quebec announced the creation of the St. Lawrence Action Plan. The major objective of this plan is the restoration of environmental health to the St. Lawrence River and estuary through a program of research and rehabilitation, and second, the establishment of a marine park at the Saguenay Fjord/St. Lawrence River estuary as soon as possible. Public meetings and discussions have occurred about the proposed marine park from the very beginning. Such early consultation has assured local users of the area that they will be included within the park and corrects the errors made in the handling of the West Isles proposal.

North Baffin Island/Lancaster Sound

Proposals for this marine park suggest both a land-based and marine national park. Boundary possibilities are literally limitless. Defining them will depend on ecological, political, economic, and social considerations.

A key to the ecological significance of eastern Lancaster Sound will be the polynyas and ice-lead systems. Such ice edges produce upwellings that bring nutrients and relatively warm, deep water to the surface. High biological productivity is the result, particularly during the spring and early summer when there is an earlier plankton bloom than in adjacent, ice-covered areas. This high plankton productivity is used by species such as amphipods and arctic cod, which in turn are preyed upon by seabirds and marine mammals.

Some areas of Lancaster Sound, in springtime, gradually develop relatively open waters, which provide a crucial migration corridor for narwhals, bowhead whales, and Arctic nesting birds. Proximity of land nesting areas to such open waters is critical for marine birds.

Because of the biological productivity of the area, there are numerous Inuit archeological sites and continued Inuit use of marine resources. Protection of the area can therefore help sustain traditional native lifestyles, so the educational value of North Baffin Island/Lancaster Sound will not only include the physical and biological features, but cultural ones as well.

The desirability of establishing a marine park in the area has been the subject of public discussions since 1987. The park has received strong support from several sections of the Government of Canada as a means of establishing Canadian sovereignty in the Arctic. Undoubtedly this is more cost-effective than buying a fleet of nuclear submarines! Initial consideration of the proposal has also begun by nearby residents of Pond Inlet and Arctic Bay through the Lancaster Sound region land-use planning exercise. Assessment of offshore mineral and energy resources is being conducted. The park-establishment process will depend on the Tungavik Federation of Nunavut land-claims settlement process, and it may be several years before a final decision is reached.

South Moresby/Gwaii Haanas

South Moresby/Gwaii Haanas is sandwiched between two distinct marine environments. In the West Queen Charlotte Islands marine region, the Pacific Ocean reaches a depth of 2000 metres just a few kilometres from shore. This allows the power of unrestrained ocean waves to reach the rugged shore, with the result that this area of the west coast receives greater wave energy than any other in Canada. On the eastern side, the Hecate Strait marine region is quite different. Sheltered from the open ocean, its near-shore waters are much calmer and home to a prolific, diverse coastal marine community.

In July 1988, Canada and British Columbia signed a federal-provincial Memorandum of Agreement to establish the South Moresby/Gwaii Haanas National Park Reserve and National Marine Park Reserve. It didn't come easily, but finally it came. The agreement defines the proposed marine park as one that extends an average of 10 kilometres from the South Moresby coast and covers an area of over 3000 square kilometres. Establishment of the park reserve will be delayed for up to five years, pending completion of offshore mineral and energy exploration. When this study is completed, it will be used by federal and provincial officials to decide on the final boundaries of the marine park.

The lesson to be learned about our new marine-park system from experiences at South Moresby/Gwaii Haanas is that it will not come easily. Government action on the park followed over a decade of public demonstrations. Even after an agreement is signed, decisions about the park will not be final until years later. Only *then* can development of park programs begin!

WHERE DOES THE NEW MARINE-PARKS SYSTEM GO FROM HERE?

One way to make predictions about the future is to look at the fate of similar initiatives.

In 1972, the United States began its National Marine Sanctuary Program. Seven marine sanctuaries have since been created, and three sanctuary candidates have been proposed for designation.

However, declining federal budgets have limited financial and human resources earmarked for sanctuary areas. The process of identifying and selecting sites has been slow. Perhaps the worst criticism of all is that the sanctuaries add little real protection for the areas.

Australia's Great Barrier Reef Marine Park Authority has operated for about as long as the U.S. sanctuaries program. Although this park is acknowledged as an example of first-rate ocean management, it has serious difficulties. Tourism along the Queensland coastline, principally targeted to the Great Barrier Reef, has grown at about 30 per cent per year. The once-remote reef is now accessible daily, by high-speed catamaran, to thousands of tourists. Financial and personnel resources for management are strained. Although this marine park continues to operate well, many are concerned about the prospects for its long-term success.

The brand-new marine-parks initiative in Canada is also a rather frail and endangered effort. Qualified staff for the new marine-parks system is available but it numbers only three. The current Minister operates in a government that has seriously cut park budgets; there is no new funding for the Canadian Parks Service to establish marine parks. Actual development of marine parks will not be accomplished until sometime in the future. Even if we were able to create marine parks now, current resources and knowledge of management techniques for these areas would quite likely result in serious problems surrounding both the conservation and the educational roles of such parks. Further, little information about marine parks has been made available to the public, and public support for the effort is minimal.

So, what can be done?

We simply cannot let the present initiative fail. Interested groups and individuals must show their support for our new marine-parks system to the Government of Canada. The Canadian Parks and Wilderness Society is currently designing a marine-parks education program to encourage public endorsement and support. But Canadian initiatives to establish marine parks have been grounded before. If we are to succeed this time, Canadians must demand that the initiative continue.

Only recently we celebrated one hundred years of our national-parks system. It began quite inconspicuously but succeeded in building a national-parks system that today is among the best in the world. No doubt when the *bi*centennial of the Canadian park system is celebrated, a new generation of Canadians will look back and marvel at the frail but important start of the marine-parks program with considerable pride. It is up to all of us to make sure that happens.

PART THREE

THE STATE OF WILDERNESS
ACROSS CANADA TODAY

BARRY MAY

Newfoundland and Labrador: A Special Place

Reaching boldly into the North Atlantic, our province fends off the arctic waters of the Labrador Current. This icy flow bonds Newfoundland and Labrador and sets its rugged lands apart.

Northern landscapes are tempered and enlivened by the sea, never far away or far from mind. Our provincial emblems symbolize this special character. The puffin, perky denizen of barren islets, brings life and mystery from the sea. The caribou roams the barrens but here comes to the shore and knows the taste of wrack and tang of brine. Here wilderness can be sea ducks in rushing river rapids, whales in sheltered bays, ptarmigan bursting up from lonely coastal barrens. It is a wild land, but it welcomes and rewards the traveller who comes and learns its ways.

NATURAL SETTING

The province's geologic history has been the subject of much study and acclaim. Labrador is the easternmost extension of the great Canadian Shield. The gneisses of its Torngat Mountains are the oldest rocks known, dated at 3.7 billion years. Many of these ancient rocks have been subject to later remelting and metamorphosis, but have been little affected by tectonic events. The Island, however, has a more exciting Palaeozoic history. As the African and European plates converged with the North American continent, there was volcanic activity and uplifting of parts of the earth's mantle. Evidence of these dramatic events is seen in Gros Morne National Park and other areas on the west coast of the Island.

With passing time, the continents spread apart again. Part of the North African plate remained behind to form the Avalon Peninsula of Newfoundland. This area escaped the upheavals of the Island's west coast and contains unique deep-water Precambrian fossils, which are more than 600 million years old and of major international significance.

A long period of geological stability with gradual erosion of the mountains followed the opening of the Atlantic Ocean. Then, repeated glaciation created many of the characteristic landforms we recognize today: great fjords, meandering eskers, scraped bedrock, and glacial boulders strewn willy-nilly. Rebounding coasts, freed of the weight of glacial ice, have created a number of scenic raised beaches, frequently the site of major archeological discoveries. Fine clays left behind in glacial till have resulted in extensive bog and fen formation. Several plant communities found in calcareous barrens on the Northern Peninsula and maritime barrens on the Avalon Peninsula support species found only here and in the Rocky Mountains, thousands of kilometres distant, indicating areas that may have escaped glacial influence.

Sweeping down from Greenland and the Canadian Arctic, the Labrador Current, more than any other natural feature, gives the province its special character. Carrying pack ice in winter and icebergs all year round, its cold northern water swirls about the Island, prolonging winter, delaying spring, and shrouding the coasts in a cool summer fog. But along the coastal shelf and over the banks, it wells up, bringing oxygen- and nutrient-rich waters to the surface, and mixes with warmer waters of the Gulf Stream. This highly productive marine environment attracts seals from the Arctic, whales and seabirds from the south, and fishermen from around the world.

Patterns of vegetation reflect the cool, damp climatic conditions. The dominant forest is coniferous, covering about half the Island and a similar portion of Labrador. Balsam fir and black spruce predominate. A few hardwoods, such as birch and red maple, and a fair variety of shrubs are found in more favoured sites, particularly the valleys of the Island's west coast. Extensive areas of barrens, bog, and tundra characterize the uplands, northern Labrador, and the Island's south coast. Of the province's 1034 known indigenous plants, 151 are known only from Labrador, 325 from the Island, and 558 from both sites. By contrast, Iceland has 450 known indigenous plants and Nova Scotia, which is smaller, 1100.

On the Island, there are only fourteen indigenous mammals. The distribution suggests that most of these species originated in Labrador, as there is a delightful, distinctly northern emphasis to the fauna, highlighted by caribou, lynx, bear, and arctic hare. Interestingly, there is recent evidence that coyotes may have successfully crossed the Strait of Belle Isle to colonize the Island. Many common animals are missing, such as the skunk, groundhog, porcupine, and raccoon. At least ten species have been introduced, including the moose, varying hare, shrew, and red squirrel.

Of the thirty-five species found in Labrador, many, such as the beaver and porcupine, reach their northern limits, which are confined by the tree line. One species — the polar bear — reaches its southern limit here. Every few years one of the big white bears turns up on the Island, perhaps having come down on the ice to hunt for seals.

A few scattered arctic char appear on the Northern Peninsula and rainbow and brown trout have been introduced locally on the east coast; however, the Island's rivers and ponds (only the largest bodies of water are termed "lakes") contain only speckled trout and salmon to attract the angler. Introduced toads and several frog species are gaining a foothold, but there are no snakes here. It is too cold. Labrador has considerably more variety in its waters, but only a few rare frogs, one species of salamander, and the garter snake.

Birds are relatively richly represented. They certainly are not much limited by the 17-kilometre Strait of Belle Isle and do quite well in crossing the 160 kilometre Cabot Strait. In fact, vagrants from Europe and the circumpolar regions make for exciting birdwatching, particularly after a big easterly storm. About 160 species breed in the province, with 20 represented only in Labrador and 60 only on the Island. Several, such as the northern waterthrush, black and white warbler, and fox sparrow, are particularly common. Ptarmigan enliven the barrens with the staccato call usually heard much farther north. Ospreys and eagles are common in favoured localities, while the gyrfalcon and peregrine may pass by on migration from the cliffs of Labrador. Still, it is the seabirds that excite most people and symbolize a crucial element of our natural heritage. The great colonies along our Atlantic coast are one of the province's most cherished international treasures and most significant conservation responsibilities.

HISTORY

As the glaciers receded about 10,000 years ago, the Maritime Archaic Indians began moving into the province, followed a thousand years later by Palaeo-Eskimos and then Dorset Eskimos. These cultures faded. By the time of Norse settlement 1000 years ago, Thule Eskimos were moving down from the North, and the Naskapi-Montagnais Indians occupied southern and interior Labrador. The Vikings who settled L'Anse aux Meadows on the Northern Peninsula almost certainly met the Beothuks, who were probably the Skraelings of the sagas, and very possibly the direct descendants of the Maritime Archaic Indians. Five hundred years later, as European fishermen began occupying the coastline, conflicts arose with the Beothuks, disease spread, and a tragic decline ensued despite serious efforts to prevent it by a number of prominent men, including naval governor Sir Hugh Palliser, who in 1768 authorized an expedition in search of Beothuks.

In 1822, a young naturalist, William Epps Cormack, made a remarkable four-month journey on foot across the Island with a Micmac guide, Joseph Sylvester. He was unsuccessful in his quest to meet Beothuks, but made many accurate and useful observations of the area's natural history. Another, shorter journey farther north, five years later, gave added credence to the conclusion that the Beothuks were extinct.

This sad history sometimes strikes a poignant chord in the wilderness traveller. Deep in the woods, it is easy to share the melancholy longing expressed so well by Newfoundland poet Tom Dawe in these lines from his poem "In There Somewhere":

Besides, I know that
deep within my island
there are austere voices
in the August birch
and slow dawns are caught
in great wooden bowls
where the meek still inherit.
And a moon is always
a moving canoe
across blue acres of the night.

And a child is always
laughing
in the splash of white water
down the long bakeapple hills.

I could not laugh
because they are
still
in there
somewhere.

Throughout most of the last four hundred years, unrestrained exploitation of resources and the view that wilderness needs to be conquered have taken their toll on our wildlife and wildlands. Polar bears, beluga whales, and walrus are now rare or absent along most of the Labrador coast. On the Island, the once-great caribou migrations have been eliminated by the railways and highways. The wolf is gone, and the easily trapped pine marten endangered here, although both are represented in healthy populations elsewhere. For our lost bird species, the evidence is less hopeful.

Captain Richard Whitebourne, who had spent forty-two years sailing the waters of Newfoundland, wrote of the great auks of Funk Island in 1622: "God had made the innocency of so poor a creature, to become such an admirable instrument for the sustenation of man." Ships from Europe regularly stopped to provision themselves as early as 1500 when the Island is thought to have been discovered by Cortereal. With time, crews were left to harvest the large flightless birds for eggs, oil, meat, and feathers. In 1785, Sir George Cartwright, an early colonizer of Labrador, warned authorities of the impending extinction. A ban on landings was proclaimed and flogging was meted out to violators, but it was too late. Cormack looked for the auks in the 1820s but did not find any. The last known birds were taken from Eldey Island, Iceland, in 1844.

At about the same time, three other species which likely visited the province were under pressure. The Labrador duck, probably never very numerous, was

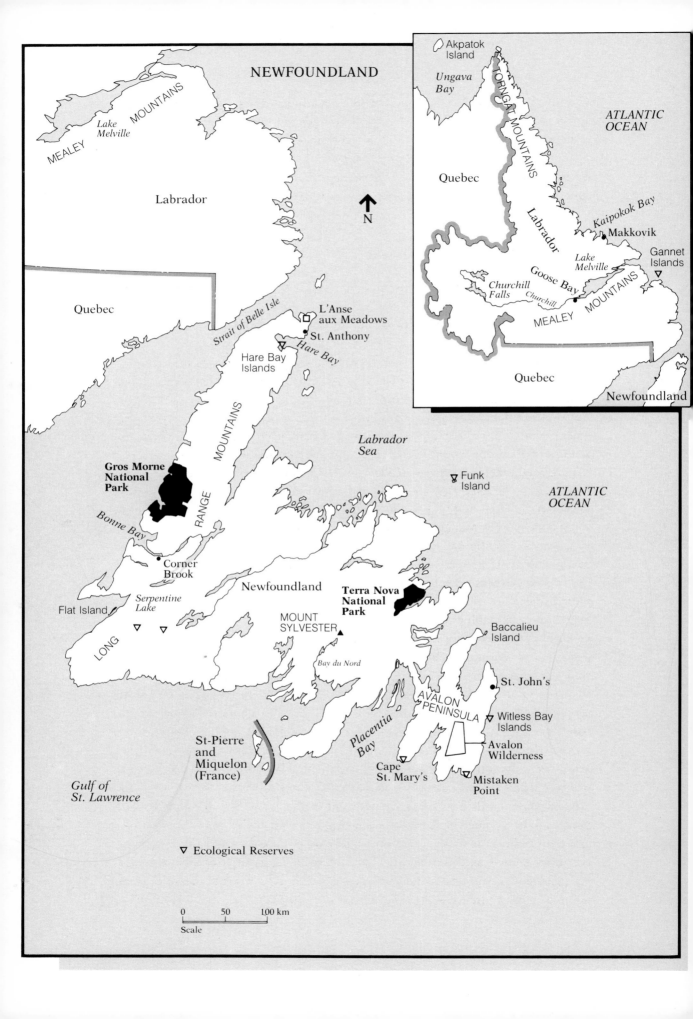

NEWFOUNDLAND

Akpatok
Island

Ungava
Bay

TORNGAT MOUNTAINS

ATLANTIC
OCEAN

Quebec

Labrador

Kaipokok Bay

Makkovik

Gannet
Islands ▽

Lake
Melville

Goose Bay

Churchill
Falls

Churchill

MEALEY MOUNTAINS

Quebec

Newfoundland

MEALEY MOUNTAINS

Lake
Melville

Labrador

Quebec

Strait of Belle Isle

L'Anse
aux Meadows

St. Anthony

Hare Bay
Islands ▽

Hare Bay

LONG RANGE MOUNTAINS

Gros Morne
National
Park

Bonne Bay

Labrador
Sea

▽ Funk
Island

ATLANTIC
OCEAN

Corner
Brook

Newfoundland

Terra Nova
National
Park

Flat Island

Serpentine
Lake

LONG

▽   ▽

MOUNT
SYLVESTER ▲

Bay du Nord

Baccalieu
Island

St. John's

AVALON
PENINSULA

▽ Witless Bay
Islands

Avalon
Wilderness

St-Pierre
and
Miquelon
(France)

Placentia
Bay

Cape
St. Mary's ▽

▽ Mistaken
Point

Gulf of
St. Lawrence

▽ Ecological Reserves

0   50   100 km

Scale

last taken on Grand Manan Island in 1871. Eskimo curlews may yet exist in very limited numbers, but passenger pigeons are gone forever, both victims of unrestricted shooting south of the provincial border. Many cliff nesters inhabiting steep rocky islands on the Atlantic coast survived. However some birds nesting on low islands, such as Funk and west coast islands, were wiped out by eggers, and eider duck populations have been drastically reduced.

CONSERVATION

As these tragedies unfolded, gradually more and more people saw the need for effective conservation measures to protect our natural heritage. In 1845, Newfoundland passed an Act for the Protection of the Breeding of Wild Fowl in this Colony, probably the first such legislation in the history of present-day Canada. Its harsh fine of £20 led to public outcry and legislative recognition of legitimate subsistence activities.

In 1890, the Game Protection Society was founded, perhaps our first environmental pressure group. It was followed in 1927 by the Fish and Game Protection Association, and later by the various rod and gun clubs under the umbrella of the Newfoundland Wildlife Federation. The Newfoundland Natural History Society, founded in 1950, has long supported conservation practices. Ecowatch and a number of groups mounted effective campaigns on single issues, such as forest management, then became dormant. Over the last ten years and more, the Salmon Association of Eastern Newfoundland in St. John's, the Salmon Preservation Association of the Waters of Newfoundland in Corner Brook, and the Environmental Resources Management Association of Grand Falls have been effective spokesmen for enlightened salmon management and protection of the environment. Similarly, members of the Tuckamore Wilderness Club in Corner Brook and the Wilderness Society of St. John's have spoken out on a variety of conservation issues.

As a result, notable progress has been made in several areas. Leadership within government has come consistently from the provincial Wildlife Division. Its first head, Harry Walters, though not a scientist himself, recognized the need for scientific management. He invited Ira Gabrielson of the Wildlife Management Institute to visit and help chart the Division's course. Shortly after, one of his recommendations was realized when Doug Pimlott, to whom this book is dedicated, became the Wildlife Division's first chief biologist.

Pimlott had become enthralled with the Island while riding the Newfie Bullet across the Island to join his unit during the Second World War. While here, he worked principally on moose research, publishing a number of papers using hunter return cards and extensive personal field-work. It was in many ways a family affair, as much of the data-processing was done by his wife, Dorothy. She and their two young children often joined Doug in the cold drafty woods camps. His work served as the foundation for the province's very successful moose-management policy. He is remembered fondly as the man who quashed the notion of introducing white-tailed deer here. They had been very successful on Anticosti

Island, a similar habitat. However, Pimlott recognized that healthy moose and deer populations do not co-exist on the same range, though he did not understand why. It is now known that the brainworm that would have been introduced as well would probably have decimated moose and caribou herds.

Doug Pimlott was a persuasive salesman for wildlife biology. Not long after his arrival here, a young pre-med student stopped by his office for a chat. Frank Manuel was all set to go to medical school, but he was one course short and had some time to pass. Under Pimlott's tutelage, it wasn't long before he switched to wildlife biology. He returned to work in the Division and eventually became deputy minister. Not long before Doug Pimlott left to return to the University of Wisconsin for graduate studies, he met another young pre-med summer student, Dave Pike, now Chief of the Wildlife Division.

Links with Wisconsin have persisted and strengthened, helping ensure the continuation of enlightened management practices traceable back to the philosophy of Aldo Leopold. This tradition has been succinctly stated by Leopold's student and Pimlott's mentor, Dr. Robert McCabe, former chairman of the department of wildlife ecology at Wisconsin: "Keep in mind that the basic responsibility as professionals is to the resources, not to resource users. If professionals exercise that responsibility, the resource user is automatically served."

RECENT PROGRESS

There have been several important developments in protection of wildlands in the province in the past three decades.

Throughout the past century, the Island's caribou herds had been declining, particularly on the Avalon Peninsula, the most heavily settled part of the province. This herd was down to fewer than one hundred animals. Recognizing the need for maintenance of habitat as well as protection from poaching, Harry Walters recommended the central portion of the peninsula be set aside as a wilderness area. In 1964, this was accomplished under the wildlife regulations. Largely through the efforts of such men as enforcement officer Mike Nolan, the people in surrounding communities came to understand and accept the importance of the reserve.

Today, 5000 caribou roam the 1070-square-kilometre reserve, a unique herd, living farther south and nearer to a major city than any other and with some of the largest animals ever recorded. Their progeny are about to be released on Mt. Katahdin in an effort to repopulate Maine with caribou. But it is not really the caribou themselves that are so important. It is because, as Yorke Edwards so aptly says, "the proof of real wildness will be whether moose still bob for plants along the shores of lakes; whether otters still play tag in the rivers; and whether bull caribou still stand curiously on wild shores watching solitary canoes cross lonely lakes." We have all of this on the Avalon.

In the same year as the Avalon Wilderness Area was established (1964), most of the province's major sea-bird nesting colonies were also protected as sanctuaries under wildlife regulations. Superlatives are necessary to describe their significance. There are nine colonies at five sites — all islands except Cape St. Mary's. Witless Bay Islands contain the greatest concentration of breeding seabirds in eastern North America. Gull Island vies with Baccalieu Island as the world's largest Leach's storm-petrel colony, and Great Island has North America's largest puffin colony. Funk Island has a growing gannetry and the world's largest common murre colony. Cape St. Mary's has the second largest North American gannet colony and is distinguished by its accessibility and dramatic aspect. Finally, the Gannet Islands in Labrador have North America's, and probably the world's, largest razorbill colony.

In all, more than three million breeding seabirds have been given protection. Several of the sites are worthy of consideration as world heritage sites. In large measure, it was Dr. Les Tuck, an outstanding ornithologist and the first Dominion wildlife officer, who laid the groundwork for the establishment of these sanctuaries.

PARKS

Newfoundland is fortunate in having two national parks, both located on the Island: Terra Nova, established in 1957, contains 405 square kilometres of boreal forest surrounding several long arms of Bonavista Bay. As well as animals of the forest, hikers are likely to see eagles, ospreys, and possibly the rare Newfoundland pine marten, which has recently been reintroduced.

Gros Morne, 1805 square kilometres of spectacular country on the west coast at the base of the Northern Peninsula, contains coastal plain and Long Range Mountains surrounding Bonne Bay. Its dramatic representations of tectonic geological events and later glacial processes are so outstanding that it has recently become the province's second world heritage site. The park's back country is mainly Long Range barrens, wilderness home to rock ptarmigan and arctic hare.

Newfoundland and Labrador are unique as a province in being bounded by three Parks Canada marine regions — the Gulf of St. Lawrence, the Labrador Sea, and the Atlantic Southeast Coast. Both terrestrial national parks are good candidates for eventually having marine components established.

The existing provincial-park system is important and extensive, though small in total area (359 square kilometres). While established primarily to serve as destination sites for vacationing Newfoundlanders and pleasant waystations for visitors, many of the parks include ecologically significant sites, such as falls on salmon rivers, beaches, and ponds. George Chafe worked nearly twenty years in developing this network of parks across the province. In 1984, his valuable contribution was recognized as he received the first Tuck-Walters Award, given by the Newfoundland Natural History Society. In 1986, the Parks Division developed a new classification system and assumed responsibility for the province's wilderness and ecological reserves.

Above: Nachvak Fiord proudly proclaims Newfoundland/
Labrador a "Special Place."   CREDIT: DENNIS MINTY.

Opposite: The Atlantic Ocean rolls in at Stephenville,
Newfoundland.   CREDIT: BRUCE LITTELJOHN.

Pages 134 and 135: The Torngat Mountains of Labrador
harbour "glacierettes" on the north side of Mount
Razorback.   CREDIT: DENNIS MINTY.

WILDERNESS AND ECOLOGICAL RESERVES ACT

Passage of the Wilderness and Ecological Reserves Act (as well as the Environmental Assessment Act) made 1980 a watershed year in the province's conservation history. Recognizing the accelerating loss of potential wilderness habitat, several members of the Wildlife Division, notably chief biologist Eugene Mercer, received support for an interdepartmental committee to develop protective legislation in the mid-1970s. Finally, with the strong backing of Deputy Minister Frank Manuel, the Minister of Culture, Recreation and Youth, Ron Dawe, brought the bill to the House where it gained easy passage after he spoke eloquently on its behalf.

The Act has a number of important features. An independent advisory council is established to hear proposals, conduct interdepartmental reviews, resolve conflicts if possible, and report to cabinet if a proposal appears to have merit. If cabinet concurs, it establishes a provisional reserve and directs the council to draft a preliminary management plan and to arrange for public hearings. Following this, the council makes a second report to cabinet, where a final decision on reserve establishment is made. If a reserve is established, there are firm prohibitions against road and facility construction, hydro development, mining, and forestry. Motorized transport is prohibited. Hunting, fishing, and trapping, as well as canoeing and camping, are permitted so long as they do not threaten the natural resources. Some non-conforming uses may continue as long as they do not increase, or threaten the integrity of the reserve. The strength of the legislation lies in the requirement that major changes in the management plan be referred to the council for its recommendation, and most importantly, that any boundary change be preceded by public hearings.

The advisory council was appointed in 1981. Its first major recommendation was to bring the seabird sanctuaries and the Avalon Wilderness Area under the Act directly, in view of their long, successful, and accepted establishment. Cabinet concurred for the seabird reserves. An interesting feature of the amendment is that the reserves include within their boundaries waters within provincial jurisdiction, a distance of three nautical miles.

Cabinet wished to undertake the full establishment process for the Avalon. Though time-consuming, this served to highlight the broad base of support existing in neighbouring communities, and it allowed for some significant boundary changes in response to resident suggestions and in recognition of new information on caribou calving areas. The area of greatest controversy lay in the management plan and restrictions on mechanized access. Cabinet recognized the importance of this valuable wilderness resource by giving it full protection, but ignored the Act's proscriptions and allowed continued aircraft access.

Several ecological reserves have been brought to provisional status, but have been held up by such issues as a need to resolve private title or water rights. Mistaken Point, a very significant Precambrian, deep-water, multi-cellular fossil site, has achieved full reserve status, and may be nominated for consideration as a world heritage site. Ten other ecological reserves are at various stages of the process.

Part of council's time was spent addressing two highly contentious issues.

More than fifty years ago, it became apparent that the Newfoundland race of pine marten had nearly disappeared. Thus, trapping of this species has been prohibited on the Island since 1934. By 1973, the situation had not improved, but a remote area of heavy timber in the Little Grand Lake area was identified as the centre of the only known significant population. This area was closed to all trapping and snaring. However, the forest was slated for harvesting, and when some of the timber was killed by spruce budworm, logging became an urgent consideration. Formal environmental assessment was recommended by council and accepted by government, a major achievement. It became apparent that data were inadequate to permit harvesting without jeopardizing marten survival. Nor was there enough information to make a useful recommendation regarding an ecological reserve. Thus, a small area of dead timber was allocated for harvesting, while disposition of the rest awaits further studies funded both by government and by the Cornerbrook Pulp and Paper Co. — a reasonable compromise.

Main River, a small river on the Northern Peninsula, was noted to have potential for canoeing by a local outfitter and conservationist, Gene Manion. When Parks Canada sent a reconnaissance team of paddlers to the river, they were very impressed by its diverse wildlife, scenic beauty, and exciting paddling. Later, in reviewing results from across the country, they ranked it among the top few wild rivers. Harry Collins, a member of the original survey team, returned to paddle it again and almost single-handedly fought to change the route of a power transmission line planned to cross the river. Soon the province's own canoeists discovered its charms and came to appreciate its significance. Unfortunately, its basin also contains extensive prime forests promised to the Kruger Company when it bought the nearby paper-mill five years earlier. Harvesting plans called for a bridge bisecting the river. Though a large coalition of conservation groups pressed for its being maintained in a pristine state, and though government conceded the necessity of environmental assessment, no independent review of the possibility of an economic harvest without the bridge was required. This battle, and the wild river, were ultimately lost.

PRIORITY AREAS — THE ISLAND

By far the most important wildlands issue for the province over the past few years has been the Bay du Nord–Middle Ridge Wilderness Reserve proposal. The country is a plateau of maritime barrens and scrub forest insinuated between myriad lakes feeding the Long Harbour, North West, Terra Nova, and Bay du Nord rivers. It is set off by several monadnocks, including the Tolt and Mt. Sylvester, by which Cormack checked his course for nearly two weeks as he made his heroic trek. Rich in game, it contains the Island's second-largest caribou herd and the best Canada goose breeding range. The Bay du Nord River is without question the Island's finest remaining wilderness river, of national significance and a prime candidate for nomination to the Canadian Heritage Rivers System.

The Bay du Nord area is now a provisional wilderness reserve. A preliminary management plan has been drafted and extensive information sessions and public hearings have been conducted in local communities. As well, boundary adjustments and management-plan compromises have been made to accommodate local concerns. Throughout this process, the advisory council has been inspired by the vision, hard work, and pragmatism of geologist Bryan Greene.

Repeatedly, at the hearings, we heard people speak eloquently of their love of the country. There was broad support for protecting natural areas from development and, at the same time, suspicion of government intentions. This feeling was well captured in the often-expressed sentiment "Protect this area for us, not from us."

The Bay du Nord Reserve is a magnificent area. Cabinet has received the advisory council's final report. Now, we await the government's decision.

Another area worthy of protection is Baccalieu Island. Lying off the Avalon Peninsula at the mouth of Conception Bay, it is home to a huge, complex seabird community. It rivals the Witless Bay Islands in numbers of Leach's storm-petrels and has the province's third gannetry (one of only six in North America). With 60,000 puffins, it is the third-largest colony and is one of only three known breeding sites of northern fulmars in the western Atlantic. Overall, it is the province's most diverse seabird site and unquestionably of global significance. It is surprising that it was by-passed when the original seabird sanctuaries were established in 1964. Formal protection is long overdue.

Sandy Point (Flat Island) is a five-square-kilometre island of sand and cobble.

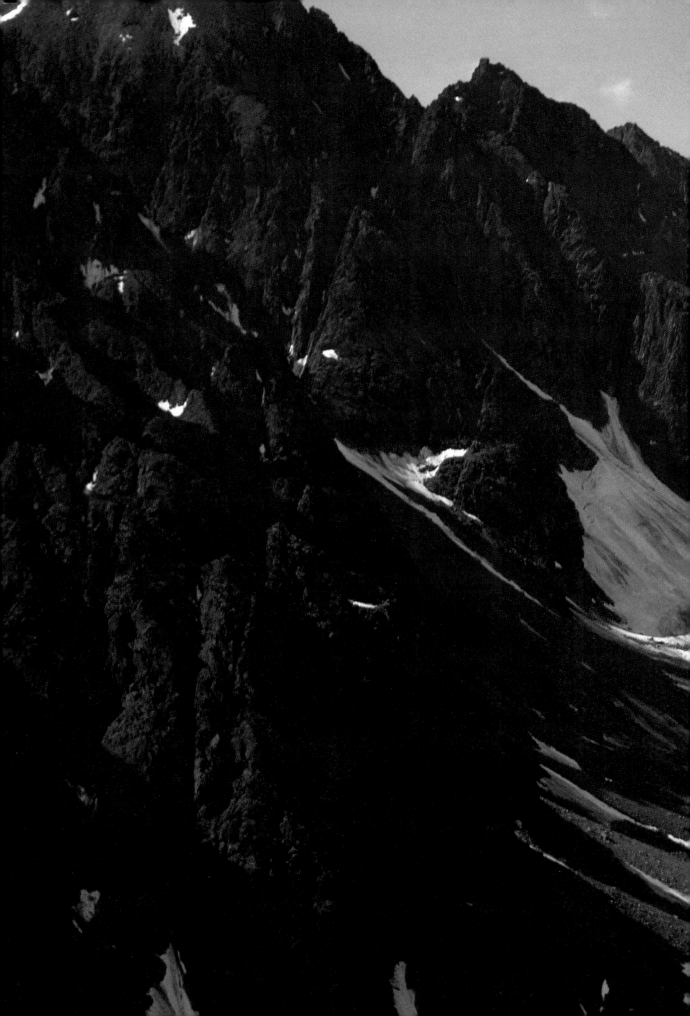

It was once the tip of the largest wave-built feature in the province, a long spit extending into Bay St. George. Formerly the site of the largest community on the west coast, it was visited by Audubon on his return from Labrador. Birds were sparse, but he brought back a pitcher plant, later added to his painting of the red-throated loon done in Labrador. During their stay, his party was escorted to a rollicking dance at a fisherman's house by "the belles of the village." But over time, commerce declined, the people drifted away, and the sea breached the barrier beach.

The old houses have nearly vanished, but summer grazing by cattle and horses preserves a lovely pastoral aspect in the old townsite. On the beaches, the birds have returned. There are now colonies of several hundred gulls and terns. Its small ponds attract large numbers of ducks. Great blue herons (uncommon in Newfoundland) are regularly seen. The very rare piping plover has been seen frequently, but is not yet known to breed there.

Residents of nearby communities have kept the memory of their former home alive, and they are proud of the island's beauty and its thriving wildlife. Recognizing the threat from unrestricted hunting and all-terrain vehicles, they have requested that it be considered for park or ecological-reserve status. Though extensive private holdings pose significant problems, everyone is optimistic that it will eventually become one of the treasures in the reserve system.

Serpentine Lake may be the prettiest lake on the island. It lies between the Blow-Me-Down plateau and the Lewis Hills, at 814 metres, the highest point on the island. Nearby peaks loom above its beaches. Awesome canyons with nearly sheer walls flank the lake. These are strange barren canyons, with brown pyridotite on one wall and grey gabbro on the other, relics of an ancient ocean mantle and crust thrown up hundreds of millions of years ago. The high valley floors carry braided streams as if from a northern glacier, while the Serpentine River flows through a broad, alluvial valley. Ten kilometres from the lake, the river drops over a beautiful two-metre falls, a resting place for salmon and a spot in which to spend some time. Below, in gentle rapids, if you are lucky, you will spot harlequin ducks cavorting in the whitewater.

As early as 1917, the tourist potential of the Serpentine Lake area was heralded. Its rugged beauty, unusual landforms, and rare plant communities should be protected for all Newfoundlanders, and for all Canadians.

PRIORITY AREAS — LABRADOR

Vast Labrador, with only 31,000 people and relatively little development, still has an abundance of wilderness and wild rivers. But dams and power corridors, mining, the trans-Labrador highway, and military expansion signal the need to identify significant natural areas now.

The Canadian Parks Service, the Provincial Parks Division, and the Wilderness and Ecological Reserves Advisory Council have surveyed rivers. Many, such as the Notakwanon, Ugjoktok, and Atikonak, to name only a few, have spectacular wild-river qualities and national significance justifying protection and eventual nomination to the Canadian Heritage River System. Some of these rivers enter the sea in long protected bays behind myriad salt-water islands, where the paddler is rewarded anew with Labrador's special beauty. Coming up Ugjoktok Bay, we camped on long sandy beaches, feasted on mussels and clams, and listened for whales spouting. We weren't so fortunate as a couple from Makkovik, who had paddled here the year before escorted one morning by a pair of killer whales.

However, wild rivers are not important just to the trapper, paddler, or adventurer. We forget that this is everyone's heritage, and to lose it would diminish us all. Wilderness-river designation and protection must begin now and proceed in step with development to guarantee our children always have more than just a memory of Labrador's wild beauty.

Even more majestic than Labrador's rivers, the Torngat Mountain region of the northern coast commands attention. These spirit mountains, home of the Inuit god of wind and storm, are the highest and most rugged range in eastern mainland Canada. Incised by icy fjord arms of the Labrador Sea, these coasts are among the most dramatic in the world. Home to seals, beluga whales, polar bears, and wolves, the region is calving ground and summer range to the world's largest caribou herd, the George River Herd. Seabirds range the offshore islands, and eiders nest unmolested. In the summer of 1988, a raptor survey party discovered a small herd of muskoxen, apparently moving in from Ungava.

The region's prehistory is also interesting. Numerous archeological explorations are slowly unravelling the story of successive early peoples. For instance, Ramah chert used for making stone tools and weapons was traded along the whole eastern seaboard. Now uninhabited, the area is visited by coastal Labradorians fishing for char and hunting caribou and seals. Increasingly, they are joined by sport fishermen, sea kayakers, hikers, and mountain climbers.

The dramatic stark beauty and ecological richness of the Torngat region have long been recognized. In 1979, federal and provincial ministers anticipated signing a five-year planning agreement to see if a national-park proposal could be developed. However, the opposition of the Labrador Inuit Association and the Naskapi-Montagnais Inuit Association resulted in abandonment of the agreement. From its inception, the Wilderness and Ecological Reserves Advisory Council has also anticipated eventual establishment of a Torngat-area wilderness reserve. This provincial initiative may be stifled as well if land-claims settlement remains an unresolved issue. It is time now for our governments to seriously address the land claims of our native peoples. In Labrador, as in much of the country, it is the only way to cast off the pall of doubt and suspicion that keeps us from working together for wilderness-area designation and management, an effort where there ought to be a natural partnership.

As probably the finest and most important unprotected wilderness area in Canada today, the Torngat region should be a top national and provincial priority for protection. Now that the South Moresby and Pacific Rim agreements have been negotiated, it is time to direct attention back to our east coast. These majestic mountains mark the boundary with Quebec. Thus there is a splendid opportunity for the two provinces and the federal government to work together to protect this internationally significant area.

FUTURE PROSPECTS

Newfoundland and Labrador have seen dramatic changes since joining Canada in 1949. Isolation has given way to education, communication, and transportation links; subsistence, to a wage economy; and rural values, to resettlement, urbanization, and outward migration.

Yet our attachment to home and province is strong. Our approach to woods and wildlife is more utilitarian than that of other Canadians, but by the same token our love for the country and its torments and charms is powerful. As we see more of the rest of the world, we better understand the value of what we have here. And we don't want to lose it.

At the same time, Newfoundlanders share with other Canadians a new respect and concern for the land. Harold Horwood describes it well as a "new sense of conscience toward the world. The sense that we are fellow-travelers with the rest of the living world is something entirely new. A hundred years ago a few people understood this in their heads; only now have millions of people begun to feel it in their guts."

Our government knows this. It believes it. We are making progress. Environmental assessment is operational and improving steadily. Forest management has been scrutinized by a royal commission. The Wilderness Advisory Council has been well supported and allowed to remain independent. We are developing a provincial conservation strategy and continue to co-operate nationally in a great number of joint conservation efforts. We have the beginnings of a wilderness and ecological reserves system.

Almost ten years ago the provincial government stated its aims and philosophy in *Managing All Our Resources — A Development Plan for Newfoundland and Labrador, 1980–1985*. It is an ambitious document. Setting out a blueprint for economic progress, it also sets a standard for maintenance of environmental quality and anticipates establishment of two wilderness reserves on the Island and one in Labrador. In the Throne Speech of 1980, the government recognized wilderness as an essential part of the social and cultural heritage of the province and pledged to preserve for all time some of the natural splendours inherited from our forefathers for the use and benefit of our people.

These have been difficult years. Achievements have been made despite a background of frustrating economic conditions. The government's courage in negotiations on offshore energy promises major new economic benefits and exciting opportunities. As we embark on these massive new world-class developments, let us hope our government shows the same courage in protecting our world-class natural heritage.

PIERRE TASCHEREAU

The Forest and the Sea: Maritime Priorities

In the eastern part of North America . . . lies a country known of old as Acadia. It covered most of that large peninsula which is nearly encircled by the great River St. Lawrence, the Gulf, and the Atlantic Ocean, with a western limit at the River Penobscot. Today it is parted into five political divisions: the Provinces of Nova Scotia, New Brunswick, Prince Edward Island and a portion of Quebec, together with a part of the state of Maine. It is a fair land, charming in summer though stern in winter, moderate in resources, varied in aspect, modest in relief, deeply dissected by the sea. Once it bore an unbroken mantle of forest, the sheltering of a wandering Indian race and nurse of a great fur-trade, while its waters have ever yielded a rich return from the fisheries.

Thus, botanist William Ganong introduces his 1908 translation of Nicolas Denys's 1672 description of the coasts of Acadia, the earliest account we have of the Gulf region, its Micmac inhabitants, vast forests, and summer fisheries for cod, which played such a large part in the early relations between Europe and northeastern North America.

No other factor has influenced the region and its people as much as has the sea. New Brunswick's shores are wave-washed by the Bay of Fundy and the Gulf of St. Lawrence. Prince Edward Island, separated by 14 kilometres from the nearest mainland, is cradled by the waters of the Gulf. Nova Scotia, almost an island, is linked to North America only by the narrow 22-kilometre lowland Isthmus of Chignecto.

The landscapes are as varied as the seas around them. The rough beauty of the exposed rocky Atlantic shores of eastern Nova Scotia contrasts strikingly with the gently sloping sandy shores of the Gulf coasts. The fertile, pastoral landscapes of the river valleys, such as those of the Saint John, the Annapolis, and the Margaree, and of the various smaller intervale meadows, contrast vividly with the rugged grandeur of the Cape Breton Highlands. The sharp rocky promontories bordering parts of the Bay of Fundy give way to the mud-flats, salt marshes, and pastured dykelands of the Bay's inland reaches. Ringed by water, Prince Edward

Island, with its red-soiled, rolling farmland of open fields and small woodlots and its miles of golden sandy beaches, little resembles its forest-clad, rocky-shored mainland neighbours.

The earliest human inhabitants of this land of contrasts were small bands of Palaeo-Indians who lived in the icy permafrost conditions that followed the retreating glaciers. Much, much later, Micmac families came to dwell in the protection of the great forests that developed over the land. In winter, the Micmac sheltered in these woods, protected from storms by the massive trees, but in summer they moved to the coastal shores, with their abundance of food and fresh sea breezes that drove back the hordes of biting flies.

Some thousand years ago, Vikings passed this land and wrote about it in their sagas. Later still, Portuguese fishermen came to fish in the region's rich waters, and stopped to dry their catch on its fine beaches.

In 1605 Samuel de Champlain sailed into a sheltered basin along the Fundy coast. Soon, he found a protected site by the shore and christened it Port Royal. There he worked on his garden, built a pond for trout, and constructed a small reservoir for saltwater fish. He wrote: "I arranged a summer garden with fine trees in order that I might enjoy the air; the birds gathered in great numbers and chirped so pleasantly that I do not think I ever heard the like."

Acadian farmers of French descent later settled in protected bays and inlets along the Fundy coast, where they dyked the low-lying land, converting its extensive salt marshes into farmland.

English settlements, established first for military reasons, soon attracted settlers drawn to the land. The English arrived first, followed by Germans, Irish, Scots, and settlers from other countries. Today's traveller in the region encounters placenames that tell of the origin of these many peoples.

LAND AND SEA: PRIORITIES
Forests

The Maritime provinces belong to what ecologists call the "Hemlock–White Pine–Northern Hardwood Region of Eastern North America" or, for short, the "Eastern Hemlock Region." The forests are, in many respects, transitional between the deciduous forests that flank them to the south and the northern conifer forests that occur along their northern borders.

Trees cover about 80 per cent of the land surface of Nova Scotia, approximately five million hectares and vast areas of New Brunswick. Virtually all of the forests, however, consist of the young second-growth descendants of earlier forests that have been cut-over. Few Maritimers have ever seen an old-growth forest; very few are even aware that such forest stands exist.

Long before the coming of the first European settlers, such forests covered much of the land. Today New Brunswick and P.E.I. have only a few scattered remnants. Some of the finest old-growth forests still occur in Nova Scotia, though the stands are small and widely scattered.

Old-growth forests are strikingly different from the familiar woodlands that make up so much of the Maritime countryside. Their trees are large and widely spaced, with the occasional much larger tree scattered among them. The older trees range in age from 150 to 350 years, with the oldest individuals perhaps up to 450 years. The larger trees may reach a metre or more in diameter towards the base and may be as tall as 30 metres.

The tall, straight white pine of the Acadian forests were early prized as masts for the English navy's ships. By 1728, however, twenty-one years before the founding of Halifax, the British government had found it necessary to reserve what remained of the better white pine. The harvesting practice of always removing the very largest and finest trees from a stand is called "high-grading." Over a period of time it depletes the genetic stock by leaving only the inferior specimens to reproduce.

Current forestry practices in the Maritimes do not sanction the protection of old-growth forests. Such stands are viewed as unproductive, reservoirs of disease, and potential breeding sites for insect pests such as the spruce budworm. Also, because of the great size of the trees, the timber available in old-growth stands is very valuable. Foresters view the notion of not harvesting such "decadent" stands of "overmature" trees as silvicultural mismanagement, and as an outright waste of a valuable resource.

Nevertheless, these relict forests are ecologically and culturally priceless. Here, in the old-growth woods, relatively undisturbed by human influence, man can study the natural processes and gain some understanding of how they work. These forests also have an historic and cultural significance. Here are examples of the forest primeval, once the refuge of the lichen-eating caribou and the shelter of aboriginal people, the culmination of nature's work over thousands of years. Their importance to the public is demonstrated by the large amounts of money citizens and governments are paying to protect forested areas as important heritage sites. In the 1980s, for example, the Prince Edward Island government purchased, at great expense, a 4-hectare woodlot at the edge of Charlottetown, to prevent the destruction of trees that were to be cleared to make way for a shopping mall. On the woodlot were a number of large red oak, the Island's official provincial tree. In 1972, the Island government purchased 104 hectares, 24 of which contain almost all that remains of the Island's once-great hardwood groves. These purchases emphasize just how priceless a part of the region's cultural heritage are the few remaining stands of virgin forest. As more and more Maritimers come to relish the natural environment, they are refusing to be alienated from this birthright of their natural heritage.

In the structure and composition of its plant communities and in the genetic make-up of its species, the old-growth forests of the Maritimes are unique, unduplicated anywhere else in the world.

River Margins and Lake Edges

Riparian zones are vegetated strips that fringe ponds and streams and clothe the banks of rivers. They are important habitats for mammals that feed and nest in these areas — beaver, raccoon, mink, ermine, muskrat, red-backed voles, meadow voles, meadow jumping mice, and woodland jumping mice. Wooded riparian zones are particularly important to brook trout, rainbow trout, and salmon. The trees provide shade and cover, and insects falling from them are eaten by juvenile and adult fish. As well as providing animal habitats, these vegetated areas protect streams from siltation and help to control soil loss from agriculture. Farming and forestry practices that disrupt this zone bring about deterioration of water and habitat quality.

The Prince Edward Island Natural Areas Survey lists three particularly important riparian sites: a 24-hectare pond on the Naufrage River, another site along the scenic Miminegash River valley, and Trout Creek.

In New Brunswick, more than half of the specialized habitats of the province's rare plants occur along the margins of rivers and lakes.

The gravelly strands along the Saint John, Restigouche, and Saint Croix rivers are among the region's most critical areas. Here, subarctic and western plants such as the milk vetches, and other post-glacial relict species, such as the Lake Huron tansy and northern painted cup, have been able to survive and reproduce. Along the banks of the upper Saint John River grows a plant called the furbish lousewort, which is officially classified as an endangered species in Canada. The plants are about one-half to one metre tall. Their two-lipped, greenish-yellow flowers occur in a cluster at the end of a dark red stem with fern-like leaves. The species is found nowhere else in the world.

Two assemblages of rare plants in Nova Scotia are associated with river margins. One is the rich hardwood flora of river intervales in northern and central Nova Scotia. The other is the coastal plain element consisting of plants occurring on the coastal plain farther south, but which in Nova Scotia are restricted to river margins and lake edges in the southwestern part of the province. Plants

A scene of water, ice and snow in the Cape Breton Highlands of Nova Scotia.
CREDIT: J.A. KRAULIS.

MARITIMES   New Brunswick, Nova Scotia and P.E.I.

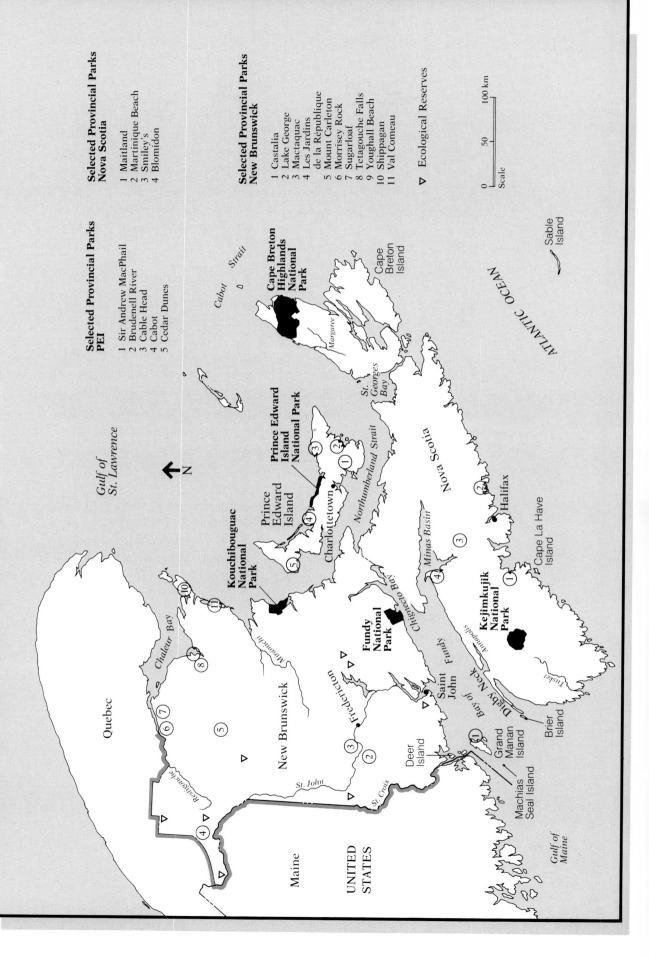

**Selected Provincial Parks
PEI**

1 Sir Andrew MacPhail
2 Brudenell River
3 Cable Head
4 Cabot
5 Cedar Dunes

**Selected Provincial Parks
Nova Scotia**

1 Maitland
2 Martinique Beach
3 Smiley's
4 Blomidon

**Selected Provincial Parks
New Brunswick**

1 Castalia
2 Lake George
3 Mactaquac
4 Les Jardins
  de la République
5 Mount Carleton
6 Morrisey Rock
7 Sugarloaf
8 Tetagouche Falls
9 Youghall Beach
10 Shippagan
11 Val Comeau

▽ Ecological Reserves

Scale

0   50   100 km

Gulf of
St. Lawrence

N

Cabot Strait

Cape Breton
Island

**Cape Breton
Highlands
National Park**

Margaree

St.
Georges
Bay

ATLANTIC OCEAN

Sable
Island

Prince Edward Island

**Prince Edward
Island
National Park**

Charlottetown

Northumberland Strait

Nova Scotia

Halifax

Cape La Have
Island

**Kejimkujik National
Park**

Tusket

**Kouchibouguac
National Park**

Miramichi

Minas Basin

Chignecto Bay

**Fundy
National Park**

Annapolis

Digby Neck

Bay of Fundy

Brier Island

Quebec

Restigouche

New Brunswick

Fredericton

St. John

St. Croix

Saint John

Deer Island

Grand Manan
Island

Machias
Seal Island

Chaleur Bay

Maine

UNITED
STATES

Gulf of
Maine

associated with the hardwoods along river intervales include Canada lily, wild leek, hepatica, and feverwort, among the rarest in the province. Other species occurring in the north include bloodroot, wild leek, yellow violets, spring beauty, Dutchman's-breeches, and blue cohosh.

In southwestern Nova Scotia, particularly in portions of the Tusket River Valley near Yarmouth, rare and endangered plants such as the Plymouth gentian and pink coreopsis are found. Plymouth gentian, classified nationally as "threatened," is about 60 centimetres tall with rose-coloured or white showy flowers and a delicate fragrance. Pink coreopsis, classified as "endangered," is a daisy-like plant about 30 centimetres or so tall, with pink ray petals and short narrow leaves. Another "threatened" coastal-plain species found in the same area is a woody shrub called sweet pepperbush. This fall-flowering, moisture-loving plant with fragrant white spikes of flowers is about 2 metres tall.

In the warm inland areas of southwestern Nova Scotia one finds isolated populations of southern flying squirrel, and relict populations of two southern reptiles, Blanding's turtle and the northern ribbon snake. These animals have persisted in small warmer pockets since the times of warmer climate that followed the retreat of the last ice age.

Sea Margins: Salt Marshes and Coastal Dunes

One of nature's beautiful gifts to the region is a garland of salt marshes interspersed with golden sands and lofty dunes. The ribbon of green growth, part land, part scurrying water, is the nursery of the sea, the birthplace and shelter of numerous small organisms that provide food for the larger.

Estuaries and salt marshes are about ten times as productive as the coastal waters upon which the commercial fisheries depend, and the coastal waters, in turn, are about ten times as productive as the open ocean. Birds and fish have evolved depending on finding such habitats along the coast. A whole system of marshes with its high productivity, rather than individual marshes, is what needs protection. Human activity damages the marsh wetlands directly by dredging, filling-in, and building, and indirectly by siltation and pollution. More and more of the frail marsh-estuary system will be inevitably destroyed unless an overall plan is developed to evaluate and protect significant marsh areas.

The most developed and spectacularly beautiful coastal dunes are on Prince Edward Island. The P.E.I. Natural Areas Survey examined more than thirty dune systems in the province and recommended that six with the highest priority be given protected status. These are areas with spectacular land and seascapes harbouring a variety of life, including birds such as the endangered piping plover.

In New Brunswick, two salt marshes and two sand-dune systems, one of them within Kouchibouguac National Park, have been recommended as protected natural areas. One salt marsh is on the Bay of Fundy side of New Brunswick, the other is on the Gulf Coast. In Nova Scotia, the International Biological Program team surveyed only three salt-marsh sites and five sand-dune sites.

Little attention has been given to these important coastal sites. However, one need only look to the coastline south of the border to see what could happen to them. In the United States, 35 per cent of the population lives within 240 kilometres of the east coast. Every year many people come to the shore at least once, and many come several times. While there is still a maximum of options, it is vital that Canadian planners, politicians, and citizens become aware of the need to protect this natural ribbon of green and gold.

Bogs, Gypsum, and Limestone

Bogs or peatlands are abundant over much of Nova Scotia and New Brunswick. They may not be the preferred habitat for most waterfowl, but information available suggests that they are used by many organisms including shrews, voles, mice, and other mammals, birds, reptiles, amphibians, fish, and invertebrates. Bogs are the prime habitat for some of Canada's rarest and most beautiful native orchids and for some of our most unusual plants, such as the carnivorous pitcher plant, sundew, and bladderwort.

In Prince Edward Island and New Brunswick only two bog sites have been recommended for protection as nature reserves. Nine bog sites in Nova Scotia have been recommended for protection as ecological reserves. Currently, only one of these sites, which happens to fall within the boundaries of Cape Breton Highlands National Park, has any protected status.

The Nova Scotia Department of Mines and Energy recently completed a very detailed field study of all the peatlands in the province. The purpose of the study was to examine areas suitable for extracting peat for fuel, but the rich data-base could be used just as well to plan sites for ecological reserves.

Gypsum and limestone outcrops in Nova Scotia and New Brunswick are habitats for some of the region's rarest plants. Among the showy orchids growing there are the yellow lady-slipper, and the Ram's-head lady-slipper.

The gypsum caves are the winter hibernacula for rare bats such as the eastern pipistrelle and the northern long-eared bat. These alkaline areas with their special flora and fauna for the most part have received little attention as candidate reserve sites. Only one site in Nova Scotia is now protected as a provincial park.

LAND AND SEA: PROGRESS

Three groups have had a marked influence on preservation efforts in the region.

The International Biological Program was a ten-year co-operative project, begun in 1964, as a response by scientists and governments in ninety-six nations to the world-wide problems of human population explosion, food shortages, and environmental destruction. The key was the setting aside of natural areas to maintain the diversity of living organisms in all parts of the world. They would serve as benchmarks by which to measure man-made changes in the ecosystem, and would be used for biological research, education, and demonstration purposes.

The Maritime provinces contributed to the program by setting up a panel of experts from government, universities, and museums. It recommended that 110 sites be established as ecological reserves: 27 in New Brunswick, 69 in Nova

Scotia, and 14 in Prince Edward Island. Now, fifteen years after publication of the panel's report, *Ecological Reserves in the Maritimes*, all three provinces have enacted special legislation to protect natural areas, and are in the process of establishing reserve systems. To date, three reserves in Nova Scotia have been established, seven in New Brunswick, and seven in P.E.I.

In 1982, the Canadian Council on Ecological Areas was established as a national forum to encourage the selection, protection, and stewardship of a comprehensive system of ecological reserves in Canada. The council draws its membership from federal, provincial, and territorial governments, non-government organizations, universities, and private citizens. Its goal is to promote a Canadian system of protected areas that would reflect the full ecological diversity of our country and serve as yardsticks for measuring damage or change to areas disturbed by man.

Ecological reserves are the responsibility of the provinces, but like the International Biological Program before it, the Canadian Council on Ecological Areas has catalyzed governments, generated enthusiasm, and injected new life into provincial efforts to protect natural areas within their jurisdictions. In Atlantic Canada, the council has already spawned a regional working group to focus on the protection of natural areas in the region, including Newfoundland as well as the three Maritime provinces.

The first priority of the Atlantic Working Group of the Canadian Council on Ecological Areas was to devise a program that would serve as a connecting link between various conservation groups in Atlantic Canada. It would facilitate communication between government and non-government groups and help to focus on the protection of both rare and characteristic habitats in the region. Like other regional conservation programs, for example, the World Wildlife Fund's Wild West and Carolinian Canada programs, Atlantic Coastal Canada is designed to stimulate conservation action by both private and government agencies, resulting in tangible conservation achievement. The program is meant to actively involve members of the general public, naturalists, Scouts, and other groups with an interest in the out-of-doors.

An interim steering committee, with representatives from all four Atlantic provinces, has been established to provide guidance in the early stages of the project, and the School for Resource and Environmental Studies, Dalhousie University, Halifax, has agreed to provide a home.

New Attitudes

In the 1960s, a sizeable segment of the Maritime population believed that parks were essentially public playgrounds for golf, various outdoor sports, and picnics. On sites developed for recreation, the untidy variety of the natural flora soon gave way to the neat uniformity of well-managed lawns. The notion of nature as the prime resource was not widespread.

Similarly, parks as areas where *all* wildlife is protected is also relatively new. Traditionally, wildlife has meant only commercially valuable species. Now, however, "wildlife" has come to include the full spectrum of wild living organisms, both plant and animal.

The changing view of the role of parks in protecting natural habitats, and all forms of wildlife within them, is reflected in the new kinds of parks to be created. For example in Nova Scotia the Minister of Lands and Forests, the Honorable Jack MacIsaac, stated in 1988 that "under the new policy, a parks classification system will be introduced. It will incorporate the following categories: Wildland Parks, Natural Heritage Reserves, Historic Parks, Natural Environment Parks, Outdoor Recreation Parks, Wayside Parks, Wildlife Parks and Park Reserves."

An objection still sometimes levied against parks and natural areas is that they fail to practise multiple use. Parks and nature reserves, it is claimed, limit the number of ways in which land can be used; they restrict resource extraction, and they lock up large amounts of productive land for a single use. The multiple-use concept applies primarily to consumptive use, and only in this limited sense can parks and nature reserves be seen as single-use. In fact, most parks and many reserves are available for hiking, canoeing, fishing, swimming, cross-country skiing, for conducted school classes, birdwatching, photography, and so on. Parks and reserves, while protecting the genetic diversity of the living organisms within them, are used for baseline research studies, obtaining genetic material for plant breeding, for ecological and behavioural studies, and soil and hydrological research.

Multiple use may be a rational approach to land utilization, but the concept must be applied with some discrimination. Some areas justify the highest, most suitable type of use, rather than the most possible kinds of use. Even though a family applies multiple use to a house as a whole, not every room is used for every purpose.

New Brunswick Priorities

The Saint John River Valley is among the natural areas in the province with highest priority for protection. The bottomlands and slopes are rich in floral elements and the rich deciduous woods are distinguished by the presence of butternut, basswood, and silver maple trees absent in Nova Scotia and Prince Edward Island.

In 1988, the New Brunswick Nature Trust was formed. One of its first activities was to produce a booklet describing the province's critical natural areas. The recent publication of the *Flora of New Brunswick*, by Hal Hinds of the University of New Brunswick, will also boost interest in conservation of this varied region.

Nova Scotia Priorities

Old-growth forests are among this province's natural areas of highest priority. In 1987, the province's first ecological reserve was proclaimed and formally announced in the village of Tusket, not far from the reserve site. Two endangered species — pink coreopsis and water pennywort, and one threatened species, Plymouth gentian, occur there in relative abundance. A local environmental committee is conducting a landowner-contact program with cottagers whose land is adjacent to the critical wetlands on the Tusket River.

In 1986, under the aegis of the School for Resource and Environmental Studies, Dalhousie University, the Nature Reserves Liaison Committee was formed. The committee members envisioned their role as helping to link various groups and agencies interested in the protection of natural areas, and to support and provide technical expertise for government agencies. This committee also serves as the provincial steering committee for the Atlantic Coastal Canada conservation program.

The most recent government action to protect natural areas is reflected in the 1988 legislation: a new Provincial Parks Act, a new Trails Act, and amendments to the Beaches Preservation and Protection Act.

The Bowater Mersey Paper Company owns much of the finest forested land in central and southwestern Nova Scotia. A leader in conservation and sound land management, the company has taken a special interest in protecting important ecological areas on its land. It has a policy of protecting ecological sites recommended as reserves by the International Biological Program.

Prince Edward Island Priorities

In Prince Edward Island 50 per cent of the land is under cultivation and the remainder consists of cut-over woodlots and old-field spruce regeneration. There are a few 3- to 4-hectare stands of white pine and one old-growth hardwood grove of 24 hectares. Most of the best natural areas are along the coast: sand-dune and salt-marsh sites. Only 10 per cent of the land is owned by the provincial and federal Crown, including a national park and some small provincial parks.

The Island's main conservation vehicle is the Island Nature Trust, a non-government agency. Established in 1984, the Trust has worked effectively in cooperation with government and in concert with other conservation agencies to secure the protection of a number of the Island's natural areas. It also undertakes educational and promotional activities related to natural areas.

In March 1988, the following legislation, of great significance to natural-area protection, was enacted: (1) the Natural Areas Protection Act, the equivalent of ecological reserves legislation in other provinces, enables the government to designate natural areas on Crown land, and on private land with the owners' agreement; (2) the Environmental Protection Act provides for the protection of sand dunes from vehicular traffic; and (3) the Forest Management Act recognizes the value of natural areas and wildlife habitat.

In August 1988, Hon. Gilbert R. Clements, P.E.I. Minister of Community and Cultural Affairs, chose the occasion of the annual meeting of the Canadian Council on Ecological Areas, hosted in Charlottetown by the Island Nature Trust, to announce the designation of seven parcels of Crown land as natural areas. Included among the designations was the remnant of original forest described by the International Biological Program as "one of the best old-growth hardwood groves in the province."

NATIONAL PARKS AND PROTECTED SITES

National Parks

In the Maritimes, there are five national parks. Cape Breton Highlands National

Park is the largest (950 square kilometres) and protects the most diverse and significant habitats. It is bounded on the west by the Gulf of St. Lawrence and on the east by the Atlantic Ocean.

Kejimkujik National Park, covering 381 square kilometres in the warm southwest interior of Nova Scotia, is a forested, gently rolling region of lakes and islands. Almost all of it has been burned or logged within the past two hundred years, but as a result of the warm, moist climate and good soils, the forest has largely regenerated and now a mixed wood covers about three-quarters of the area.

Fundy National Park covers 206 square kilometres along the Fundy shore in southern New Brunswick. The Bay of Fundy is a bird-migration route. In spring and fall large numbers of migrating birds stop over, and the elusive eastern cougar has been sighted within the park and may be surviving there.

Kouchibouguac National Park covers 239 square kilometres consisting of coastal and inland habitats, along the Gulf coast. Named after one of the park's three rivers, Kouchibouguac is a Micmac Indian word meaning "river of the long tides." Prince Edward Island National Park is a narrow coastal area of 32 square kilometres along the Gulf of St. Lawrence. The park protects areas of coastline and associated dunes, but is particularly valued for its fine recreational beaches.

Natural Areas of Canadian Significance

As part of its planning for a representative national parks system, Parks Canada identifies natural areas it considers representative of the natural region in which they are situated. These areas, called "Natural Areas of Canadian Significance," have no legal or protected status, but by making a public register listing the sites, Parks Canada hopes to draw attention to their importance and enlist public support for their protection.

Four Natural Areas of Canadian Significance have been identified in the Maritimes. Deer Island Archipelago consists of some forty islands, and numerous shoals, passages, and ledges close to the New Brunswick shore, near the mouth of the Bay of Fundy. The islands support numerous seabird breeding colonies and serve as feeding ground for vast populations of migrating and wintering waterfowl and shorebirds. The waters are inhabited by large numbers of harbour porpoise and harbour seals, while the endangered right whale and humpback whale, as well as finback and minke whales, are regular visitors to the area.

Grand Manan Archipelago is adjacent to Deer Island in the Bay of Fundy. It consists of fifteen major islands and numerous islets, ledges, shoals, and tidal flats. The waters about Grand Manan support a rich abundance of marine life, while the island itself is a staging area for migrating shorebirds. The landscape of Grand Manan is marked by its spectacular basalt cliffs. Bald eagles and osprey nest on these cliffs and on bluffs throughout the archipelago.

Brier Island is located at the tip of Digby Neck in southwestern Nova Scotia. Its abundance of fish and zooplankton makes it a vital feeding area for an exceptionally large number of migrant seabirds. A diversity of seals and whales feed and winter in these marine waters. The Nature Conservancy of Canada has recently purchased a large part of Brier Island to be maintained as a protected natural area.

The Cape La Have Islands and mainland fringe represent the irregular and diverse coastline of southwestern Nova Scotia. Particularly well represented are fine sandy beaches, shingle beaches, and a mainland landscape characterized by a series of drumlins overlooking the coast.

Canadian Heritage Rivers

The St. Croix River in southeastern New Brunswick has been accepted by Parks Canada as a candidate heritage river. Its special features include nature observation, outdoor recreation, and novice white-water canoeing. Nova Scotia, one of the participating provinces in the Heritage River Program, is presently considering several rivers for nomination.

National Wildlife Areas and Migratory Bird Sanctuaries

Originally, the National Wildlife Area program was restricted to migratory-bird habitats, but it now includes the habitats of other wildlife. Twelve national wildlife areas are in the Maritimes: seven in Nova Scotia and five in New Brunswick. The New Brunswick sites, ranging in size from 439 to 1990 hectares, encompass fresh- and salt-water marsh habitats, wetlands, woodlands, and sand-dune communities. The Nova Scotia sites range in size from 41 to 1020 hectares. Habitats within these areas include salt marshes, woodlands, and marine and fresh-water wetlands. The major species protected in these areas are migrating and nesting waterfowl, shorebirds, and various other birds, muskrats, and ungulates. Hunting is permitted in most national wildlife areas, and an area's natural condition may be altered by blasting out ponds for waterfowl breeding sites, planting trees and shrubs as covers for birds and deer, or otherwise altering the landscape to increase the food and shelter for wildlife.

The Canadian Wildlife Service of the federal Department of the Environment administers the Migratory Birds Convention Act, which gives the federal government authority to acquire and manage habitats for migratory birds, and in agreement with the provinces and territories, for other species of wildlife.

There are eleven migratory-bird sanctuaries in the Maritimes: eight in Nova Scotia, two in New Brunswick, and one in Prince Edward Island. In contrast to practice in the national wildlife areas, hunting is not permitted and no activity is allowed that might be harmful to migratory birds or their eggs, nests, or habitat.

Migratory-bird sanctuaries in Nova Scotia range in size from 100 to 433 hectares with one 2350-hectare sanctuary on Sable Island. Habitats within the sanctuaries include barrier beach ponds, floodplains, mudflats, salt marshes, estuaries, wetlands, fields, forests, beaches, and dunes. Some of the major bird species protected include piping plovers, Ipswich sparrows, and arctic terns.

In New Brunswick a 250-hectare sanctuary on Grand Manan Island protects eider ducks, Brant geese, and various migration waterfowl. Ten hectares of Machias Seal Island, with its heath meadow and rocky shore habitats, are also protected as a sanctuary. Prince Edward Island's Black Pond, a pond and barrier beach sanctuary of 130 hectares, protects Canada geese, black ducks and various other waterfowl.

TOWARDS A SYSTEM OF NATURE RESERVES

Today each Maritime province has in place legislation to protect its natural areas as nature reserves.

Within the last year, there has been a great increase in activity to establish these reserves. To date, however, the sites set aside as reserves are too small and too few. Perhaps, because they are special, reserves are looked upon as islands or oases amid man-modified environments. They are seen as apart from, and often in competition with, other kinds of land use. Instead of being but a fraction of land zoned specially for preservation, research, and education, reserves ought to be looked upon as integral components of most major land-use categories. Thus envisioned, reserves would be a part of such categories as subsurface resource lands, agricultural land, multiple-use forestry and recreation lands, and other natural to semi-natural, more or less manipulated lands used for hunting, fishing, and wildlife management.

In the Maritimes, as elsewhere, there has been an understandable emphasis on defending the irreplaceable, in the belief that the replaceable is better able to look after itself. This has inevitably led to an emphasis on the special rather than on the commonplace. One approach being used in the Maritimes to achieve protection of representative as well as rare habitats is the use of systems employing ecologically defensible subdivisions of the land as a basis for site selection. Nova Scotia uses its "Theme Regions" as a biophysical base, New Brunswick has "ecoregions," and Prince Edward Island makes use of various "habitat categories." Ecological subdivisions of land are mapped and with this visual approach, areas inadequately represented by nature reserves quickly become apparent.

Public appreciation of reserves in the Maritimes has come largely from the involvement of citizens and non-government groups in the process of reserve creation. Virtually all of the currently legislated nature reserves owe their existence to the persevering interest and work of unpaid individuals and groups. Public perception of nature reserves — their function, value, importance for wildlife, and relevance to mankind — continues to be critical. Landowner contact and private stewardship have been essential in Prince Edward Island, which is 90 per cent privately owned. Nova Scotia and New Brunswick have more Crown land than does Prince Edward Island, but some of the finest natural areas in these provinces are on privately owned land. Here, as on the Island, landowner contact and private stewardship are important ways of protecting natural areas. In addition, this approach heightens public awareness of the need to protect segments of the landscape, and deepens public appreciation of nature reserves.

HARVEY MEAD

Quebec's Natural Heritage

Quebec's history marks it off in many important ways from that of the other provinces. Its traditions of hunting, fishing, and trapping are still deeply rooted. These traditional activities were not until recently paralleled by the non-consumptive activities associated with natural areas so common throughout anglophone North America. And the overwhelming dominance of extractive industries, particularly the pulp-and-paper industry, has, in the eyes of the population, made of much of Quebec a land of timber concessions used secondarily for hunting and fishing.

The notion of protecting wildlands in Quebec from all kinds of resource exploitation effectively dates only to 1977, when the Parks Act was adopted. Previous to this legislation, the notion of parks as protected areas was almost unknown in Quebec. Large areas known as "parks" — the Parc du Mont Tremblant and the Parc des Laurentides, for example — were essentially forest reserves that had been exploited since their creation in the late nineteenth century.

The St. Lawrence River, the major axis of transportation and settlement, has a history with corresponding overtones. Drainage and urban expansion schemes have led to the loss of wetland habitat along major sections of the river corridor. At the same time pollution from the ever-present pulp-and-paper mills, and more recently from industrial complexes, has slowly degraded the quality of the water and of the river-bottom sediments. A tremendous increase in human population, and in "wealth", has had impacts in Quebec analogous to those encountered elsewhere since the Second World War. As with the land, the province's (and indeed Canada's) major waterway has been taken for granted.

None the less, "development" in many of its contemporary forms came to Quebec later than it did to other provinces, and there is reason to believe that public awareness of the need for protected areas to complement development is expanding at a rate that is making up for the lateness of official and popular recognition.

The questions that need to be asked are whether and how it will be possible, even with the change in attitude, to adequately protect the "endangered spaces" of Quebec in the coming years. These questions are all the more crucial in that scarcely 0.3 per cent of the land surface of the province — perhaps 1 per cent of the southern area — is currently protected from development. A potential obstacle lies in the recently adopted Forest Act. Under the terms of this legislation, almost all the forested areas of Quebec will be allocated in the coming years to private forestry companies on a long-term basis. It should be noted that much of the original deciduous forest, especially that of the St. Lawrence flood plain, has long since been converted to agricultural land. On the other hand, the St. Lawrence River system is the subject of major federal, provincial, and non-government programs of protection, restoration, and more sensible development. Finally, a major thrust in the agricultural sector towards intensive cropping would seem to have peaked, confronted by serious problems of erosion, compaction, lowered productivity, and rising costs.

WHAT'S AT STAKE?

It's important to keep in mind just what Quebec has to offer to a pan-Canadian effort to protect our natural heritage. In keeping with its status as the country's largest province, Quebec has a diverse landscape.

One basic division of the territory can be made via the major drainage basins, of which there are three, almost of equal size. These are the St. Lawrence basin (673,000 square kilometres), the James Bay and Hudson Bay basin (518,000 square kilometres), and the Ungava Bay basin (492,000 square kilometres). This division of the province is of some significance, because it ecologically identifies the entire southern and most populated part of the province as the drainage basin of the St. Lawrence River.

In terms of vegetation, a second division more or less overlaps the first, with tundra and taiga constituting almost the entire land area of the two northern drainage basins, and boreal or mixed forest covering the entire southern part associated with the St. Lawrence basin. Approximately 5 per cent of the latter has been converted to agriculture and human settlements.

The St. Lawrence River itself flows for approximately 1300 kilometres from its entry into Quebec at the Ontario border near Cornwall, to the point (not clearly defined) where it becomes the Gulf of St. Lawrence and merges with the Atlantic Ocean. In the section east and west of Montreal, several important enlargements offer unique natural features; these enlargements are known as "lakes" (Lac Saint-François, Lac Saint-Louis, Lac des Deux Montagnes, Lac Saint-Pierre), although they are integral parts of the "flowing" river.

At Batiscan it becomes a tidal river, at a distance of more than 1050 kilometres from the ocean. The influence of the tides becomes more and more marked as it continues its flow, with tides over 6 metres occurring in the Quebec City area.

Just east of Quebec City, the St. Lawrence enters a new phase, becoming for the first time saline. The degree of salinity continues to increase until the river merges with the gulf and the ocean.

The non-tidal part of the river which simply "flows" was originally the bed of the Champlain Sea 10,000 years ago, when the most recent glaciation was receding and the meltwaters flooded the area. In more recent times, this fertile sedimentary basin was the heart of an impressive deciduous forest of which only remnants remain today. The shallow "lakes" and large numbers of islands add to the natural importance of this section of the river, offering some chance for finding representative sites worthy of protection. The historic variations in flow also meant that flood plains were an important natural feature, although this was changed in significant ways by the construction of dams and the St. Lawrence Seaway. Lac Saint-Pierre is unique as it retains interesting flood-plain areas.

The fresh-water tidal area of the river marks the beginning of the shoreline characterized by bullrush marshes, such as those at Cap Tourmente National Wildlife Reserve. With the beginnings of salinity at this point, the marshes continue, but are dominated by more salt-water–adapted species. The latter are well known as a result of the efforts to protect them in the Kamouraska area. Wetlands are, then, still important throughout the reach of the St. Lawrence, even if a large percentage of the marshes have been destroyed or seriously affected by various human activities.

South of the St. Lawrence, the Appalachian Mountains reach their northernmost extension. These mountains are characterized by mixed forest dominated by sugar maple in the southern and western part of the region. To the north and east, Parc de la Gaspésie, whose summits rise to 1200 metres, protects seven different vegetation zones, including tundra and taiga at the higher elevations.

North of the St. Lawrence, the Laurentian Shield, harbouring the oldest mountains on Earth and extending into Newfoundland and Labrador on the east and Ontario and Manitoba on the west, lies at varying distances from the river itself. The Shield abruptly joins the St. Lawrence at Cap Tourmente, marking the end of the deciduous-forest lowlands and the fresh-water river basin.

Heading north, the forest passes from mixed forest to spruce-fir forest. Numerous river valleys drain the area in the direction of the St. Lawrence. Their history has been radically shaped by glaciation, frequently leaving deep gorges of spectacular beauty. The Lac Saint-Jean area constitutes a major enclave of relatively fertile soils in the interior. Transformed by human development over the past century, the area is drained by the Saguenay River. This "world-class fjord" joins the St. Lawrence estuary at Tadoussac, site of a thriving whale-watching industry and a proposed national marine park.

At approximately the fifty-second degree of latitude, the spruce-fir forest gives way to the taiga. These scattered trees and lichens finally disappear into the tundra of the high northern area. This area, New Quebec, encompasses close to two-thirds of the province's land surface.

It should also be noted that Quebec possesses an enormous coastline extending for 4645 kilometres, from James Bay to the Labrador Coast, and for 4500 kilometres along the St. Lawrence and the Saguenay. In addition, bogs scattered throughout the province and covering large areas reflect the province's moist climate and its geology. Important bogs in the south are in imminent danger of disappearing.

THE LEGAL FRAMEWORK

A great deal remains unknown with respect to the province's ecosystems and special places. The Ministry of Recreation, Fish and Game, responsible for the parks system, has identified in the official parks policy forty-three natural regions that merit recognition via the creation of parks representative of the ecological values of each region. The Parks Act also foresees the creation of parks for the protection of exceptional natural areas and for recreational purposes. In addition, the federal government's program could permit the creation of several more national parks to complete its system.

Other approaches to protection or preservation exist, although on a limited scale or for specific types of territory:

- Following a carefully developed ecological evaluation that identifies areas of value for their genetic and ecological diversity, the Quebec government plans to ultimately set aside more than 100 ecological reserves, usually of very small size.

- Several national wildlife areas administered by the Canadian Wildlife Service offer substantial protection for wetlands against traditional threats from agricultural drainage, urban development, or simple "trashing."

- There is some movement towards more careful logging practices in the provincial wildlife reserves. A recent and important political decision was made to retain these reserves, covering some 7 million hectares, following opposition to proposed privatization.

- A shoreline-protection policy has been adopted recently that may prevent, on a broad scale, further degradation of these non-tidal areas, without isolating specific sites for special protection. The policy has yet to be tested, however.

- A recently adopted amendment to the Wildlife Conservation Law will further enhance conservation of habitat for approximately a dozen species or groups of species; for example marine bird colonies.

- A Law on Endangered and Vulnerable Species was adopted in the spring of 1989, designed in part to permit protection of habitat for species of plants and animals not recognized in the previous amendment to the Wildlife Conservation Law.

A major challenge, in the context of this rather substantial legislative and regulatory activity, involves identifying rapidly those areas — perhaps 3 to 4 per

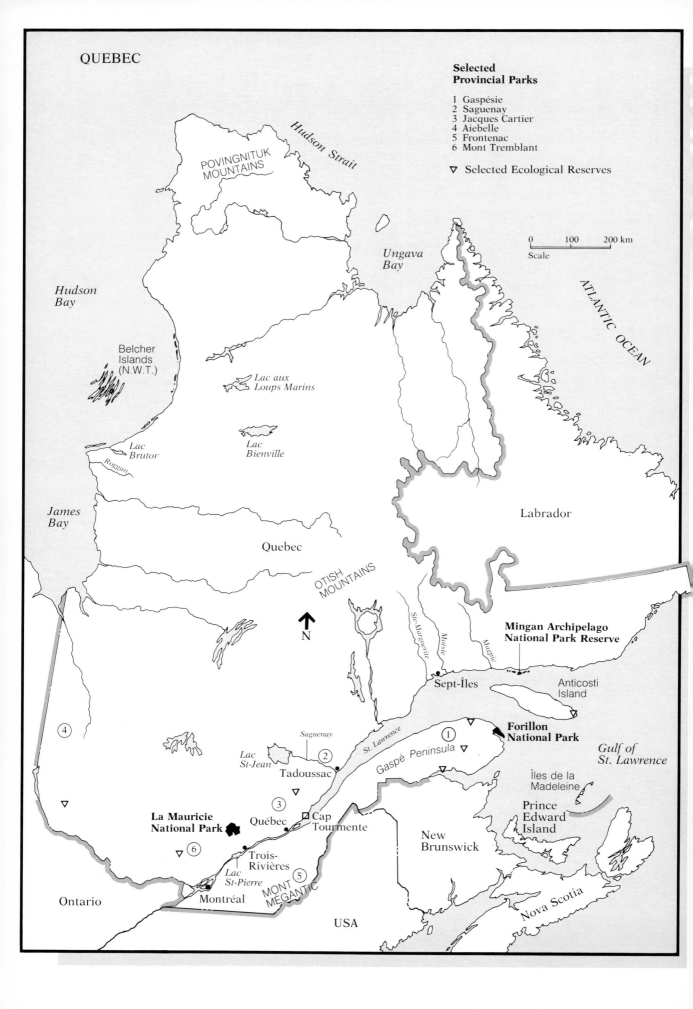

QUEBEC

**Selected
Provincial Parks**

1 Gaspésie
2 Saguenay
3 Jacques Cartier
4 Aiebelle
5 Frontenac
6 Mont Tremblant

▽ Selected Ecological Reserves

POVINGNITUK
MOUNTAINS

Hudson Strait

*Ungava
Bay*

0   100   200 km
Scale

*Hudson
Bay*

ATLANTIC OCEAN

Belcher
Islands
(N.W.T.)

*Lac aux
Loups Marins*

*Lac
Brutor*

*Lac
Bienville*

Roggan

Labrador

*James
Bay*

Quebec

OTISH
MOUNTAINS

N

Ste-Marguerite

Moise

Magpie

**Mingan Archipelago
National Park Reserve**

Sept-Îles

Anticosti
Island

④

▽

St. Lawrence

Saguenay

①

▽

**Forillon
National Park**

*Gulf of
St. Lawrence*

②

*Lac
St-Jean*

Tadoussac

Gaspé Peninsula

▽

Îles de la
Madeleine

③

▽

**La Mauricie
National Park**

Québec ◻ Cap
Tourmente

**Prince
Edward
Island**

▽ ⑥

Trois-
Rivières

New
Brunswick

*Lac
St-Pierre*

⑤

Montréal

MONT
MÉGANTIC

Ontario

USA

Nova Scotia

cent of the total land mass of the province — that merit special attention in terms of preservation, i.e., complete protection, and developing the means of protecting them adequately. There is reason to hope that adequate enforcement of the new legislation will also permit a beginning in the field of conservation, i.e., management for sustainable use, on the remaining 96 per cent of the land base.

The Nature Conservancy of Canada has just launched an important three-year inventory program in collaboration with the Quebec Ministry of the Environment designed to identify Quebec's natural areas of great significance. The results of the work, a pilot project based on an American model and to be applied later in other provinces, will only be known in three or four years. This chapter is in some ways an intuitive attempt to sketch what the Nature Conservancy's ultimate conclusions might be.

COMPLETING THE PARKS SYSTEM

As mentioned earlier, Quebec's park system dates only to 1979, with the creation of two recreation parks. The first conservation park, Parc de la Gaspésie, was established in 1981. For the past two years (1986–88), the provincial government has imposed a moratorium on any further additions. It is possible that the sixteen extant recreation and conservation parks will constitute almost the total system. These parks protect approximately 400,000 hectares in only eleven of the forty-three regions identified by the parks policy documents.

Quebec has little chance of embarking on the strategic land-use planning exercise that Ontario went through in 1982–83. None the less, Ministry studies have tentatively identified a large number of sites that could constitute appropriate inclusions in the parks system, beyond federal suggestions. Fifteen natural regions remain unrepresented in the southern area of the province. There are at present no parks in New Quebec, where the ministry has identified seventeen natural regions.

With intensifying pressures for development in the north and south, the government will have little choice but to move quickly if it is going to make any realistic effort to complete the system envisaged by the official parks policy. It must proceed by identifying "park reserves," leaving any plans for developing these areas for visitor use to a later date when funds become available. This option is not one favoured by the Ministry, since investments will provide few publicly recognized benefits in the short term.

Such an approach, however, is consistent with the rationale behind the protection of "representative areas of natural regions," which is the mandate of the Parks Act. Protecting areas of exceptional interest and areas having important recreational potential are also part of the mandate. A brief look at sites presently identified as candidates for the park system gives some idea of the diversity of Quebec's landscapes and ecosystems.

Several mountainous regions in the south remain in a state sufficiently pristine to permit their recognition. Mont Magloire and Mont Mégantic (both in the

Appalachian chain, south of the St. Lawrence River) as well as Mont Valin and Mont des Eboulements in the Shield, are all of considerable interest. Another valuable candidate, Mont Pinnacle, has recently been lost to a private resort and luxury housing development.

An exceptional site in the Laurentian Shield is the upper gorge of the Malbaie River, long mentioned as a candidate for park status. It has recently been given regional park recognition by the local municipal authority, but such protection does not have any established legal precedents in terms of long-term protection. The provincial government has no coherent policy with respect to such regional parks.

Among island areas of the St. Lawrence River and Gulf, Pointe de l'Est on the Magdalen Islands, the Sept Iles Archipelago, the north strand of Ile d'Orléans and the Montmagny Archipelago merit recognition. The provincial and federal governments, as well as private conservation organizations, are making plans to acquire other island groups near Montreal, including the Sorel Archipelago. The two governments signed an agreement in 1988 to permit the eventual creation of the Saguenay National Marine Park in the St. Lawrence/Saguenay estuary.

The federal national wildlife area system already protects other extremely important areas, which might otherwise merit recognition as parks, particularly along the St. Lawrence corridor. Lac Saint-François, Cap Tourmente, and what remains of the Kamouraska salt marshes are in this system. The Quebec branch of the Nature Conservancy and the Société Duvetnor have also been acquiring sites on a private basis, although some of their acquisitions may eventually end up in provincial or federal parks.

One or more of the majestic rivers on the Quebec North Shore (Moisie, Magpie, Sainte-Marguerite, for example) should constitute a high priority, particularly with Hydro-Quebec planning to dam every one of them. Coupled with the recently created Matamek Ecological Reserve, they would provide valuable recognition of this remarkable region, some 800 kilometres north and east of Quebec City. Time may be of particular importance in this region, as extensions of the road along the lower North Shore are opening it up to development.

An exceptionally rich riverine system nearer population centres is the Méta-betchouane-Metaskouac system in the Laurentian Shield triangle formed by Chi-coutimi, Quebec, and Montreal. While rarely mentioned as a candidate area, its undeveloped state (save for forestry operations), and its proximity to large numbers of people, both residents and tourists, indicate its considerable value.

A preliminary estimate of the area covered by this selection of sites in the southern part of the province would suggest the need to protect approximately 1 million hectares in addition to the 400,000 hectares already protected. The total would still amount to only 1 per cent of Quebec's land area, and approximately 2.6 per cent of the St. Lawrence River drainage basin.

The lack of population centres makes it possible to "think bigger" in the North. The type of ecosystems found there — fragile, extensive, with relatively little diversity — makes such an approach biologically appropriate as well. Approximately 5 million hectares would be required to adequately protect the sites associated with a completed parks system.

Perhaps the crown jewel of the area is the Torngat Mountain Range, which reaches an altitude of 1300 metres, an exceptional elevation in the ancient Shield formation of northern Quebec. The Koroc River draining it is one of the most beautiful rivers in the province. Several other mountainous regions would offer extremely important additions to a complete park system. These include the Otish Mountains, the Colline Blanche, and the Povungnituk Mountains.

Based on available inventories, the shores of James Bay, Hudson Bay, Hudson Straits, and Ungava Bay have been divided into five different regions by the Ministry. Baie aux Feuilles, Cap Wolstenholme and Douglas Harbour, Kovic Bay, Boatswain Bay, and Lac Guillaume-Delisle are exceptional sites and could represent these regions. Six other northern regions are associated with lakes and also merit some form of recognition. These could include Lac Assinica, Lac Mistassini, Lac Bienville, Lac Colombet and Eaton Canyon, Lac Cambrian, Lac Burton, and Roggan River as well as Lac aux Loups Marins.

The James Bay lowlands present a special case, with major hydro-electric projects presumably limiting options. The Keewatin Peninsula is an area of special interest, constituting a major staging area for the greater snow goose.

While far from Quebec's population centres, and thus not conceived in terms of large numbers of tourist person-days, many of the sites indicated above are none the less exceptional in their importance for wildlife, especially migratory waterfowl. This, in turn, can increase the interest of the southern population for their protection.

THE ECOLOGICAL RESERVES SYSTEM

After the Parks Act, the second major legislative authority for protecting natural areas of importance is the Law on Ecological Reserves, adopted in 1974. Following up on and applying the work of the International Biological Program, ecological reserves in Quebec are established in fifty bioclimatic zones.

Generally, the sites selected are neither well-known nor publicized. Their protection seeks to maintain genetic diversity. In contrast with the parks system, "development" of these sites for public access is completely foreign to their intention. The reserves are thus generally small and totally protected from direct human intrusion except for carefully controlled research and education projects.

Overall, the Ministry of Environment, which is responsible for this program, has outlined plans to establish some one hundred ecological reserves, supplementing the original fifty representative sites with an equal number of special areas. As an indication of their distinct, scientific character, the total area protected by the reserves in the southern part of Quebec would be smaller than 200,000 hectares.

Because of their uniqueness and their suitability for status as ecological reserves rather than parks, the bogs of southern Quebec merit special mention. One of the most important sites was recently lost to a highway. Development pressures from agriculture and urban expansion are ever-present, as these areas are located primarily in the regions south of Montreal, where 45 per cent of the population resides. The valley of the Richelieu River is the site of several key bogs, among them the Clarenceville Bog.

In the northern part of the province the Ministry sees a need to protect approximately twenty sites. These cover close to 1.5 million hectares, two-thirds of which overlap those selected as potential park candidates by the Ministry of Recreation, Fish and Game.

The two systems, parks and ecological reserves, are quite complementary, particularly in the north where public access need not be a high priority. If and when completed, the two systems, as sketched in the preliminary documents, would ultimately provide approximately 5.5 million hectares of protected space in Quebec. The fact that only 400,000 hectares are currently in the two systems makes clear the enormity of the task facing the two agencies.

THE CHALLENGE AHEAD

After close to four hundred years of European colonization, little of the southern part of the province remains in a pristine state. For example, only remnants remain of the majestic pine forests originally covering a great deal of southern Quebec. Large virgin spruce and fir are now found only in tiny, isolated places suitable for ecological reserve protection, but not for parks.

The Quebec Union for the Conservation of Nature has just produced an inventory of 180 priority wetlands in southern Quebec, 140 of which are currently unprotected. A major axis of the sites identified is the St. Lawrence River corridor. Programs of both the federal and provincial governments have as their objective the protection and improvement of some of these sites. Of the areas on the QUCN list, thirty-five sites in the Montreal area would seem to be most threatened by continuing urban development and agricultural pressures. These sites are normally small, excluding them from consideration as provincial conservation parks, and without the uniqueness that would entitle them to consideration as ecological reserves. It is thus likely that their protection will involve regional and private commitment and new categories of protected status.

The recent opportunity to provide complete protection to an entire untouched river basin, that of the Matamek River, gives some indication of the need for innovative ideas. After a decade of operating a research station on the north shore of the St. Lawrence, near Sept Iles, the Woods Hole Oceanographic Institute decided to terminate its operation at the Matamek Salmon Research Station in 1985. The battle was on.

Ultimately, an ecological reserve was established in 1989 protecting a virgin river basin with an area of more than 70,000 hectares. The settlement was unusual, in that an area the size of a typical park received a protected status normally reserved for much smaller sites. Indeed, Matamek Ecological Reserve is larger than all twenty of the other existing or proposed reserves combined.

History and politics were behind this anomaly. Other river basins could have been seen as more desirable, had they not been subjected to forestry operations or scheduled for major hydro-electric development. Clearly, the area could have been a valuable contribution to the parks system, probably fitting into an un-occupied niche in the representation of natural regions. Most important, however, the basin was within weeks of being leased out for total harvesting. This urgency brought the area to the fore, whether or not it fit into some grander plan.

Many other efforts to protect important sites in recent years have also been last-minute responses to development pressures. Such was the case for the Beau-port Flats (an urban freeway), the Kamouraska Salt Marshes (agricultural drain-age), the Grands Jardins Park (forestry operations), Lac Saint-Pierre (agricultural drainage), and the Longueuil shoreline (urban water-treatment facilities and recreation). In this regard, it is worth noting that environmental pressure groups were simply non-existent until the early 1970s, and outside of Montreal until the 1980s. Until the late 1970s, there were no public institutions with a mandate to seek protection of natural areas. By the late 1980s, that situation has changed in terms of both non-government and government agencies. The new government agencies responsible for natural area protection are, none the less, seriously underbudgeted and understaffed, constituting "junior" portfolios in the eyes of the government.

With barely 0.3 per cent of the total province (1 per cent of the southern area) presently protected, the two government agencies responsible for the two prin-cipal systems of protected areas — parks and ecological reserves — should none-theless be aiming to preserve 3 per cent of Quebec's land base. By way of comparison, Ontario's park system already protects 8 per cent of that province's land area. And 75 per cent of this is preserved from all development. Quebec, therefore, has an enormous task ahead. On the other hand, the fact that other provinces have made major commitments to overall conservation strategies may serve to provide an incentive to the Quebec government, which is at present dragging its feet.

Accomplishments to date in the province have been too time-consuming. It has taken years, for example, to bring government involvement of any substantial kind to the protection of the St. Lawrence. The time remaining to recognize the currently unprotected terrestrial sites simply will not allow such delays. The failure to complete the park and ecological reserve systems will constitute not only a loss to Quebec, but also to Canada.

Quebec's population seems to be entering an era of growing understanding of its natural heritage. This involves a parallel understanding and concern about protecting representative and spectacular natural places. At the same time, this new awareness is confronted by significant development pressures, primarily hydro, forestry, agriculture, and urban housing and transportation.

Realistically, it is becoming more and more difficult to foresee the protection

Above: Quebec's Magdalen Islands represent unique and still wild ocean habitats in the Gulf of St. Lawrence.   CREDIT: BRUCE LITTELJOHN.

Opposite, above: The Dumoine River in Quebec, one of Canada's premier canoeing experiences, photographed by one of Canada's finest canoeists, the late Bill Mason.

Opposite, below: The trees and wildlife of Quebec's Laurentian Mountains are threatened by acid rain.   CREDIT: J.A. KRAULIS.

of major terrestrial areas not already identified for some protected status in Quebec. Costs will be substantial in future efforts to "withdraw" forested areas. A large percentage of wetlands have already been lost, and much more will undoubtedly be lost in the Montreal area. Less development pressure offers some chance for protection of wetland sites elsewhere in the province. Peat bogs cover immense areas in the north and small areas in the south of the province. Inventories will perhaps permit identification of important candidate areas before some form of development impacts on them, though in the south, it is almost too late.

The government needs to act rapidly on several fronts:

• An overall strategy for parks and ecological reserves is needed to avoid the danger of administrative infighting between the two agencies responsible for administering the two systems.

- Funds for "consolidating" the current parks system should be allocated to the Ministry. The primary intention of this step would be to increase public awareness of the value of parks. Otherwise, the public is in danger of discovering the value, and the need, too late.

- The overall system of parks and ecological reserves should be completed now. The costs of such a step later may be prohibitive. At the present time, it would constitute an upgrading of the two ministries involved, a move compatible with present concern both inside and outside government for the environment.

- The importance of protected areas should be made a clearer part of an overall provincial conservation strategy. The initiative of the Council on Conservation and Environment to hold hearings in the fall of 1988 on such a strategy was encouraging; the first chapter of the supporting document addresses the issue of protected areas.

- Wetlands, including bogs, merit special recognition and emergency action. Agreements with various non-government organizations have already been developed by the provincial and federal governments. It is imperative that these initiatives not be abandoned.

- Negotiations and discussions with native peoples, primarily but not exclusively in the North, should proceed with respect to implementing an overall strategy for parks and ecological reserves. This step cannot be left until the non-native population has reached its conclusions on the issue, given the necessity of including native peoples in the management of some parts of the system.

Other areas of potential conflict must be addressed. For instance, mining interests may be difficult to resolve in certain areas, such as the Parc de la Gaspésie or the northern park candidates. A debate is already brewing over a proposal to remove an important area from Parc de la Gaspésie in order to permit mineral extraction. This is simply history repeating itself. The area has been identified for "true" park status on previous occasions, only to see that status withdrawn under pressure from forestry or mining interests.

Hunting is another area of potential conflict. However, carefully worked-out arrangements, for example for traditional hunting of migratory waterfowl by local communities in the off season, could be compatible with some forms of protected status. Trapping, on the other hand, impacts directly on resident species, and thus could be seen as a form of competition with natural predators.

The chances of protecting Canada's endangered spaces, including those of Quebec, are bleak indeed as society continues to associate wildlife exclusively with material benefits. In light of past, and even contemporary experience, it seems unreasonable to insist on permitting consumptive activities everywhere. The purpose of protecting a small portion of the planet is to permit sensible development on the rest. It seems like a fair bargain, and the very least we can do.

ARLIN HACKMAN

Ontario's Park System Comes of Age

Shortly after Toronto's CN Tower was topped off at 549 metres, a provocative handbill appeared on downtown hydro poles and store windows. It showed the potential zone of impact should this massive feat of engineering topple over like a dead tree in the forest primeval. Though tongue-in-cheek, the message elegantly reflected what is probably a nation-wide perception: the only untamed wilderness remaining in Ontario is the urban jungle around King and Bay streets.

It's a mistaken view. Beyond the chrome and glass of the "Golden Horseshoe," catcalls still give way to wolf howls; Canada's second-largest province still harbours countless opportunities for solitary encounters with a vast and varied green inheritance. Many of these result from the Ontario government's announcement, on June 2, 1983, that it would add roughly 2 million hectares of provincial lands and waters to an already outstanding provincial park system. This commitment, largely implemented, brings Ontario's network of protected areas close to the goals of many jurisdictions only now embarking on a similar venture. Therefore the first question to ask in assessing Ontario's agenda for conservation lands and waters is simply "Do we really need more?" A close look reveals that much remains to be accomplished and that the clock is ticking.

WHAT'S WORTH SAVING?

To a visitor from western Canada, especially one who endures the wearying journey by train across the virtually unbroken spruce and jack-pine forests of Northern Ontario, the landscape may lack the dramatic appeal of the Rocky Mountains, the Pacific coast, or the expanse of the prairies. Save for the Lake Superior shoreline and Niagara Escarpment, few jagged edges remain. Still, Ontario's four vegetation regions — deciduous, Great Lakes–St. Lawrence, boreal, and tundra — support a spectacular natural diversity.

In the southern part of the St. Lawrence Lowlands, where the underlying limestone carries a rich mantle of glacial till supporting Ontario's agricultural heartland, we can still glimpse remnants of Carolinian Canada. Once a continuous band of dense hardwoods stretching from Windsor to Toronto, this forest zone and its exotic southern species, such as tulip trees, possums, and Carolina wrens, are only preserved in a few locations, most notably Rondeau Provincial Park. Here, too, we find Niagara Falls thundering over the brow of the 725-kilometre-long Niagara Escarpment, the site of Ontario's first park (1887).

Moving inland, away from the mild shoreline winters, a transitional zone of beech and maple groves draws us into the Great Lakes–St. Lawrence forest zone. Its towering red and white pine fell to the axe of early loggers and its mix of maple and birch in the canoe country of Algonquin Park furnished a fall palette of colours for celebrated paintings by the Group of Seven. Here we encounter glacier-polished domes of pink granite marking the Precambrian shield, which leads us on a northern journey across the face of Ontario, through myriad lakes and rivers, to the Manitoba border. This is the land of moose and black bear, porcupine and snowshoe hare. Because of the rich ores contained in the oldest metamorphic and volcanic rocks of the shield, it is also home to Ontario's vital mining industry. A host of small communities, dependent for survival on this fragile resource economy, lie scattered along the thin ribbons of highways and hydro lines linking this remote hinterland to the larger cities.

Far to the north of Lake Superior, across the height of land where rivers such as the Albany begin their long subarctic journey, lies a wide band of Boreal Forest dominated by black and white spruce trees, the mainstay of Ontario's giant forest industry. This region contains the breeding ranges for the Canada goose, great gray owl, and white-crowned sparrow. Other common species include the red squirrel, deer mouse, porcupine, timber wolf, and lynx. Harsh winters drive 80 per cent of the breeding birds south and keep amphibian species to a minimum. Only one reptile, the garter snake, is widely distributed.

Isolated native reserves are scattered across the region, bleak reminders that the land was occupied long before our roads and machinery revolutionized the "harvest" of forests, fish, and other wildlife that had sustained the nomadic hunter-gatherers for generations.

Only as we emerge from this mossy forest onto the expansive limestone-floored Hudson Bay lowlands, do we leave civilization behind, gazing across kilometre upon kilometre of lichen-carpeted peatlands to the thin strip of subarctic tundra bordering the freezing coast. Here lies Polar Bear Park, Ontario's and one of the world's largest parks. Its barren 2.4 million hectares, more than one-third of Ontario's total park system, protects habitat for arctic loons, snow geese, eiders, willow ptarmigan, and arctic fox, as well as the marine mammal for which the park is named.

While the salt-water bays off Ontario's northern shore are beyond provincial jurisdiction, the inland lakes and Great Lakes provide a tremendous recreational resource for literally millions of Ontarians. Ontario's only marine park, Fathom Five, off the tip of the Bruce Peninsula, was recently acquired by the Canadian

Parks Service in association with the newly established Bruce Peninsula National Park, one of five national parks in Ontario.

For those who keep score, the natural diversity of this vast province yields impressive numbers: some 3000 species of vascular plants; 450 mosses and liverworts; 1000 fungi, lichens, and algae; and 600 vertebrates, including 302 breeding birds, 84 mammals, 24 reptiles, 24 amphibians, and 150 fishes.

A FRAMEWORK FOR ACTION

Ontario's Ministry of Natural Resources (MNR) is responsible for the inventory, disposition, and protection of this natural treasury. Though major parks such as Algonquin, Rondeau, and Quetico were established many years ago, the Ministry's conservation effort was a halting and ad hoc affair through the first half of this century. But in the past few decades it has developed an impressive system for setting conservation targets, influencing approaches taken elsewhere in the country. The overall goal has been to protect representative areas reflecting the full natural landscape across the province.

During the 1950s, the MNR became interested in protecting a spectrum of forest stands for genetic conservation and research. Angus Hills laid the foundation by classifying the province into thirteen "site regions" representing the main forest associations encountered along the journey from the warm Carolinian zone to the cold boreal forest and tundra. A government nature reserves committee followed in 1961, prompting the first lists of candidate protected areas. Later in the decade, this initiative was given a boost by the world-wide inventory of key natural areas under the International Biological Program (IBP). By 1973, an inventory of more than 600 sites was completed.

Even with the wider circle of academic scientists involved in the IBP program, and a growing constituency of naturalists, very little conservation action occurred. The 1970 Wilderness Areas Act was the one legislative outcome traceable to the IBP exercise. Though its vision of statutory protection for ecologically important areas pre-dated any other ecological-reserves legislation in Canada, its application was restricted to areas of 260 hectares or less — a result of resource-industry lobbying and an entrenched senior bureaucracy in the MNR. Consequently, the IBP program remains a largely technical effort and sits on the shelf gathering dust to this day.

Fortunately, however, the ecological land-classification work of Hills and other experts, such as Paul Maycock, found a more effective channel for action in the emerging provincial-parks program. The stage was partially set in 1954 with the passage of the Provincial Parks Act and the creation of the Parks Branch, a move that brought all existing parks under one administration. This action was followed by the creation of nearly one hundred parks throughout the 1950s and 1960s.

Although many of these areas contained interesting features, their selection was driven by a surge in demand for outdoor recreation, not by an overall plan for biological conservation. The government did introduce a park-classification

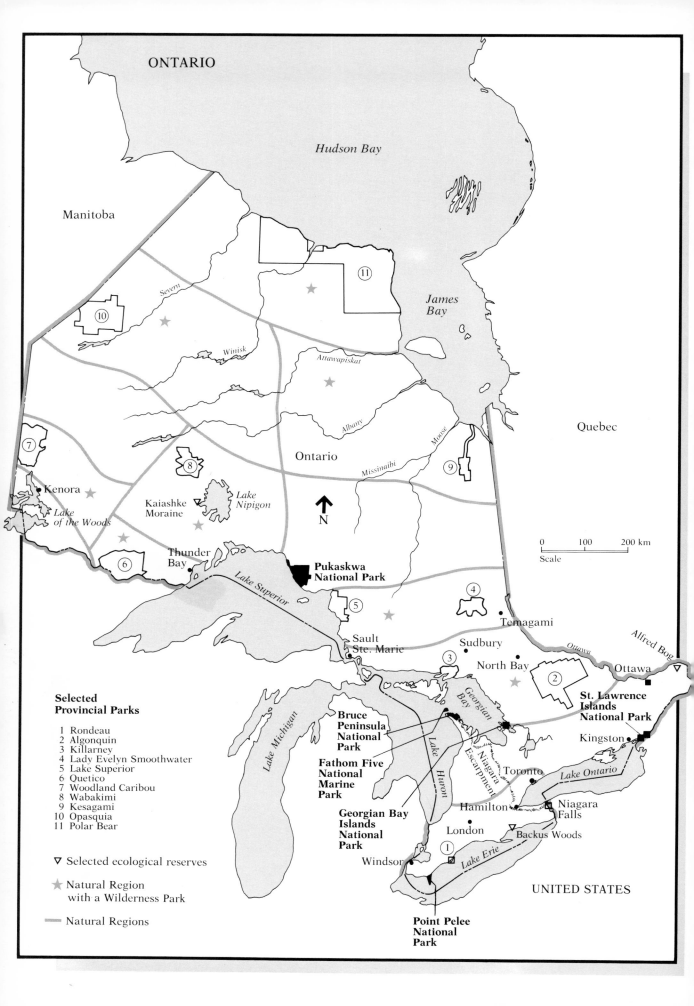

ONTARIO

Hudson Bay

Manitoba

James Bay

Quebec

⑪

Severn

⑩

Winisk

Attawapiskat

Ontario

⑦

Albany

Moose

Missinaibi

⑨

Kenora

Lake of the Woods

Lake Nipigon

⑧

Kaiashke Moraine

N

Alfred Bog

0   100   200 km
Scale

⑥

Thunder Bay

Lake Superior

Pukaskwa National Park

④

Temagami

⑤

Sudbury

Sault Ste. Marie

③

North Bay

②

Ottawa

Ottawa

St. Lawrence Islands National Park

Kingston

Lake Michigan

Georgian Bay

Bruce Peninsula National Park

Selected Provincial Parks

1 Rondeau
2 Algonquin
3 Killarney
4 Lady Evelyn Smoothwater
5 Lake Superior
6 Quetico
7 Woodland Caribou
8 Wabakimi
9 Kesagami
10 Opasquia
11 Polar Bear

Fathom Five National Marine Park

Lake Huron

Toronto

Niagara Escarpment

Lake Ontario

Hamilton

Niagara Falls

Georgian Bay Islands National Park

London

Backus Woods

▽ Selected ecological reserves

☆ Natural Region with a Wilderness Park

━━ Natural Regions

Windsor

①

Lake Erie

UNITED STATES

Point Pelee National Park

and -zoning scheme in 1967. However, it was not until 1978 that a formal cabinet-approved parks policy appeared, mandating the completion and permanent protection of a park system representing the full natural and cultural heritage of Ontario.

By itself, the dull-grey policy brochure was unremarkable. Its real impact was that it sanctioned the release of the Ontario Provincial Parks Planning and Management Policies, which were bound in a thick blue binder and became known simply as the "blue book." Little could cabinet have guessed the impact that this bureaucratic-sounding document would have on land-use and public opinion across the province.

Prior to this time, provincial-government efforts regarding protected areas were largely piecemeal and site-specific as a result of the ever-dominant influence of logging and mining. Parks policy was residual to industrial policy. Decision-making remained obscure. This piecemeal approach also fragmented the efforts of conservation groups.

But the "blue book," for the first time, brought all the pieces together into one blueprint for a comprehensive, province-wide conservation system. In simple terms, it spelled out why we need to set up different types of parks, how many such areas we need, how to identify the best sites, and what we need to do to keep them in good condition *after* they become parks. In doing so, it somewhat unwittingly united a broad conservation constituency behind a common agenda.

Six classes or types of parks were identified — wilderness, nature reserve, natural environment, waterway, historical, and recreation — each serving a special role and thereby creating a true park system. Hills's landscape classification underlay the process of setting regional targets and selecting candidate areas to meet them. For example, the "blue book" called for one wilderness park of no less than 50,000 hectares in each of Hills's thirteen "site regions."

By 1978, the landscape analysis was based on a more precise calibration of ecological variables than Hills had sketched out. An earth-science classification scheme, based on rock strata, fossil assemblages, and landforms, was added. This refinement was due largely to the efforts of two park-system planners within the MNR, Bob Davidson and Tom Beechey. They organized a provincial earth- and life-science inventory, which enabled an assessment of the adequacy of the current park system and a region-by-region selection of candidate natural areas needed to fill the gaps. As a result, conservationists were, and still are, able to pinpoint and defend candidate parks with a far greater degree of scientific authority than before.

This fact has tremendous importance in the context of the political decisions necessary for land or resource allocation in Ontario. Not only can conservationists respond to proponents of alternate land uses, we can also demonstrate that there are limits to the amount of land needed to complete the system of protected areas we are working to achieve. It's not a bottomless pit or "unfinishable agenda."

This technical capability was one essential pre-condition for the Ontario government's decision to establish 155 new parks in 1983.

PUBLIC CONCERN: THE DRIVING FORCE

Although the evolution of the MNR's parks program followed rapid advances in the science of biological conservation during the 1970s, it also responded to public concern about the loss of wilderness and wildlife habitat, both outside and inside the park system of the day.

In a talk he gave to the 1966 annual meeting of the Ontario Federation of Anglers and Hunters, Doug Pimlott asked, "Should we be proud of Ontario's park system?" and answered with a resounding "No!" His concern was this: "Are you satisfied that in all of Algonquin Park's 3000 square miles there is not one single area that is protected by regulation, which is sacrosanct, inviolate from the

Above: The Carolinian Zone of Canada, now 90 per cent gone, is home to southern species such as the opossum.
CREDIT: J.D. TAYLOR.

Centre: A remnant of the Carolinian forest is protected in Rondeau Provincial Park, Ontario.
CREDIT: G.W. CAULFEILD-BROWNE.

Below: A successful crested flycatcher delivers dinner.
CREDIT: LEONARD ZORN.

Opposite, left: White-fringed polygala stretch for spring sunlight near Paris, Ontario.
CREDIT: MARY W. FERGUSON.

Opposite, right: The rare eastern bluebird now needs help with artificial nest boxes due to the loss of natural cavities.
CREDIT: R. BARRY RANFORD.

chainsaw or from the bulldozer? Is this the heritage of nature you want Ontario to pass on to your grandchildren in its parks? If it isn't, you had better start arguing and making your objections known because this is what you are getting for them."

The chainsaws still buzz in Algonquin and, ironically, the organization to which Pimlott spoke later joined forces with the forest industry to bitterly oppose the park system envisioned by the "blue book." But Pimlott's challenge was heeded by thousands of citizens across the province who penned a letter, formed new organizations, or simply signed a cheque to demonstrate that they shared his concern. Their collective energy, voiced in the public arena by organizations such as the Algonquin Wildlands League, Federation of Ontario Naturalists, National and Provincial Parks Association (now the Canadian Parks and Wilderness Society), Sierra Club of Ontario, and World Wildlife Fund brought about major changes in the way government viewed and served its parks mandate.

Though a great deal of effort was spent fighting, losing, and winning a few pitched battles over management issues in individual parks (such as logging in Quetico), the impact was system-wide. For the first time, proper park master plans were prepared, addressing biological conservation as well as recreation interests. Public comment was solicited through formal hearings under the auspices of a permanent Provincial Parks Council. At the same time, the MNR recruited parks planners and managers with training in environmental studies.

Conservation groups evolved as well, transferring the knowledge gained from personal experience into broad policy positions set down in publications such as *Wilderness Now* and *Wilderness in Ontario*. The latter comprehensive report, prepared by Bill Addison and David Bates of Thunder Bay, had a formative influence on the "blue book" policies for wilderness parks.

Any lingering doubt that Doug Pimlott captured the imagination and conviction of a generation of Ontario residents was dispelled by the MNR's own Gallup poll in 1981: A solid majority, in every region of the province, was against logging, mining, and sport hunting in provincial parks.

SLUP: THE RUBBER MEETS THE ROAD

Well before the "blue book" was released, a host of other land-use conflicts made it clear to the government that a larger set of land-use policies was needed for the province as a whole. In the south, wetlands were disappearing at a ferocious rate and the Niagara Escarpment was being nibbled to death by piecemeal development. In the boreal region, the forest industry was gobbling up hundreds of thousands of hectares of virgin timber each year, displacing wildlife and traditional users without discussion, and jeopardizing its own future by cutting more trees than it planted. The mercury-pollution tragedy befalling the native people at Whitedog and Grassy Narrows, and the bid for enormous new cutting rights in the region by the same paper company responsible for this pollution, provoked a fierce public outcry across Canada and prompted the longest, most expensive royal commission in Ontario history. Quite simply, in this period Ontario reached the end of its frontier.

In response, the province initiated two far-reaching planning initiatives: Design for Development, a short-lived regional economic strategy, and the Strategic Land-Use Planning program (SLUP). Announced in 1972, SLUP was to become the testing ground for the 1978 parks policy and the "blue book."

At first, the conservation community was barely equipped to address this planning program, involving fully 87 per cent of the province, almost a million square kilometres of Crown Land. But then, neither was the MNR, the agency responsible for carrying it out. Never before had any province in Canada developed an objective, public process for setting long-range (twenty-year) resource-management goals. Consequently, the effort sputtered along from 1972 to 1981.

Quite likely SLUP would still be lumbering (or slumbering) along today, if Alan Pope hadn't been appointed Minister of Natural Resources. Young, impatient with bureaucracy, and ambitious, Pope took firm command of his portfolio and directed his officials to complete the SLUP program in the space of two years. By the end of 1982 he wanted to see the final products of the process in place, including detailed land-use plans for each of the Ministry's forty-six administrative districts across the province! The shock waves woke up civil servants from Toronto to Moosonee.

It was a David-and-Goliath situation for the conservation community (as well as for Pope and his department run by Deputy Minister Bill Foster). Only one organization, the Federation of Ontario Naturalists, had a securely paid, full-time person to work on the case. The Algonquin Wildlands League, where I worked, operated with a total annual budget of less than $50,000; the tireless workers in Thunder Bay, where much of the action took place, were all volunteers. By contrast, the advocacy budget of the well-organized forest industry must have run into six figures, while the Ministry's budget for publications, public meetings, and other promotional work ran higher still.

For a time, even the meagre forces we commanded were scattered, each conservation group focusing on this or that park proposal. But the need to mount a co-ordinated province-wide campaign and maintain a common front at Queen's Park, the seat of government, drew us together. At the initiative of long-time wilderness advocate Bill Addison of Thunder Bay, the Wildlands League organized a key meeting of conservation-group representatives in the spring of 1982 at the office of World Wildlife Fund Canada. This meeting produced an informal coalition that tracked the progress of SLUP until the final decisions were announced on June 2, 1983. Supported by a far-flung network of volunteers in naturalist clubs, recreation associations, environmental groups, universities, local tourism associations, and social-planning agencies, we were able to provide a reasoned critique of Ministry land-use and parks proposals in every corner of the province. In addition, we provided a steady stream of material to Government and Opposition party members in the legislature, met with the Minister on half

Above, left: Red fox bejewelled by fireweed.
CREDIT: STEPHEN J. KRASEMANN.

Below: The big waters of Lake Nipigon, Ontario, whose forested islands are home to woodland caribou.
CREDIT: G.W. CAULFEILD-BROWNE.

Above right: Swamp maples show the first signs of fall in Ontario.   CREDIT: PETER VAN RHIJN.

Opposite: This unique flower-pot formation is protected forever by a national park on Georgian Bay, Ontario.
CREDIT: G.W. CAULFEILD-BROWNE.

a dozen occasions, and made two presentations to the premier.

In hindsight, our strategy was quite simple:

- try to capture the public imagination with what was at stake on a province-wide basis;

- position our parks proposals in the context of an overall concern for the future economic and social well-being of the region concerned, establishing public alliances with other stakeholder groups from these areas;

- prepare well-reasoned arguments, proposals, and submissions for parks in every district plan, based on the Ministry's own stated goals, broad conservation principles, and targets;

- cultivate media coverage at regional and provincial levels by a core of well-informed journalists across the province;

- work with legislators from *all* political parties;

- support the Minister's personal leadership in the face of bureaucratic resistance and offer him help in working out compromises on specific issues.

A major effort was made to face head-on the hypocritical claim by industry that condominium conservationists were bent on a northern land grab at the expense of local jobs. The Wildlands League, for example, held directors' meetings in Thunder Bay and other northern locations, inviting representatives of local agencies to attend and present their concerns. We also assisted other local user groups to gain access to the Minister. Though these efforts seldom resulted in joint follow-up action, they were at least successful in convincing the Minister that our aims were not self-serving, a perception he never came to hold of the industry lobby.

There were two milestones along the road to the 1983 decisions, both testament to the effectiveness of the conservation lobby. The first was the public release by the Minister on March 12, 1982, of the *Report of the Task Force on Parks System Planning*. Chaired by MNR mandarin Richard Monzon, the task force had been assigned to translate the "blue book" park-system targets into a list of specific candidate parks for consideration through SLUP.

In this one hurried step ordained by Alan Pope, the possibility of actually completing the provincial-park system leapt off the pages of planners' textbooks into the real world. The report was flawed and its list incomplete because of hasty preparation, but the Minister's high-profile announcement ensured that decisions on the 245 candidate parks would be taken. It also tied his personal reputation to the outcome.

Predictably, the announcement of 245 specific candidate parks provoked dismay and outrage among the forest and mining industries. A virtual firestorm of public debate followed. The seven public forums that followed later that year, over which the Minister personally presided, drew crowds as large as 750. In 1982 alone, 184 open houses were held across the province at which more than 10,000 people made their views known. More than 10,000 written submissions were received by the Ministry. There wasn't much time to enjoy the wilderness we were fighting for.

The second milestone was a low-profile but influential, closed-door meeting in January 1983. Presided over once again by the Minister, it was attended by representatives of twenty-seven stakeholder groups, including half a dozen conservationists. Here the Minister sought compromise on a number of issues, primarily related to wilderness parks, which formed the hottest items on the parks agenda.

By all accounts the case for parks and wilderness protection was well argued by conservationists at the meeting. Led by Monte Hummel, park proponents were also the only ones to open the door to compromise, not on the number of parks but on permitted uses in wilderness areas. It was proposed that logging should be flatly prohibited, that mineral exploration should be low-impact (aerial) with the added proviso that any subsequent mines would be removed from the park and compensated by adding comparable parkland elsewhere, and that sport hunting and commercial tourist operations should only be considered on a park-by-park basis, under strict conditions, to avoid damaging the special features to be protected in each wilderness area.

The final decisions, made public on June 2, 1983, revealed that the Minister, given an inch, had taken the proverbial mile. Of the 245 original candidate parks, 90 were dropped and many of the remaining 155 were whittled down in size, due to resource conflicts, for a total reduction of 3 million hectares! No mechanism was established for recovering this lost ground through future park proposals. Some of the dropped candidates were renamed Areas of Natural and Scientific Interest (ANSI), but the one-page hastily assembled ANSI policy offered the vaguest assurance of protection. Though logging was to be excluded from the promised parks, mining, sport hunting, and commercial tourism would be allowed in most, including the wilderness parks, with no mention of the special conditions Hummel had proposed at the January meeting. "Blue book" management policies were cast aside. The whole business was exempted from environmental assessment, against the recommendation of the government's own Environmental Assessment Advisory Committee. And land-use plans became land-use guidelines of little force. As a result, the announcement drew faint praise and barely made the evening news.

To give Alan Pope some benefit of the doubt, his headstrong approach to the job did provoke a backlash within the provincial cabinet, especially from Northern Affairs minister Leo "King of the North" Bernier. In a seven-page letter to Pope, the powerbroker from Kenora scolded his challenger from Timmins, agreeing with the forest industry that Pope was proposing "excessive" amounts of land for wilderness use, which "particularly cannot be justified in terms of loss to the local economies." He also said it would create a better "public image in the north" if the plans were called "guidelines."

PERSISTENCE PAYS OFF

Hopes for redress were rekindled when the new Liberal government was elected in 1985, especially since environmental protection was a key issue during the election and the new government promised a strong agenda for reform. However, the new Minister of Natural Resources, Vince Kerrio, was content with the status quo. He even added possible hydro development to Pope's list of non-conforming uses in wilderness parks.

With Kerrio turning a deaf ear, conservationists took their case to his colleagues and discovered that there were some new attitudes as well as faces around the cabinet table. It took almost three years of effort, but on May 17, 1988, Kerrio was moved to restore the "blue book" vision of wilderness as government parks policy. He also committed the government to dedicating, within a year, the last big batch of the parks promised by Pope in 1983.

When this action is complete, Ontario will have 270 provincial parks covering 6.3 million hectares. More than 80 per cent of this area will be managed as pure wilderness or nature reserves where no logging, mining, hunting, trapping, or hydro-electric development are permitted. A long chapter in conservation history will have ended as a qualified success. Through persistence, we will have obtained a reasonably favourable result on the allocation issue — that is, getting the land set aside for parks — as well as a satisfactory response on the management issue — that is, the prohibition of non-conforming uses on those lands.

But the story cannot end here.

THE WAY AHEAD

Ontario's network of protected natural areas, including wilderness parks, remains incomplete. Is it possible to finish the job?

The short answer is "no." For example, however hard we look, there is no potential wilderness park to be found in southwestern Ontario. More to the point, the government's commitment has lagged: work on system planning within MNR simply ground to a halt in 1983. Apart from one unpublished report prepared by the Wildlands League, no systematic attempt has been made to assess the achievement of "blue book" park targets since then. The prevailing attitude in MNR management circles is that SLUP provided our one "kick at the can," at least until the year 2000. Mere mention of adding new parks now causes officialdom to quiver in disbelief and industry to become apoplectic.

Conservation groups have also taken a breather. Our forces were sorely taxed by the intense effort needed to win the 155 new parks in 1983 and to restore "blue book" management policies in 1988. However, in the last two years, public concern has once again reached critical mass in the fight to protect old-growth forests around Lady Evelyn-Smoothwater Wilderness Park. The Federation of Ontario Naturalists' Breeding Bird Atlas project, as well as the Natural Heritage League's private stewardship program, also reveal that a broad constituency of dedicated volunteers can be mobilized for conservation province-wide when given clear direction and a specific focus. What is this future road map?

One key element of the endangered-spaces agenda is clear. MNR should be convinced to finalize its aborted park-system plan, if we are to have a clear picture of the gaps remaining in the park system or a roster of natural areas that might fill them. Second, as far as deficiencies in wilderness parks are concerned, conservationists might adopt the approach of the Temagami Wilderness Society. This would involve developing proposals for extending some form of protection to carefully managed buffer zones around smaller existing parks in natural regions where no satisfactory wilderness park has been, or is likely to be, established. Research is showing that to survive as self-regulating ecological units, wilderness areas need to be at least as large as Quetico (475,800 hectares). Extending protection beyond existing park borders in this fashion would greatly contribute to wilderness protection in Ontario's park system.

This effort will inevitably take time. The Ontario parks centennial in 1993 should provide a catalytic date for some interim achievements. Priority attention should be given to Wabakimi Wilderness Park, which was drastically reduced in size from the original Ogoki-Albany proposal and is being encircled by logging. The Albany Peninsula in Lake-of-the-Woods, a wilderness candidate dropped entirely during SLUP, also deserves special management, perhaps along the lines of the regional trust proposed for the Madawaska Highlands west of Ottawa by the Canadian Parks and Wilderness Society.

Third, we need a more coherent province-wide effort to protect significant ecological sites through a mix of public- and private-sector strategies. The baseline earth- and life-science inventory backing this effort is still proceeding within MNR under the Areas of Natural and Scientific Interest (ANSI) program. More than 600 relatively small but significant sites have already been identified, including former candidate parks, primarily on private lands in Southern Ontario where large wilderness areas no longer exist. Under the program, the Ministry shares responsibility for securing protection with many other agencies, as appropriate to each case. A range of public and private sector approaches have already been used. For example:

• Backus Woods, an outstanding tract of old-growth Carolinian forest near London, has been protected through a conservation easement, inter-agency management plan and endowment fund raised by public and private contributions;

• In eastern Ontario, 1370 hectares of Alfred Bog have been purchased by the Nature Conservancy of Canada, which will transfer the property to a local conservation authority for management;

- Kaisashke Moraine, a forested interlobate moraine in northwestern Ontario, has been protected in a government-industry forest management agreement;

- Along the Niagara Escarpment, about fifty sites have been protected through "natural area" zoning and development controls.

Though a promising initiative, the ANSI program is dogged by a number of problems. Ministry policy on managing ANSI is vague and has low priority within the MNR's own field offices. Only two of the Ministry's eight administrative regions have completed the inventory. There are no clear standards for mapping, sampling, and reporting, or for determining what constitutes adequate protection. Promised funds have not been allocated. Setting priorities for action on identified sites is a major challenge for the host of agency partners, linked through the Natural Heritage League, a loose coalition of government and non-government conservation organizations operating under the Ontario Heritage Foundation.

The Conservation Lands Act, which provides tax relief to ANSI landowners through a signed protection agreement, is one recent initiative that will alleviate some of these problems. Still, more discipline must be brought to the program. First, the 1993 parks centennial should be established as the deadline for completing the inventory. Second, the Ministry must not be allowed to renege on its modest annual $500,000 funding commitment for protection and management. Third, after winding up efforts to protect the thirty-eight priority sites under the $3.8 million Carolinian Canada program conceived by World Wildlife Fund, the Natural Heritage League should set Southern Ontario wetlands as its top-priority sites for protection, especially those along the Great Lakes where 70 per cent have already been lost. Fourth, the approval/renewal of Forest Management Agreements between the MNR and forestry companies in the North should be contingent on exclusion of ANSIs from cutting areas. Fifth, the Provincial Parks Act should be overhauled. At present, this legislation merely confers authority for establishing and operating parks. As critics Paul Eagles and John Swaigen have proposed, the Act needs to nail down management objectives so that they are not subject to another rollercoaster ride of arbitrary policy changes by ministers or bureaucrats, such as those approved by Alan Pope in 1983. It needs to assign responsibility for management planning, with the maintenance of "ecological integrity" as first priority as the recently amended National Parks Act now stipulates. Public involvement and access to information need to be guaranteed with the burden of proof shifted from those who wish to protect resource values to those whose actions would degrade them.

New ecological reserves legislation being drafted by the Ministry may address a few of these concerns, as well as the failure of the Wilderness Areas Act. It would do so by taking over and strengthening protection for existing nature reserves in the park system as well as other provincially significant ANSI identified in the earth- and life-science inventory. However, the Provincial Parks Act and program should always remain the centrepiece of Ontario's protected areas network and it must be backed by a much more explicit legal conservation mandate.

The prospects for completing this agenda are dimmed by two major issues:

First, the Liberal government has failed to inject fresh ideas or funds into the natural-resources field. The forestry environmental assessment is but one example. After more than a decade of stalling, the MNR has finally submitted itself to an independent hearing on its forest-management program. Having penny-pinched until it finally was forced to move, the Ministry is now sparing no expense in deluging the hearing process with paper patter, taking a year just to make its opening presentation — all in support of business as usual by the bureaucracy and industry. Meanwhile conservation budgets are cut. The premier and his cabinet seem to have drawn an arbitrary line between pollution and resource-conservation issues, perhaps convinced that such a line reflects public opinion or ensures northern rural and business support.

The second problem hindering further park creation is the tension among the resource "user groups" with a direct stake in conservation. These include hunters, trappers, naturalists, native peoples, fishermen, tourist outfitters, and outdoor recreation groups. Of particular concern are the steadily deteriorating relations between hunters and naturalists, which reached a flashpoint in the battle over Temagami. Differences in priority are inevitable because the two camps are grounded on the familiar squabble over the "wise use" and "preservation" definitions of conservation. However, taking extreme positions on either side opens up a very wide and dangerous gulf indeed. Sadly, despite the obvious merits of joining forces to present industry and government with a common conservation agenda, the real world prospects for reconciliation appear bleak.

Up close, there may be more grounds for optimism. In large measure, future action depends on individual leaders of the different conservation organizations. Ontario is still small enough that one or two changes in leadership or leadership attitudes makes a major difference. The trick is to find a few proverbial win-win opportunities for competing conservation organizations so that the leadership sees some benefits from co-operation.

Experience amply demonstrates that local support for protected areas is the main factor in their success or failure, both in getting them in the first place *and* in keeping them healthy later. The prospects for community consensus on land use are often bleak, and pitched battles may be unavoidable. However, conservation groups would be wise to look ahead now to local areas where wilderness proposals might be launched, or where park-management plans are to be prepared. Community links should be set up as soon as possible, and proposals developed that meet local as well as provincial interests.

Woodland Caribou and Atikaki wilderness parks may be such a testing ground. Linking together across the Manitoba/Ontario border, these two parks afford an opportunity to protect half a million unsung hectares of wilderness in the middle of Canada. Management plans for both parks are underway, affording an opportunity to achieve interprovincial co-operation and, in Ontario, set the tone for other management plans in the new parks. Tourism development related to these parks is one of the regional concerns that will have to be resolved through local involvement.

THE "UNFINISHABLE AGENDA"
Ontario's new parks mark a significant advance towards provincial conservation goals, by any standard. But the hard work is not over yet. In the south, it's a rush against time to protect remnant wetlands and Carolinian woodlots. In the north, important sites on the Hudson Bay lowlands have only just been mapped.

Gaining these areas will not be easy. There is no SLUP process in motion today, being led by a "take charge" Minister. If anything, governments are stepping back from centre-stage, challenging private conservation agencies to play a larger role in meeting the public interest. And there's one final factor to reckon with, a sleeper.

In a recent issue of the *Logging and Sawmilling Journal*, Ron Arnold, a former U.S. Sierra Club director turned strategic adviser to anti-wilderness groups, analyses the tactics of the wilderness lobby. Our fundamental aim, in his view, is to create an "unfinishable agenda," goals for protected wildlands which allow for an ever-enlarging geographic claim.

In one way, Arnold is right. In our lifetime, the major effort has been to designate as much wilderness as possible. Furthermore, since wilderness depends, to a certain extent, on the eye of the beholder, it is likely that each generation will replay a similar struggle with whatever naturalness is still available.

But Arnold is also dead wrong in two ways. First, protected-area systems are based on securing a representative sample of biological diversity, following Aldo Leopold's profound insight: "The key to intelligent tinkering is to keep all the parts." There are scientific techniques to identify and limit requirements for protected areas, and conservationists in Ontario were prepared to accept such limits in SLUP. The problem was that while resource harvesting scored close to 100 per cent, parks targets made only a passing grade.

Second, efforts to add to the roster of conservation lands and waters are taking place in a much larger context of wilderness destruction. In other words, our gains are only relative. It's like throwing a ball in an airplane. The important measure of its speed is taken relative to the ground, not the airplane. The real force creating Arnold's "unfinishable agenda" is the relentless extension of industrial development across the land.

Right or wrong, Arnold's challenge will become more insistent as land-use pressures mount. The upshot is that park advocates must increasingly acknowledge and respond to the immediate local impacts of our proposals. Coupled with declining government leadership, this means that we must find practical ways to overcome conflicts with other stakeholder interests; we must be prepared to help pay the direct costs; we must bring Thoreau's "In wildness is the preservation of the world" down to the level of day-to-day human needs.

DAVID A.GAUTHIER & J.DAVID HENRY*

Misunderstanding the Prairies

> Within one human lifetime, the prairies have passed from wilderness to become the most altered habitat in this country and one of the most disturbed, ecologically simplified and overexploited regions in the world.
>
> Dr. Adrian Forsyth

Adrian Forsyth's incisive criticism is an indictment of the way we have treated the prairies over the past century. Successive waves of explorers and settlers, each eager to harvest the impressive productivity of a grasslands ecosystem, have eroded the natural processes that underlay the great fertility of the prairie landscapes. And this massive alteration of the prairies continues to this day.

To examine this transformation, we must first know what the Canadian prairies looked like at the time of the arrival of the first Europeans. In August 1691, Henry Kelsey was travelling overland north of the Touchwood Hills of present-day Saskatchewan. In his journal, he described the prairies in this manner: "Today we pitched to ye outermost edge of ye woods. This plain affords nothing but short round sticky grasses and buffalo and a great sort of a bear which is bigger than any white bear and is neither white nor black but silver-haired. . . . "

La Vérendrye explored southern Manitoba between 1738 and 1739, describing the long-grass prairie as follows: "it is all very level, without mountains, all fine hard wood with here and there groves of oak; that everywhere there are quantities of fruit trees, and all sorts of wild animals; the savage tribes are there very numerous, and always wandering. . . ." Later that summer in his journal, he states: "I found the water [in the Assiniboine River] very low, as there had been no rain all the summer. There are fine trees along the banks, and behind these a boundless stretch of prairies in which are multitude of buffalo and deer."

Edward Umfreville explored the prairies adjacent to the Saskatchewan River in 1790. He described the northern edge of the prairies:

* Order of authorship decided by a toss of a coin.

The fruits, which spontaneously shoot up, are not in such great variety in the wildernesses of Canada, as in the country, I am speaking of. . . . Raspberries, strawberries, currants, cranberries, and an infinity of other kinds which I know not the names of, are to be found everywhere. . . . In the valleys and humid situations, the grass grows to a great height, which fattens our horses in a short time; but the buffalo usually makes choice of hilly, dry ground, to feed on, the blades of grass on which are small, short and tender. When a numerous herd of these animals stay any length of time in one place, the ground is absolutely barren there for the remainder of the season, the grass being ate off. . . .

Thus, the early European explorers were deeply struck by the natural productivity of the Canadian prairies. The massive herds of bison, the scattered groupings of elk, the ubiquitous pronghorn antelope combined with the packs of prairie wolves and scattered plains grizzly bears left a lasting impression upon these early travellers. Despite the harshness of its climate, the rich prairie soils together with the abundant wild fruits and plentiful wildlife deepened their conviction that this was a land of great endemic productivity.

Unfortunately, the northern prairies has always been an ecosystem that can be easily impacted, and it took surprisingly few years and remarkably few Europeans to leave an indelible mark on these abundant wildlife populations. In his famous travel classic, *The Great Lone Land*, William Francis Butler described the Canadian prairies as he encountered them between 1870 and 1872:

Around it, far into endless space, stretch immense plains of bare and scanty vegetation, plains seared with the tracks of countless buffalo which, until a few years ago, were wont to roam in vast herds between the Assiniboine and the Saskatchewan. Upon whatever side the eye turns when crossing these great expanses, the same wrecks of the monarch of the prairie lie thickly strewn over the surface. Hundreds of thousands of skeletons dot the short scant grass; and when fire has laid barer still the level surface, the bleached ribs and skulls of long-killed bison whiten far and near the dark burnt prairie. . . . There is not a sound in the air or on the earth; on every side lie spread the relics of the great fight waged by man against the brute creation; all is silent and deserted — the Indian and the buffalo gone, the settler yet to come.

This drastic alteration of the prairies was largely promoted by the leaders of the time. Removal of the bison provided a simultaneous solution to what was referred to as "The Indian Problem." In the United States, this unsanctioned policy of the U.S. Government was perhaps most baldly stated by General Philip Henry Sheridan of the U.S. Cavalry. In 1875 he stated: "The Buffalo Hunters have done more in the past two years to settle the vexed Indian Question than the entire regular army in the last thirty years. They are destroying the Indian's commissary. Send them powder and lead if you will, and let them kill, skin and sell until they have exterminated the buffalo!"

Farley Mowat in *Sea of Slaughter* points out that General Sheridan later told Congress it should strike a medal honouring the buffalo hunters, with the imprint of a dead buffalo on one side — and a dead Indian on the other.

Humans have been present on the Canadian prairies for the past 12,000 years. This amount of time — a fleeting moment in terms of geological time — has been marked by several successive waves of increasing exploitation across the North American grasslands. In the ancient "dog days" before they acquired horses, native hunters would have had little effect upon prairie wildlife populations. The low numbers of native hunters, their reliance on large, shifting big-game populations, their relative lack of mobility, and their lack of firearms meant a harsh, nomadic lifestyle. During the nesting season they hunted waterfowl, but the plains Indians were primarily bison hunters.

By the early 1700s, hunting efficiency and movements of plains tribes had become affected by the introduction northward of horses that had been brought into the southern plains by Spaniards. The expansion of the fur trade into the Canadian West also affected native lifestyles by providing voracious trading partners in the form of the competing Hudson's Bay and North West companies. The companies required substantial supplies of food to feed the men stationed at a growing number of posts. In turn, they provided native people with new tools, including firearms, that helped to reduce the harshness of their lives. It became readily apparent that the prairie and parkland regions, with their abundance of wildlife, could serve to meet that growing demand and that plains tribes and a growing Metis population could be used to obtain that food.

Beginning in the 1820s and over the next sixty years, organized bands of Metis hunters and settlers from the Red River colony set off each summer to hunt the large buffalo herds that lay to the west. The hides were sold for blankets, coats, and leather; the meat was turned into pemmican and dried meat, then sold to the fur companies. These organizations used the meat to support their fur transportation routes and trading posts located farther north.

It has been estimated that 100,000 to 300,000 plains bison may have been slaughtered annually to meet the food needs of the trading companies and Metis and Indian communities. But the numbers of plains bison so greatly exceeded those numbers, that the slaughter for food was not regarded as a serious threat to the survival of the bison herds. The tragic story of the extinction of the plains bison really begins after 1830, when the buffalo-robe trade developed further and increased settlement eliminated the great herds in settled areas from Manitoba to Kansas. In addition, the early 1870s brought forth a process for making commercial leather from buffalo hides. Each year the buffalo hunters had to extend their range farther to harvest sufficient numbers of animals. Then in 1883 the Red River carts of the hide hunters returned home from the buffalo range with empty wagons, and the hunt was never again attempted.

In the incredibly short span of forty years, the plains bison became extinct in Manitoba. By the 1870s, remnant herds were found only in southern Alberta and southwestern Saskatchewan. These were soon to be killed by settlers and starving Indians. The plains Indians whose hunting lifestyle had been based largely on a single resource were reduced to extreme poverty and growing dependence on government assistance.

After the hide hunters quit, the bone pickers came. Buffalo bone commanded six to ten dollars per ton. The bones were ground up and used in refining sugar; horns were fashionable as buttons, combs, and knife handles; and hooves were salvaged and turned into glue. The bone-and-skull trade was over by the 1890s. And the great herds had vanished forever.

Bison had dominated the prairie landscape, but with their loss other wildlife also suffered. The plains-dwelling wolves and grizzly bears were eliminated with the loss of their prey. Elk and deer became overhunted as traders tried to replace their losses of bison with other animals. By the early 1880s the fur-trading era was over, but the ability of prairie wildlife to survive was to be strongly affected by even more significant impacts.

ESCALATING EXPLOITATION

Buffalo harvesting was only the first wave of exploitation initiated by Europeans to roll across the Canadian prairies. Since then, ranching, agriculture, and mining have successively swept the region. The formation of the Province of Manitoba in 1870 opened the region to agricultural settlement. Settlers moved into the region in large numbers, facilitated by the completion of the Canadian Pacific Railway in the 1880s.

Demands escalated on wildlife populations, as elk, moose, mule deer, and other animals were hunted for food, driving their numbers even lower. Corridors of agricultural development appeared along the main and spur rail lines. As land was cleared and planted, vegetative cover was altered significantly. White-tailed deer moved north from Minnesota into this new preferred habitat with no fear of competition from bison and elk. The greater prairie chicken also moved north into the prairie region of Manitoba and Saskatchewan, occupying the islands of untilled rocky habitat set in a growing sea of cultivated lands.

Between 1901 and 1913, two million more people settled on the prairies. In the same time period, cultivated land increased from 2 million to 25 million hectares. Wildlife habitat became severely modified. Pronghorn disappeared from Manitoba and were seriously reduced in Saskatchewan. To meet hunter demands, exotic upland game birds were introduced: ring-necked pheasant, gray partridge and chukar, and the wild turkey.

Waterfowl are one of the great natural resources of the prairies. The prairie pot-hole region has traditionally been productive habitat for waterfowl in the breeding season, with larger lakes and marshes used in the post-breeding period and migration. In the early days of agriculture, before farms became mechanized, waterfowl adapted to human impacts without substantial losses. With time, however, available habitat decreased, idle lands became cultivated, wetlands were drained, and farming practices were intensified. Lost wetland habitat has been placed at 1.21 million hectares.

The faunal complex of the prairies developed in an environment subject to overgrazing by bison, fire, and drought. With settlement by immigrants, the prairies underwent drastic changes. Cattle replaced bison as the dominant grazer on the prairies. Large prairie fires had maintained the prairie ecosystem by removing dense vegetation, recycling nutrients, and stopping aspen trees from spreading and multiplying. With fire suppression, aspen groves soon became established in the northern prairies, surrounded by developing grain fields and a road-and-rail system. The original stable condition of soil and grass — maintained by large grazers, fire, and periodic drought — had given way to an intensively managed, inherently unstable system, and widespread deterioration of the landscape ensued.

The net result has been that the Canadian prairies have become one of the most endangered natural habitats in Canada. Human efforts have been directed towards maximizing economic return. The natural productivity of the soil and precious water resources has been viewed as a bank in which the emphasis has been on withdrawals, not deposits.

Unfavourable global markets for certain agricultural produce (especially wheat), global subsidy wars, soil erosion and nutrient losses, massive debt loads for agricultural operators, and contradictory federal and provincial government resource policies have all led to significant social and economic problems for farm operators. Biological diversity has decreased, as only a few highly productive crop and pasture seed strains are planted. Organic matter and biomass have been reduced by 50 per cent since the first land was broken, a fact masked by the current heavy use of commercial fertilizers.

Increased mechanization in terms of larger tractors and equipment results in larger areas of land being ploughed. This equipment-oriented farming encourages the removal of shelterbelts, whose loss reduces snow accumulation and soil moisture. Native wildlife habitat has been reduced by agricultural encroachment, increased urbanization, industrialization, pollution, construction of roads, and overexploitation of remaining wildlife resources. More and more marginal lands are being converted to agricultural use, even though such lands are highly susceptible to soil erosion, salinization, and nutrient loss. The failure rate for farmers occupying these marginal lands has increased as small family operators are replaced by larger corporate agricultural interests.

Over the past seven hundred years on the Great Plains, there have been thirteen drought periods lasting five or more years, with an average duration of thirteen years and a cyclic recurrence of about twenty years. The drought of the "Dirty Thirties" is well documented. However, the worst wheat drought during the past fifty years occurred in 1961. The 1980s has again seen a period of extended drought. Abnormally hot, dry conditions have resulted in destruction of agricultural crops and grazing pastures. Unseeded and even seeded soils are blowing

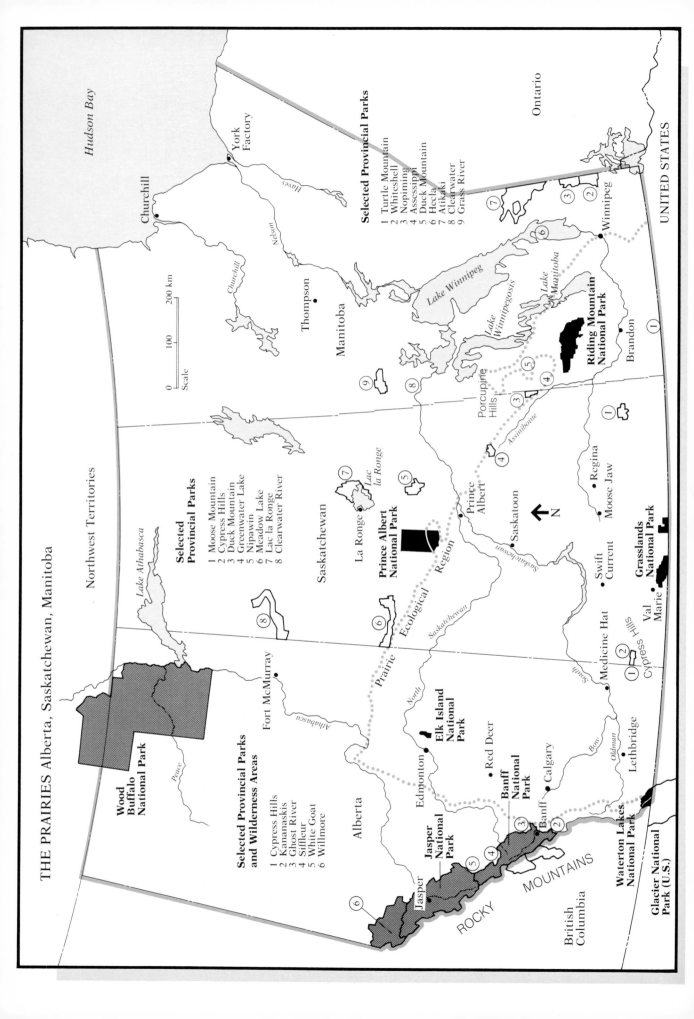

THE PRAIRIES Alberta, Saskatchewan, Manitoba

Hudson Bay

York Factory

Churchill

Thompson

Manitoba

Lake Winnipeg

Lake Winnipegosis

Lake Manitoba

Winnipeg

Brandon

Riding Mountain National Park

Porcupine Hills

Assiniboine

Prairie Ecological Region

Saskatchewan

La Ronge

Lac la Ronge

Prince Albert National Park

Prince Albert

Saskatoon

Swift Current

Medicine Hat

Moose Jaw

Regina

Grasslands National Park

Val Marie

Cypress Hills

Fort McMurray

Lake Athabasca

Northwest Territories

Wood Buffalo National Park

Peace

Athabasca

Edmonton

Red Deer

Elk Island National Park

Calgary

Banff National Park

Banff

Jasper National Park

Jasper

Red Deer

Bow

Oldman

Lethbridge

Waterton Lakes National Park

Glacier National Park (U.S.)

ROCKY MOUNTAINS

British Columbia

Alberta

Ontario

UNITED STATES

N

Selected Provincial Parks
1 Turtle Mountain
2 Whiteshell
3 Nopiming
4 Assessippi
5 Duck Mountain
6 Hecla
7 Atikaki
8 Clearwater
9 Grass River

Selected Provincial Parks
1 Moose Mountain
2 Cypress Hills
3 Duck Mountain
4 Greenwater Lake
5 Nipawin
6 Meadow Lake
7 Lac la Ronge
8 Clearwater River

Selected Provincial Parks and Wilderness Areas
1 Cypress Hills
2 Kananaskis
3 Ghost River
4 Siffleur
5 White Goat
6 Willmore

Scale
0   100   200 km

Hayes

Nelson

Churchill

North Saskatchewan

South Saskatchewan

away. Adding to the concerns about cyclic short-term drought, are fears raised by long-term climatic changes caused by the "greenhouse effect": a trend to higher temperatures caused by increased accumulation in the atmosphere of gases generated by human activities. Studies of the effect of increasingly higher temperatures on the prairies all predict substantial adverse effects as a result of greater frequency and duration of droughts.

Today, the wildness of "prairie wool" has been succeeded by field after field of tidy furrows. It is a highly geometric, checkerboard landscape measured out by roads into sections and quarter-sections. It is indeed one of the most altered environments found on the face of our planet.

PRAIRIE PRODUCTIVITY

Where did the natural productivity of the northern prairies come from? How was it that this region could support an estimated 60 million buffalo, 30 million pronghorn, plus millions of deer, elk, and waterfowl? To understand this endemic productivity, we must begin by understanding what natural processes interact to cause it.

We should start by probing the fertility of grassland soils, a resource which is highly dependent upon the sedimentary geology of the region. As time passed, ancient seas alternately inundated and retreated over the area of the present plains, leaving sediments that, as a result of accumulated weight and uplifting pressure, hardened into layered sedimentary rock, often as much as 3000 metres in depth.

Approximately 150 million years ago the Cordilleran mountains to the west began to form, an event with monumental effects on the prairies. Without the sheltering effect of the Cordilleran ranges, the plains would not have become as warm or arid, and the grasslands would never have developed. The mountain-building process also caused rivers to flow easterly, carrying sediments from these mountains to be deposited in vast blankets over the plains. These deposits would alternately be scoured and redeposited by the action of huge continental icesheets that flowed and ebbed over the plains area, finally disappearing from the plains approximately 10,000 years ago.

The wasting away of blocks of ice entrapped in sediments created the pot-hole topography of the Canadian prairies. Today, this legacy from the last continental icesheet has left a maze of sloughs, teeming with insects and invertebrate aquatic life — a habitat responsible for more than 50 per cent of all ducks born in North America. Prairie sloughs also attract red-winged and yellow-headed blackbirds, grebes, herons, bitterns, avocets, and willets as well as many different kinds of shorebirds. These prairie wetlands are also essential as resting areas and staging areas for the migration of many other waterfowl species which nest on the tundra farther north.

The meltwater channels created by the massive amount of water pouring off the wasting glaciers are also responsible for creating the deep river valleys that dissect the prairies. These river valleys offer wooded coulees and sheltered micro-habitats, which become extremely important to wildlife, especially during the harsh prairie winter.

Wayne Lynch aptly describes in *Married to the Wind* the debt that prairie farmers owe the glaciers. As the glaciers melted, they:

> retreated in a northeasterly direction, forming a barrier to the normal drainage of the land, so that water was ponded between the glacier and the higher ground in the west. The ponded water formed glacial lakes that filled with sediments up to 6 meters thick. The flat, silt and clay bottoms of Rosetown, Indian Head, and Regina lakes were to become the prime wheat-growing areas of Saskatchewan. The glacial lakes of Saskatchewan and Manitoba tended to spread out and cover large areas. Lake Agassiz, which formed in the Manitoba Lowlands, was the largest of all the glacial lakes and was probably the largest lake of any type that the Earth has ever known. The lacustrian clays formed on the bottom of Lake Agassiz constitute the belt of heavy lands — the most fertile agricultural lands across Manitoba and into southeastern Saskatchewan.

PICKING UP THE PIECES

Agriculture, and to a lesser degree urbanization, have transformed more than 80 per cent of the native prairie landscape. Some 90 per cent of the rough fescue grassland in Canada has been ploughed, and much of the remaining 10 per cent has been significantly modified by livestock grazing and haying.

Almost all of the tall-grass prairie is gone — one of the few sizeable plots remaining (about 10 hectares) is within the city limits of Winnipeg. A 1978-82 census indicated that only 18 per cent of the once-abundant short-grass prairie remains in its native state, about 24 per cent of the mixed grass prairie, and 25 per cent of the aspen parkland. About 1.2 million hectares of wetland habitat in the prairie region have been converted to agricultural use — a loss of 40 per cent of the original wetlands.

These losses are not just in quantity; they are losses in quality. The areas of tall-grass, parkland, mixed grass, and short-grass that go under the plough are usually the most fertile, productive areas. What remains in an undisturbed state are either the drier or the water-saturated sites, lands considered marginal for agriculture. Now, under increased economic pressure, even these marginal sites are under siege.

What can be done to pick up the pieces? Given the radical transformation which the Canadian prairies have seen during the last century, how should we proceed to protect what is left of the prairie natural heritage?

Part of the answer certainly rests in changing our attitudes. We must learn to think in terms of ecological concepts and evolutionary processes. For example, the prairie provinces were built on agriculture, and farming depends heavily upon genetic diversity. Native plant species are the prime source for new strains of domesticated forages and cereals. Native species are valuable for their adaptability to severe environmental conditions such as drought, and for their natural resistance to insect pests. Yet, commercial agriculture focuses the interest of most farmers on only a few highly productive strains: four varieties of wheat account for 75 per cent of the Canadian wheat crop. We know very little about the values that prairie species may hold for future foods, forage crops, pharmaceutical, and other uses. A larger effort should be made to preserve prairie plant species *in situ*; that is, in representative, undisturbed ecological reserves with a mandate for preserving benchmark communities of the Canadian prairies.

Loss of habitat is the most critical issue facing prairie wildlife. The potential for species extinctions on the prairies is a matter of serious concern. Nine Canadian species are known to have been lost in the last two hundred years, several of these from the prairies. The swift fox and the black-footed ferret have been extirpated, and the passenger pigeon is extinct. Subspecies such as the plains wolf and the plains grizzly have also been lost. Today, the few remaining herds of buffalo found on the prairies are no longer free-roaming. Only two national parks in Canada (Wood Buffalo and Prince Albert) can claim to contain free-ranging buffalo.

Many more species are now on the brink. About one-quarter of the bird and mammal species designated on the 1988 list of the Committee on the Status of Endangered Wildlife in Canada are found in the prairie provinces. Most of these live in the grasslands or aspen parkland. The status of many other prairie species is unknown, but certainly more species will join the list if action is not taken soon to conserve much of the remaining native prairie wildlands.

Over the short term, our goals are clearly definable. Since 1986 the World Wildlife Fund has brought together scientists, resources managers, and leaders from the business community to focus on the ecological degradation that has taken place on the Canadian prairies. It has been an effort to apply the global objectives of the World Conservation Strategy — maintaining essential ecological processes, preserving genetic diversity, and ensuring sustainable utilization of species and ecosystems — to the grasslands region of Canada. The World Wildlife Fund's analysis concludes that the terrestrial and wetland ecosystems of the prairies are indeed endangered spaces. The Prairie Conservation Action Plan produced by the WWF outlines an urgent five-year blueprint, which, if carried out through co-operative endeavours by government, universities, environmental organizations, and the private sector, would accomplish much towards the ultimate goal of re-establishing the biological diversity of the Canadian prairies. Conservation goals of this plan are organized around six initiatives, and specific implementation on a region-by-region basis is derived from these conservation objectives. The six objectives are:

• Complete the inventories of the remaining native prairie and parkland where necessary for conservation purposes;

- Protect at least one large, representative area in each of the five major prairie ecoregions;

- Establish a system of protected native prairie ecosystems across the three prairie provinces, including representative samples of each ecoregion and habitat subregion;

- Prepare management and restoration plans for threatened ecosystems and habitats;

- Prepare and implement recovery and management plans for every prairie and parkland species designated nationally or provincially as vulnerable, threatened, endangered, or extirpated;

- Ensure that no additional species become threatened, endangered, or extirpated.

We fully endorse these objectives of the WWF's Wild West program, as outlined in the Prairie Conservation Action Plan. We cannot imagine conservation priorities that have a more pressing urgency to be achieved during the immediate future. However, we are convinced that over the long term a more fundamental reorganization of our economic enterprises and resource management must be undertaken if the natural productivity and biological diversity of the Canadian prairies is to be reclaimed.

A century and a half of land and water management on the prairies have resulted not in preservation, but in massive ecological degradation. We have departments of wildlife and agriculture, water agencies, and a seemingly endless list of administrative units ranging through municipal, provincial, and federal levels of government. These are "cells" of a larger honeycomb of human efforts intended to wisely manage our resources. But on what ecological basis were these management cells formed, and on what basis do they operate? Do they place high priority on maintaining ecological processes and preserving biological diversity? If they do, why have we lost so much of our natural heritage?

It is easy to understand why decision-makers would opt for goals that have immediate political payoffs but long-term costs. Yet, the past century of our misunderstanding of the prairies must be accounted for. Will the processes and institutions that led us to our current state of ecological degradation be the means to lead us out? We think not. Innovative and integrative approaches to resource management are required, approaches that put the highest priority on maintaining ecological processes and preserving biological diversity.

The prairies cannot continue to be arbitrarily administered as provincial or municipal units. The current organization of the federal and provincial bureaucracies must no longer be imposed on the ecology of the prairies. We must integrate our management using ecological principles. We must manage the remaining resources and surviving productivity of the prairies as functional ecological entities.

Imagine that we could redesign our government administration to reflect ecological processes. We might structure it according to ecoregions; for example, a department of fescue grasslands, a department of mixed-grass prairie. Each department would operate according to a similar set of priorities; for example, those of the World Conservation Strategy. All land, air, and water management — all utilization of resources — would be incorporated under these priorities.

This management model is not as fanciful as it seems. Yet a reorganization of priorities will happen in one of two ways. Either wise people will recognize the need to integrate our demands on the environment with the capability of the environment to sustain those demands, and consequently design creative means for the integration; or, environmental disaster will compound upon environmental disaster until the costs of our action exceed even the short-term benefits and we will be forced to react, albeit too late to regain much of what we have lost. In essence, we can create for the future, or we can be forced to react to an increasingly impoverished environment.

The Prairie Conservation Action Plan of the World Wildlife Fund is a call for creative measures. But it is only a start. We must build on that initiative and numerous other ones, such as those related to interprovincial parks, the establishment of Grasslands National Park, the Alberta-Saskatchewan interprovincial parks, ecological-reserve and wilderness-area provincial legislation, acquisition and protection of critical wildlife habitat, the Prairie Farm Rehabilitation Administration initiative to reduce the overuse of marginal agricultural lands, and other water and soil conservation strategies. But despite these valuable initiatives, the larger arena of political decision-making does not adequately reflect the ecological processes that form the basis of much of the prairie economy. We must frame our entrepreneurial proposals, government policies, and decisions within a larger context of environmental ethics. We must all try to find moments in the hurried pace of our short lives on this planet to consider our legacy. As Rachel Carson states in *Silent Spring*: "Why should we tolerate a diet of weak poisons, a home in insipid surroundings, a circle of acquaintances who are not quite our enemies . . . Who would want to live in a world which is just not quite fatal?"

Above: Snow geese during fall migration.
CREDIT: KARL SOMMERER.

Centre: The swift fox, last seen in Canada in 1938, is now being reintroduced to the prairies.   CREDIT: WAYNE LYNCH.

Below: The decline of antelope motivated legislation to protect some of the first wildlife areas in the West.
CREDIT: TIM FITZHARRIS.

Left: A precious glimpse of tallgrass prairie; less than 1 per cent remains.   CREDIT: JOANNE JOYCE.

BRISTOL FOSTER

The West Coast: Canada's Rain Forest

Spawned in the Gulf of Alaska, a series of low-pressure weather systems sweep across the vast Pacific Ocean to encounter Canada's westernmost ramparts. Here, the scudding clouds sneak among thousands of islands and up the walls of steep fjords to collide with a barrier of mountains up to 4000 metres high. As the rising air cools, prodigious amounts of rainfall result. Fog, mists, rain, drizzle, and snow are prevalent for most of the year. They water one of the most spectacular ecosystems on the planet — Canada's rain forest.

In Canada true temperate rain forest is confined to the Pacific coast where the ocean moderates the climate. I shall refer to this forest as "primeval," "old-growth," or "ancient" forest. These terms refer in this chapter to the virgin, old, large-size trees and their ecosystems found on generally deep soils in the moist, cool environment of North America's Pacific coast.

DIVERSE BUT VULNERABLE

Foresters define an acre of old growth as having at least 2 species of tree, varying in age and size, with at least 10 trees over 200 years old and 1 metre in diameter, with 20 tons of downed logs, 10 snags over 3 metres tall and 4 snags much taller, and a shade-tolerant understory of smaller plants. In short, it represents a rich ecosystem providing habitat for everything from salamanders to swifts, eagles to bats, woodpeckers to long-horned beetles.

The feeling created in this ancient rain forest is one of awe at the great age that has spawned such an exuberance of natural life. These forests contain more gigantic trees than any other ecosystem on Earth. As the glaciers shrank, first pioneer, then a larger diversity of plants appeared on the glacial rubble. Over the millennia, a complicated web of adaptations developed among a growing number of different plants and animals. Only natural forces have controlled the destiny of the old-growth forest, and the result is inspiring.

Inside this world all is soft greenness. Branches, trunks, logs, snags, and rocks are festooned with cushions, curtains, and wisps of moss and lichen. One stands in reverence of the enormous sitka spruce, Douglas fir, western red cedar, and western hemlock that are reaching for the sky, or standing dead but full of other life, or lying quietly for hundreds of years under their blanket of moss as they sustain new growth in the forest.

The intricacies of life in an old-growth forest are far more complex and much less understood than life in a large city. There are undoubtedly many species in these forests that are not yet known to scientists. But we do know that their interlocking, symbiotic relationships are necessary to sustain the new forests we create today — and the forest industry of tomorrow.

Take fungi, for example. Some of us receive pleasure in the autumn searching for mushrooms. But industrial foresters are likely to complain about the attacks on live trees by the honey mushroom (*Armillaria mellea*). They, like most of us, have little grasp of the importance of fungi to the forests. Yet the coniferous trees that industry wants cannot exist without fungi. Fungi coat the root tips of healthy conifers. They penetrate the outer cellular layers and perform like sponges, absorbing water, minerals, and nitrogen from the soil and feeding them to the tree's root tips. From there, these nutrients rise to the top of the tree. A healthy Douglas fir has thirty to forty species of fungi attached to its root system.

Usually we hunt for above-ground fungi to eat, such as boletuses or chanterelles. Wind disperses their spores at random, and in very dry or cold years there is a poor survival rate. However, truffles and other kinds of fungi fruit below ground. Since their spores cannot be dispersed by wind, they have evolved other means of transport — they are eaten by small mammals. Ripe truffles give off distinctive odours, which help rodents find them. The mice and squirrels eat the fungi and later defecate the spores on the forest floor. Flying squirrels feed almost exclusively on these fungi, which are associated with wet, rotting wood. The rare northern spotted owl's favourite food is the flying squirrel. Therefore, spotted owls are usually found only in old-growth forests, for only here can rotting logs be found to support the fungi that feed the squirrels that feed the owls.

The fungus story is just one example of the unseen and generally unknown ecological webs that keep the rain forest healthy. It is one example that should give us food for thought, especially as industrial foresters spend millions of dollars to kill seed-eating rodents and to coat conifer seedlings with fungicides.

There are countless other ecological connections in the old-growth forest, most we know nothing about. There are more organisms in a healthy cubic metre of forest topsoil than there are people on Earth. These organisms are interconnected and critical to the flows of energy and nutrients that keep the forest healthy.

Even after a tree dies, it provides a home and sustenance for other life forms. An 800-year-old tree will take about 400 years to completely decompose. As it dies, the tree is invaded by fungi and wood-boring beetles. Then woodpeckers make their homes, later tenanted by ducks or owls. Eventually the top and branches fall off. The cracks and loose bark can now harbour bats. Finally, after about 150 years, the tree falls to the forest floor, where it becomes a nurse log for tree seedlings. Salamanders lay their eggs in the moist chambers of the disintegrating wood until, at last, it exists no longer as a tree, but has been completely transformed into other life.

As the old growth is logged, these blueprints for healthy, productive forest ecology are destroyed. It is like throwing away some of the cogs and wheels before we even know how the watch works. And while foresters call logging "multiple use" since mining, hunting, and fishing may still be possible, others would call this "multiple ABUSE" since many other forestry, recreational, and scientific options are forgone, as are "non-game" species of wildlife — from owls to bats.

CANADA'S UNIQUE TREASURE

The Canadian rain forest reaches its greatest stature on the deep soils left by glaciers and rivers. Here the sitka spruce and Douglas fir attain 4 metres in diameter and over 90 metres in height. Western red cedars can grow to 6 metres in diameter! Elsewhere, the trees struggle on the shallow soils of the walls of fjords, or survive, in declining stature, in the less hospitable environment of the subalpine regions. Sometimes, as in the boglands, the impeded drainage results in an elfin forest populated by bonsai trees of outstanding beauty. The result is a diverse tapestry of both giants and midgets.

While British Columbians generally take their magnificent primeval rain forests for granted, such forests are actually rare in the world. These cool, wet forests grow only in southern Chile, Australia, New Zealand, Norway, and in northwestern North America from California to Alaska. Today not much old-growth forest remains in Norway, Chile, Australia, or New Zealand. The forest industry itself acknowledges that less than one-third still exists in British Columbia, where the largest trees and greatest expanse of these ancient forests are still to be found. But even this estimate is misleadingly high.

Apart from size, our rain forest has many unique attributes. Many of its species are not found elsewhere in the world. They include not only the very obvious plants such as sitka spruce, but also less obvious species such as some kinds of mosses and liverworts.

There are other forms of life that depend on the survival of ancient forests; for example, the sitka deer, which survive in winter on the fallen arboreal lichens; the marbled murrelets, which nest high in the branches on cushions of moss; the cavity-nesting birds, the petrels, auklets, and ancient murrelets, which nest among the roots of old-growth trees; and the bald eagles, which reach their maximum density in the world on this coast due to the abundance of fish and the presence of ancient trees large enough to support their huge nests.

Also unique in these temperate rain forests are the aboriginal people: the Salish, Nootka, Kwakiutl, Haida, and Tsimshian. While their lives were and still are largely sustained by the rich marine life of the coast, the resources of the forest, particularly western red cedar, allowed them to develop dwellings, totem poles, and masks, which today are a triumph of aboriginal architectural and artistic achievement.

The aboriginal people of the coast were hunters and gatherers — hunters of gray whales and salmon, deer, bear, and sea otter; gatherers of mussels, clams, herring roe, and berries. The supply of food was so prolific and predictable that

B.C.'s coastal native peoples were among the most numerous of hunter-gatherer societies in the world. The rain forest provided nursery streams for the salmon and nutrients for the growth of algae in the ocean, which in turn supported endless ocean food webs. The forest also provided protection for the thin soil from heavy rains sweeping down the steep slopes. Rarely were there the mass erosions smothering spawning beds and marine life that we find today.

SUSTAINABLE USE OR LIQUIDATION?

Modern man, with his insatiable appetite for wood products, has upset the delicate balance of Canada's rain forest. Today, forestry is the application of brute strength to remove the huge trees of the old-growth forest as quickly and cheaply as possible. The reason given for the speed is that our virgin rain forest, the legacy of thousands of years of evolution, has become, in the words of the forest industry, "a cellulose cemetery." True, an old-growth forest contains trees of all ages, including the dead and dying. Foresters call this "decadent" or a "silvicultural slum" to justify its rapid removal. They argue that we must replace the old growth with a young, vibrant, rapidly growing forest.

But the primeval forest contains some of the finest trees for forestry in the world. These old veterans, hundreds of years old, with their close, straight, knot-free grain, are the cream of the forest, producing the highest-value wood. We shall never see the likes of them again, since foresters plan to log areas every 60 to 120 years. The smaller, coarse-grained, new forest has far less value as lumber, and as a home to rain-forest wildlife. Maximized profits now, through liquidation of old growth, means forgoing far greater benefits, both economic and ecological, in the future.

Since the old-growth forest is so commercially valuable, one would think that foresters would have an accurate idea of how much has been logged, and how much is left. Unfortunately this is not so. The cynic would say this ignorance is intentional because it is easier to justify logging the old growth quickly if we do not realize how fast it is running out. In general, foresters' estimates of timber volumes available for logging are exaggerated because they include areas that are too small or difficult to log at a profit. Nevertheless, such areas are left in estimates of trees available for cutting to justify a high annual harvest. This rapid rate of logging is further justified by the prediction that a new man-designed forest, with its genetically improved trees planted in monocultures, will outproduce the old. The consequences of this conceit cannot be known for many decades, long after all unprotected old growth is gone. Should we not at least take out an insurance policy, by protecting a significant portion of what's left?

Considering how little we really know about the ecology of the forest, growing evidence that the productivity of so-called managed forests is falling world-wide should not be surprising. The monocultures of Norway spruce in Europe, for example, are subject to far more diseases than are several species of trees in a mixed forest. In China, a plantation of Chinese fir cannot be grown more than two or three times on the same site because the soil can no longer support normal

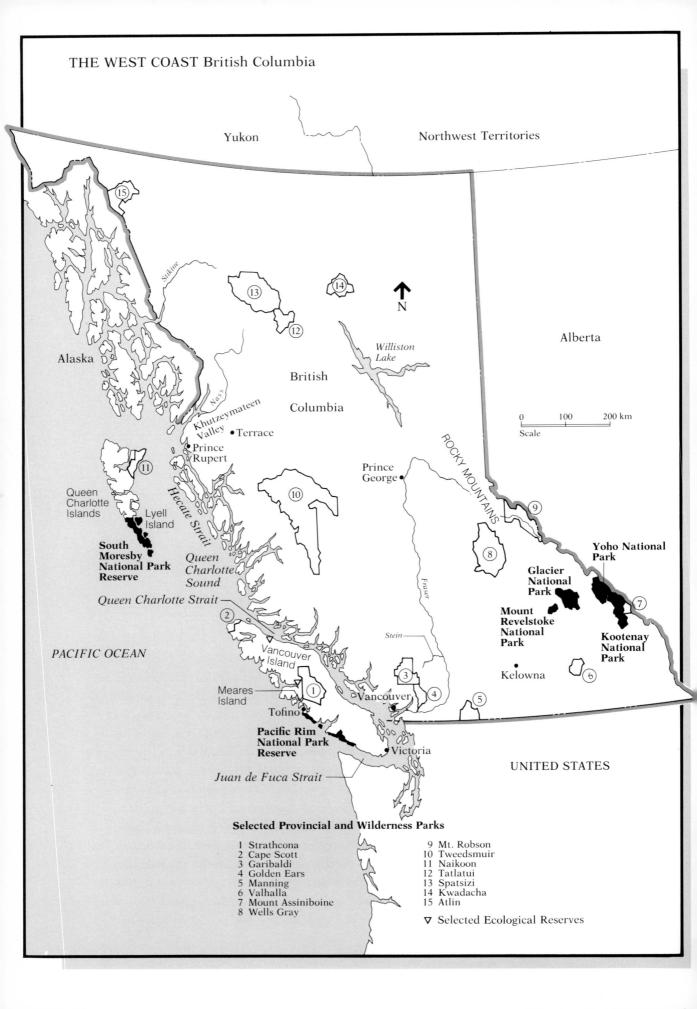

THE WEST COAST British Columbia

Yukon

Northwest Territories

⑮

Stikine

Alaska

British

Columbia

Williston Lake

Alberta

N

Nass

Khutzeymateen
Valley
• Terrace

ROCKY MOUNTAINS

0   100   200 km
Scale

• Prince
Rupert

Prince
George •

⑪

Queen
Charlotte
Islands

Lyell
Island

Hecate Strait

**South
Moresby
National Park
Reserve**

*Queen
Charlotte
Sound*

Queen Charlotte Strait

⑩

⑨

Yoho National
Park

⑧

**Glacier
National
Park**

**Mount
Revelstoke
National
Park**

**Kootenay
National
Park**

⑦

Fraser

Kelowna •

⑥

②

Stein

PACIFIC OCEAN

▽ Vancouver
Island

③

⑤

Meares
Island

①

④

Tofino •

Vancouver

Victoria •

**Pacific Rim
National Park
Reserve**

UNITED STATES

Juan de Fuca Strait

Selected Provincial and Wilderness Parks

1 Strathcona
2 Cape Scott
3 Garibaldi
4 Golden Ears
5 Manning
6 Valhalla
7 Mount Assiniboine
8 Wells Gray

9 Mt. Robson
10 Tweedsmuir
11 Naikoon
12 Tatlatui
13 Spatsizi
14 Kwadacha
15 Atlin

▽ Selected Ecological Reserves

growth. The same could occur with Douglas fir in Canada. Given this evidence, one might think that foresters would insist on saving permanent samples of old-growth forest for study. But, with rare exceptions, they do not.

WHAT'S LEFT?

There are about 3.7 billion cubic metres, 88,000 square kilometres (9.3 per cent of the area of B.C.) remaining in original old-growth forest. These virgin forests, "green gold" to the logging companies, are being mined at the rate of about 75 million to 91 million cubic metres per year. The long-run sustained yield from all commercial forest lands in the province is calculated to be about 50 million to 58 million cubic metres per year. But in 1986, 79.9 million cubic metres (2,320 square kilometres) of timber were logged, 35 per cent of which was virgin rain forest. The high-priced old-growth Douglas fir, sitka spruce, and red cedar are being logged into oblivion and replaced by a "managed forest" dominated by the lower value fast-growing monocultures.

Against this onslaught, 1,860 square kilometres or 2.6 per cent of the original ancient forest has been permanently protected and big old trees are scarce.

Provincial Parks

While 5.6 per cent of the province is given some protection in the form of provincial parks, only 22 per cent of the area of all coastal parks represents old-growth forest. Most are composed of bogs, subalpine, and alpine habitats. Even when the rain forest exists in provincial parks, it is not secure from the logger. The provincial cabinet can change the boundaries of most parks at any time. Mining is not only allowed, but encouraged.

The B.C. government has a tradition of trading valuable timber within a park to logging companies in order to obtain a new park with less valuable timber. This happened when prime timber in Strathcona Park was traded to the Raven Logging Company in exchange for Cape Scott Park. The pressure to log the small amount of valuable timber in provincial parks is certain to increase as the old growth disappears elsewhere and the second growth is not ready to cut.

National Parks

There is only one national park protecting virgin rain forest in Canada: Pacific Rim National Park. Even here, in the Long Beach section, 80 per cent of the merchantable timber was logged before the park was created. The park was to contain only 6000 hectares of ancient forest before conservationists waged a long fight to include the Nitinat Triangle, which added 9000 hectares.

Unlike provincial parks, national parks are more likely to be protected forever. Hence, conservationists on the Queen Charlotte Islands fought for the South Moresby National Park Reserve, which includes about 33,500 hectares of rain forest. However, islands always have fewer species than comparably sized mainland areas. Clearly, national parks or other permanent protection are needed on the mainland coast to conserve representative samples of the greater diversity found there.

Above: Two grizzlies frolic in a rain forest understory.   CREDIT: DENNIS W. SCHMIDT.

Below: Clearcut logging near Pacific Rim National Park, B.C.   CREDIT: ADRIAN DORST.

Opposite: Some of the tallest trees in Canada are found in the Carmanah Valley of British Columbia. Will they be protected?   CREDIT: ADRIAN DORST.

Ecological Reserves

Provincial ecological reserves are natural areas set aside for research and education. They serve as outdoor research laboratories for studying natural benchmark areas, and they help protect genetic diversity. Above all, they ensure that we will be able to answer future questions about our natural environment, questions that have not yet even been asked or even conceived. In particular, we know relatively little about how an old-growth forest functions and therefore how to grow forests in perpetuity. We must acquire this knowledge if forestry is to remain a mainstay of B.C.'s economy.

Since protected natural areas have such an important economic application, one might conclude that there would be a good sampling of the natural diversity of B.C.'s virgin rain forest protected in ecological reserves. In fact, only 5071 hectares of old growth is protected in the reserve system (out of a total reserve area of 154,670 hectares — mostly ocean, bog, and alpine habitats). Many other valuable ecosystems are not yet protected. Some never will be.

For certain forest ecosystems on southeastern Vancouver Island, and near Terrace, it is already too late. They have long since been completely logged. Other jurisdictions have done a far better job of protecting their old-growth forest. After fifteen years of struggle, B.C. has finally protected tiny Nimpkish Island (16 hectares), containing perhaps the tallest Douglas fir in Canada. However, California and southern Oregon have already protected relatively enormous areas of redwoods. While we struggle to increase our national and provincial-park coverage a percentage point above 6.4 per cent in B.C., we are surrounded by jurisdictions that protect more area: Washington State has already protected 11.3 per cent of its area, Alberta 8.2 per cent, and Alaska, an astounding 37.9 per cent.

WILDERNESS DEFENCE

Individuals and private agencies have been instrumental in protecting some of the old growth of the province, and they continue to be the first line of defence of these areas. The most far-sighted accomplishment in recent times has been the creation of a national park in South Moresby on the Queen Charlotte Islands. In this case, the Council of the Haida Nation, the Islands Protection Society, and countless individuals waged an unrelenting battle for fourteen years. Apart from the $106 million that the federal government promised to the province for the creation of South Moresby Park, there are additional costs. Important federal environmental programs have been jeopardized in order to raise this money. The logging and mining industry, and some government officials, have hardened their resolve to halt further wilderness preservation in B.C. This attitude has resulted in accelerated logging of proposed parks, reserves or native land claims such as the Nass, Kispiox, West Chilcotin, Stuart Lake, Liard, and the remaining Queen Charlotte Islands.

The Nature Trust and the Nature Conservancy of Canada have been instrumental in protecting tiny but priceless pieces of old growth. These small protected areas have the same deficiency as many ecological reserves, namely the "island effect" — small islands of naturalness in a sea of development invariably and permanently lose species. This is why we must better understand the minimum critical area needed to protect genetic resources, and strive for parks and reserves that are as large as possible as a hedge against further species loss.

Opportunities Lost and Pending

There have been many lost battles. One of the most prominent involved the Tsitika River Valley, proposed as an ecological reserve to protect major old-growth forest ecosystems. This valley was the last, major untouched valley on northeastern Vancouver Island. The government of the day allowed public hearings on the issue, but the following government committed most of the area to logging. As an "integrated plan," it has been largely a failure.

Subsequently, it was learned that Robson Bight at the mouth of the Tsitika River was considered to be the best place in the world for the public to see and scientists to study killer whales. In spite of this, the forest industry continues to clearcut the valley with the exception of a few small ecological reserve proposals and a small reserve bordering the ocean. The logging will affect large populations of salmon that spawn in the river, which could in turn adversely affect the salmon-eating whales. Logging will certainly degrade the very scenic panorama of this unique tourist attraction. Already boaters and tourists complain of the wasteland they see from the water as they pass by B.C.'s coast.

Many other proposals in the old-growth rain forest are pending. First among them is the Khutzeymateen Valley. While it is best known for its large population of grizzly bears, it also supports diverse ecosystems, four kinds of salmon, pockets of large sitka spruce, and a pristine estuary. A major problem in setting aside ancient forest is the resistance of logging companies whose logging rights must be bought out, usually at enormous expense. Since conservation is a low priority with the government of British Columbia, the money for such buy-outs is rarely available. However, in the case of the Khutzeymateen, the forest and land are uncommitted. The cost of logging this valley is likely to exceed any financial return, not to mention the losses incurred by destroying ancient ecosystems for all time. For "the Khutz," there is still hope, as the World Wildlife Fund works with local groups to make this the first grizzly reserve in Canada.

Other longstanding proposals to protect old growth are hampered since the companies that own licences to log the trees demand compensation, and prefer to trade for other trees rather than receive cash. But as the last of the ancient forests is felled, it is becoming impossible to find trees to trade.

The ancient forests of Meares Island received national attention when protesters hammered spikes into trees to stop logging. The controversy is now before the federal courts as part of a larger native land claim. There are many relevant issues at stake on Meares Island: the scenic backdrop to the tourist town of Tofino, the land claim by the Indians, and the untouched old-growth ecosystems.

During the summer of 1988 yet another controversy broke out in Canada's rain forest at Sulphur Passage, northwest of Tofino. Here the Friends of Clayoquot Sound, backed by the Tofino Chamber of Commerce, have confronted B.C. Forest

Above: A beautiful pink fawn lily from Honeymoon Bay, Vancouver Island.
CREDIT: DON McPHEE.

Centre: In 1988, oil spills rendered Pacific Rim National Park an endangered space.
CREDIT: DON McPHEE.

Below: In the fate of the Pacific salmon lies the fate of grizzlies and eagles.
CREDIT: DENNIS W. SCHMIDT.

Right: Killer whales cruise Clayoquot Sound.
CREDIT: ADRIAN DORST.

Products' road-building crews in this outstandingly scenic wilderness. Protesters have suspended themselves from hammocks and built treehouses to block the blasting. Thirty-five people have been arrested and some jailed for thirty days. Nobody in the community is against logging. It is a question of how and where it is done, and whether it is sustainable. The road to the tourist town of Tofino passes through denuded mountains with massive landslides. B.C. Forest Products says that the company has learned from its mistakes and can do a better job now, but few are gullible enough to believe this old refrain. The conflict continues.

Recommendations for old-growth areas warranting protection can be found languishing in the files of the provincial-parks and ecological-reserves programs. Many proposals have been approved by all government resource agencies, including the Ministry of Forests, yet they sit for years unsigned on the Minister's desk: Kokanee Creek, Slim Creek, Tahsish-Kwois spruce, Hellroar Creek, Jack Swart Creek, Tsitika River, Stein River, Molly Creek — more than twenty in all.

Ecologists, environmentalists, and naturalists are overwhelmed by the task of informing the public and government about the highest-priority proposals, with little time left for those of lower priority. Defending existing parks, such as Strathcona where mining proceeds apace, or ecological reserves, such as Mt. Tuam where a logger wants to put a road through the reserve, takes a considerable amount of time away from badly needed new areas.

Finally, there are valuable areas that do not appear to be under immediate threat, then suddenly logging plans change and we have yet another crisis. Carmanah Creek for example. This valley runs to the Pacific Ocean through Pacific Rim National Park and probably contains the largest trees in Canada. MacMillan Bloedel, the province's largest logging company, is poised to level them. Suddenly, Carmanah Creek is raised to a very high priority. Another potential confrontation looms.

Are Solutions Possible?

Lurching from crisis to crisis is the norm in B.C. when it comes to protecting samples of natural environments. This can be attributed to the lack of application of professional ethics by industrial foresters, to a particularly development-oriented provincial government, and to the resulting climate of polarization and confrontation when it comes to conservation efforts.

The Association of B.C. Professional Foresters has a code of ethics that includes "protecting the productive capacity of the forest and managing the forests in a wise and scientific way to maintain economic, social and cultural benefits in perpetuity." The forester should not subjugate such professional principles to the demands of employment, and must be free to advise his or her employer regarding any course of action that is not sound forestry practice.

Unfortunately, the code is frequently not followed. We are cutting down forests much faster than they are being replaced. In the process, an unbelievable amount of valuable wood is being wasted. Recently, for example, MacMillan Bloedel was caught leaving double the amount of legal "waste" on their logged areas. And they may not be the worst offenders.

While we are planting more trees than ever before, we are also logging faster than ever, and many seedlings will die. There are about 3.6 million hectares of land in the province that are not sufficiently restocked with a new forest, as a result of insufficient replanting, invasion of brush, and soil erosion.

Frequently foresters, ignoring their code, approve logging even when they know the soil is likely to slide into the river after the trees have been removed. When such landslides occur, not only is the productive capacity of the land diminished for centuries, but the destruction of salmon and other resources ensues.

Ironically, the lack of adherence to the code of ethics means the province will soon be running out of the best timber, while the new forest will not be ready in sufficient size and quality to sustain the industry, given today's rate of logging. Only 2 per cent of the remaining old-growth forests is sitka spruce, 8 per cent Douglas fir. The cream of the forest is almost gone.

Dr. Peter Pearse, a well-known forestry consultant, estimates there may be only seventeen years' worth of logging remaining in the ancient forests on our coast. As a result, forest companies do everything they can to ensure that no more old-growth rain forest is "locked up" for "single use" in parks or reserves. Yet very little has been done to compare the value of international tourist trade of such wilderness areas with the value of cutting the forest now and losing the benefits associated with preservation in the future. What *will* B.C. wilderness be worth in 2050?

It is time for someone in the forestry industry to break ranks and provide leadership by arguing for a balance of sound silvicultural management on lands identified for cutting and preservation of wilderness areas. Both are needed, but to date industry has chiefly promoted maximum short-term financial gain.

The need for a comprehensive land-use strategy in B.C. has been noted for several decades. Of course the current chaos does not have to be, nor should it. In 1986 the province's Wilderness Advisory Committee deplored the frustration, alienation, and polarization endemic to making decisions about resource development that effect preservation in the province. The committee pointed out some serious weaknesses in the land-use decision-process in B.C.: lack of government flexibility, poor communication and co-ordination, delays of more than a decade on some park and ecological-reserve proposals, decisions made without a long-term strategy and without co-ordination with policies of other sectors, and reluctance to consult the views of the public at large. The committee concluded that a "revitalized approach to decision-making" is urgently required.

The Wilderness Advisory Committee outlined an approach that could provide an orderly process for resolving wilderness land-use conflicts:

First, there is a need for a clear and consistent policy, together with explicit management guidelines, for wilderness. The committee defined wilderness as an expanse of land, preferably greater than 5000 hectares, retaining its natural character, affected mainly by the forces of nature, with the imprint of modern man substantially unnoticeable.

Second, there should be publicly available system plans and master plans for parks and other protected areas in concert with an overall land-use strategy. In the absence of such plans, decision-making is inevitably ad hoc.

Third, there needs to be a much more open system for planning and policy-making. Often an existing protected area's boundaries have been altered without consultation with interested parties, and new park proposals are similarly treated.

Finally, the committee strongly recommended the establishment of a Natural Areas Advisory Council to seek the resolution of conflicts arising from new park and ecological-reserve proposals as well as changes to their management and boundaries. By making the process public, much of the mistrust and misunderstanding that has marked resource conflicts to date would be alleviated.

Prospects

Unfortunately, none of the recommendations outlined above has been accepted. My personal involvement with the ecological-reserves program illustrates the problem further. We had an Ecological Reserve Advisory Board, as envisaged by the Wilderness Advisory Committee. However, it was abolished in 1983, because it was giving advice the Minister did not want to hear. Bluntly stated, cabinet did not want boards, planning teams, or councils offering advice that, if ignored, could make government decisions seem arbitrary (which they were and are).

Perhaps the Wilderness Advisory Committee should have made one more recommendation: that since wilderness is a rapidly declining and irreplaceable resource of immense economic, recreational, and scientific value, politicians should try to imagine the wishes of their grandchildren before making land-use decisions. We must realize that we are the last generation with an opportunity to protect more of Canada's rain forests.

In the thick of environmental controversies, it is hard to imagine that the situation will ever get better. But there is hope. National surveys indicate "environment" has become the number-one priority with most Canadians. In B.C. there are a growing number of dedicated people and organizations that put pressure on government, such as the Sierra Club, the Western Canada Wilderness Committee, Friends of Strathcona Park, Friends of Ecological Reserves, and the World Wildlife Fund. One, the Heritage Forests Society, is specifically concerned with the subject of this chapter. There are two additional groups that are chiefly involved with purchasing ecologically valuable land for its permanent protection: the B.C. Nature Trust and the Nature Conservancy of Canada. All these individuals and groups are part of a groundswell that must be recognized as a major force by politicians.

One thing is certain: protection of significant samples of Canada's rain forest in British Columbia is a public issue that will increasingly become more urgent until either endangered spaces are protected or the last tree is levelled. History is littered with the shards of civilizations that have lost their forests forever, and have utterly failed to adapt to their environment. There is still a chance that we can learn from the mistakes of others rather than repeat them. Will we?

FRANÇOIS BREGHA

Conservation in the Yukon and the Northwest Territories

Canadian geographers have debated the question "What is the North?" for decades. According to freelance writer Lyn Hancock, the North "is more a region of the soul than a region of the country." Using Environment Canada's classification of Canadian ecozones, the North comprises seven different ecological regions, spanning two territories and parts of seven provinces, covering well over half of Canada's land mass. For the purpose of this chapter, I shall restrict myself to that part of the Yukon and the Northwest Territories "North of 60."

Canada's two northern territories represent approximately 40 per cent of Canada's total land and freshwater surface area, an area of almost 4 million square kilometres. They span a distance of almost 3000 kilometres from east to west, and as much again from north to south. Together, these two territories share a "northernness" that makes them different from the rest of the country. This northernness can be seen in the distinctive landscapes that wind, ice, and snow have created, and in a unique fauna and flora found only in other polar countries, if at all. Permanently frozen ground (permafrost) and the presence of ice on land and in the water for most if not all of the year are responsible for simple ecosystems with low rates of biological productivity. Northern plants and wildlife must make the most of the short summers and are highly dependent on favourable conditions at critical times of the year. In this harsh, arid environment, "oases" can be found, areas where topographic features combine to produce uncommonly rich habitat. Because these areas are few and highly localized, they are susceptible to disruption. They are endangered spaces, and their protection is critical.

The North's distinct identity is reinforced by the presence of ecosystems functioning still, with minimum human interference; long, dark winters and cool, nightless summers; a low human population, in majority of native ancestry; a resource-based economy ranging from the pursuit of traditional hunting and trapping activities to the large-scale extraction of minerals; and the presence of some of the continent's last large, remaining free-ranging wildlife populations.

The Yukon and the Northwest Territories, however, are also very different from each other, both physiographically and culturally.

The Yukon is a rugged land dominated by mountain ranges (Canada's tallest mountains are found in the St. Elias range in the southwest corner) and with only a short coastline on the Arctic Ocean. The territory's small population (24,000) is two-thirds white, and concentrated in the capital, Whitehorse.

Seven times the size, the NWT is a mostly flat land of rock and lakes largely underlain by permafrost and is characterized by stunted black-spruce forests in the south, the treeless tundra of the barrenlands, and the mountainous Arctic islands farther north. With two-thirds of Canada's coastline, the territory is extensively influenced by maritime conditions. The majority of its 53,000 population is of aboriginal ancestry (Dene, Metis, and Inuit) and is broadly scattered across sixty-two communities.

CONSERVATION ACHIEVEMENTS TO DATE

The North's first protected area was established surprisingly long ago, in 1918, when Victoria Island was designated as a hunting reserve for the exclusive use of native peoples. The creation of this reserve, however, was not so much an example of far-sighted conservation policy as a belated response to an alarming decline in the wildlife populations upon which the native people depended, brought about by an influx of whalers, trappers, and traders. In 1926, the reserve was expanded considerably with the creation of the Arctic Islands Preserve. Chiefly designed to protect the native hunting economy, the preserve was also meant to affirm Canadian sovereignty over the Arctic archipelago — a goal that still drives the establishment of northern protected areas today. The preserve was gradually increased over the following twenty years until it covered over a third of the Northwest Territories. It is a paradox that northern protected areas reached their maximum size when there was the least threat to the North's wildlife or landscape. After 1948, the preserve was gradually dismantled until it was abolished altogether in 1966.

Today, the North's protected areas fall into a dozen categories, more or less depending on the classification system used. The most important are below.

National Parks

There are now two full-fledged national parks North of 60 (Wood Buffalo, straddling the Alberta/NWT border, and Northern Yukon on the shores of the Beaufort Sea) and four national park reserves (Kluane in Yukon, and Nahanni, Auyuittuq, and northern Ellesmere in the Northwest Territories). National park reserves are "parks-in-waiting," whose final boundaries and management regime are to be set after the settlement of the aboriginal land claims to the area. These six parks and park reserves cover a surface of 105,649 square kilometres and account for about 2 per cent and 6.7 per cent of the NWT's and Yukon's land surface, respectively. In addition, lands have already been withdrawn for the future establishment of two other parks (Old Crow Flats in Yukon and the East Arm of Great Slave Lake in the Northwest Territories).

Environment Canada estimates that at least five other parks — all in the NWT — will be necessary in order to represent fully the North's environmental diversity. Although there are no plans to complete the northern national-park network in the near future, consideration is being given to the early designation of a national park on Banks Island and, at the other end of the Northwest Passage, a park reserve on the northern tip of Baffin Island and an adjoining marine-park reserve in Lancaster Sound.

Migratory-Bird Sanctuaries

Migratory-bird sanctuaries do not enjoy the same high degree of protection as national parks because their purpose is restricted to protecting migratory birds and their habitat. Some non-renewable resource activity, such as oil exploration, is therefore allowed under controlled conditions. There are thirteen bird sanctuaries in the Northwest Territories North of 60 (three more in James Bay) ranging in size from a modest 2 square kilometres to the gigantic 63,000-square-kilometre Queen Maud Gulf Bird Sanctuary. There are no bird sanctuaries in Yukon. Three more sanctuaries in the eastern Arctic are in the final stages of designation. The Canadian Wildlife Service of Environment Canada has identified sixty-one other key habitat sites it believes should be protected, but does not contemplate immediate formal measures to do so.

Territorial Parks

Because the federal government still owns the overwhelming percentage of the land surface of both territories, the territorial park network is small. In the Northwest Territories, these parks exist primarily to provide facilities for local residents or to support tourism. The NWT network covers 5300 hectares. Conservation in these parks focuses on protecting the basic biological or physical resources around which the park is developed. There is one territorial park in Yukon, Herschel Island, in the Beaufort Sea.

International Biological Program Sites

The International Biological Program (IBP) identifies significant ecosystems for monitoring and eventual protection. By 1974, 151 IBP sites had been identified in the two territories. Although these sites do not have any legal protected status except for those that happen to lie within national parks and bird sanctuaries, they are protected in the Northwest Territories (but not in the Yukon) through the land-use regulations of the Department of Indian Affairs and Northern Development (DIAND).

National Wildlife Areas

Only one national wildlife area has been designated so far in either territory: Polar Bear Pass, on Bathurst Island in the Arctic archipelago. An IBP site, Polar Bear Pass became a *cause célèbre* in the 1970s because its exceptional ecological richness appeared to be threatened by industry plans to drill for oil and gas in the area. It became a national wildlife area in 1986 after a tortuous ten-year

Above: Lake Hazen in the N.W.T. cleanly reflects an arctic sky. CREDIT: STEPHEN J. KRASEMANN.

Right: The ecologically rich Peace–Athabasca Delta, N.W.T. CREDIT: GREG STOTT.

Centre: The arctic tundra is more like a garden than a barrenland. CREDIT: PETER VAN RHIJN.

Below: Musk-oxen on Banks Island have rebounded in numbers. Now the island itself is a candidate for national park status. CREDIT: STEPHEN J. KRASEMANN.

Opposite: The Donjek Glacier in Kluane National Park, Yukon Territory. CREDIT: J.A. KRAULIS.

process. Industrial activity is allowed in national wildlife areas provided it does not compromise the purpose for which these areas were established.

Wildlife Sanctuaries and Preserves

There are two game sanctuaries in the Yukon (Kluane and McArthur) where non-renewable-resource activities are allowed as long as they do not compromise wildlife habitat and population protection. There is also one game preserve (Peel River), which is essentially a native-only hunting area.

Three wildlife sanctuaries (Thelon, Bowman Bay, Twin Islands) and one bison sanctuary (Mackenzie Bison) have been established in the NWT. Mining is allowed in all but the Thelon Sanctuary. There are also three wildlife preserves in the NWT (Peel River, N.W. Mitchener, James Bay) and one reindeer grazing preserve, for a total surface area of over 40,000 square kilometres.

In total, 15.9 per cent of the Yukon and 3.2 per cent of the Northwest Territories enjoy a high level of environmental protection (defined as excluding non-renewable-resource activities). The percentage for the Yukon overstates, in fact, the area of the territory under long-term protection, because it includes the 8 per cent of the Yukon's land area that is temporarily protected, pending full implementation of the Inuvialuit and Yukon Indian final land-claim settlements.

While small compared to Alaska (where national parks, national wildlife refuges, and wilderness amount to 35.6 per cent of the state's surface), this total is large enough that it has led to much criticism in the North, particularly by the mining industry, for "locking up" northern resources.

POLICY CONSIDERATIONS

The uninitiated observer can be forgiven if he or she sees the field of northern conservation as an exasperating version of the children's game of Snakes and Ladders. The large number of players involved and the overlapping processes dealing with conservation make it appear that luck plays a greater role in the designation process than does any purposeful planning. That impression is not entirely incorrect: anyone who has followed the innumerable workshops, task forces, public consultations, policy reviews, ministerial statements, planning processes, and inventories over the last fifteen years knows that the process is truly complex, highly politicized, frustratingly slow, and decidedly non-linear.

In developing a strategy for the establishment of northern protected areas in the 1990s and beyond, two factors, above all others, need to be kept in mind. The first is that protected areas have a different role to play in the North than they do in southern Canada. Second, there are many legitimate stakeholders in northern conservation: their interests need to be accommodated if any progress is to be made.

WHAT ARE PROTECTED AREAS FOR?

In parts of the country where expanding economic activity has left few areas untouched, the designation of protected areas is obviously important for environmental and other reasons. Most of Canada's North, however, remains close to its natural state. It is in this context that the questions "What are northern protected areas to be protected from?" and "For whom are they to be protected?" become relevant.

These are not academic questions. Many native peoples are still hunters, trappers, and fishermen. Not surprisingly, they see the protection of wildlife as the chief goal of conservation. Northern parks, however, are not established primarily because of their wildlife values but rather to represent Natural Areas of Canadian Significance (NACS). In a region whose economy still depends in significant measure on wildlife harvesting, the geophysical criteria primarily used for park establishment accentuate the fact that parks are a foreign concept to native peoples. It is not surprising, therefore, that many native people feel ambivalent about protected areas, parks in particular. On the one hand, they recognize that these areas can often provide jobs and increased economic activity. On the other, they are concerned that protected areas may become impediments to their livelihood, particularly by restricting access to wildlife.

The proposed use of jetboats in the Nahanni National Park Reserve exemplifies the conflicting perceptions that Environment Canada must reconcile in establishing and managing northern parks. A few years ago, a local native corporation sought to capture some of the park's economic benefits by applying for authorization to transport tourists on the Nahanni River by jetboat. The park's management plan, which emphasizes the area's wilderness character, however, precludes the use of jetboats for this purpose and the application was denied. This decision left Environment Canada open to the charge that northern parks are designed more for the benefit of a handful of southern canoeists and naturalists than for local inhabitants.

Ultimately, the question "What are northern protected areas for?" raises the fundamental issue of legitimacy. If there is no broad agreement about the answer, it will be more difficult to establish new protected areas. In this regard, it is important to note that the legitimacy of northern conservation initiatives has suffered because they have not always been advanced on their own merits. For example, it is well known that part of the government's current interest in the establishment of the proposed Lancaster Sound marine park results from the belief that the park would help to demonstrate Canadian sovereignty over the Northwest Passage.

The fact that the establishment of protected areas has sometimes responded to "other agendas" has made many northerners cynical of the federal government's commitment to northern conservation. It has also meant that, until recently, protected areas have not been designated to meet local needs. Their establishment has suffered on both counts.

The legitimacy of protected areas has also been questioned for other reasons. The Thelon Game Sanctuary, for example, was set aside in 1927 to protect endangered muskox populations. It has long since outlived this purpose (the muskox is alive and well in many parts of the North) but continues to restrict all mineral activity. IBP sites, which have never received official status, nevertheless may be protected under land-use regulations. In 1986, the ambiguity surrounding IBP sites and the perceived lack of purpose behind the continued existence of the Thelon sanctuary led to a successful backlash by the northern mining industry. In its Northern Mineral Policy, the federal government undertook to "clarify the disposition of potential IBP sites within the next two years to remove the uncertainties related to the current situation"; review resource utilization in the Thelon sanctuary "with the objective of ensuring the wide range of activities compatible with the original goal of muskox protection"; and review the boundaries of all migratory-bird sanctuaries "to ensure that the lands they contain are necessary to achieve the conservation objectives for which they were established."

Although the northern mineral industry will never be accused of unbridled support for conservation, its frustration at the absence of a protected-area–system plan, setting out clearly the objectives of northern conservation and the criteria for the designation of protected areas, is understandable.

THE IMPORTANCE OF BARGAINING
A survey of the northern conservation-policy landscape quickly reveals three

overriding characteristics: *a large number of stakeholders*, several avenues of implementation, and differing objectives among the stakeholders.

The stakeholders include the territorial governments, federal departments, aboriginal organizations, the resource industries, conservation groups, and local communities. They all exert some influence on northern conservation policy. This influence, however, is often a negative one: if none of the stakeholders can impose its agenda unilaterally, each frustrates the efforts of the others.

An unfortunate example of this multiple veto is the long delay surrounding the designation of a national park reserve in the vicinity of the East Arm of Great Slave Lake. Although over the years it has garnered the support of the federal and territorial governments and the relevant native organizations (the Dene and the Metis), it has been held up by the persistent unwillingness of the neighbouring settlement of Snowdrift to take a stand on the park's fate.

Although all stakeholders in northern conservation are important, some are more equal than others. Environment Canada has the lead federal responsibility for establishing protected areas in the North. Its mandate over national parks and migratory birds gives it a pre-eminent role in northern conservation. But its record, as the decade closes, has fallen far short of the expectations it aroused in the late 1970s and early 1980s when it committed itself to "actively pursue, as a matter of top priority, the completion of the national park system in the North" and "the protection of significant wildlife habitats."

In fairness, the Department's effectiveness during this period has also been hampered by the fact that a consensus-building process can only move as fast as its slowest member. At a time of rapid political change in both territories, the territorial governments, and the native organizations in particular, have often been so preoccupied with fundamental issues such as the settlement of native land claims and the transfer of federal responsibilities to the North that they have had little time to devote to such secondary issues as the establishment of protected areas.

Environment Canada's inability to follow through with its agenda, and DIAND's expressed policy to wind down most of its northern programs, have had the result of effectively devolving the leadership on northern conservation issues to the two territorial governments and the three major northern aboriginal organizations. This devolution has major implications for the future establishment of protected areas. While it is obviously essential that northerners be directly involved, they are poorly placed to fill the leadership vacuum left by Environment Canada: the territorial governments do not control the majority of northern lands and have limited legislative instruments to protect them. For their part, the major aboriginal organizations are not in the business of creating protected areas and cannot be expected, therefore, to champion the implementation of national programs.

In any case, there are no hard-and-fast rules to establish protected areas in the North. To date, these areas have been protected by federal fiat (everything before 1980), land-use regulations (IBP sites), federal-territorial agreements (Northern

Above: The Tombstone Range in the Ogilvie Mountains of the Yukon Territory.
CREDIT: PAT MORROW.

Centre: Fall fireweed ignites a Yukon landscape.   CREDIT: PETER VAN RHIJN.

Below: A tundra wolf saunters across its autumn home. Canada has the largest remaining population of wolves in the world.

CREDIT: KARL SOMMERER.

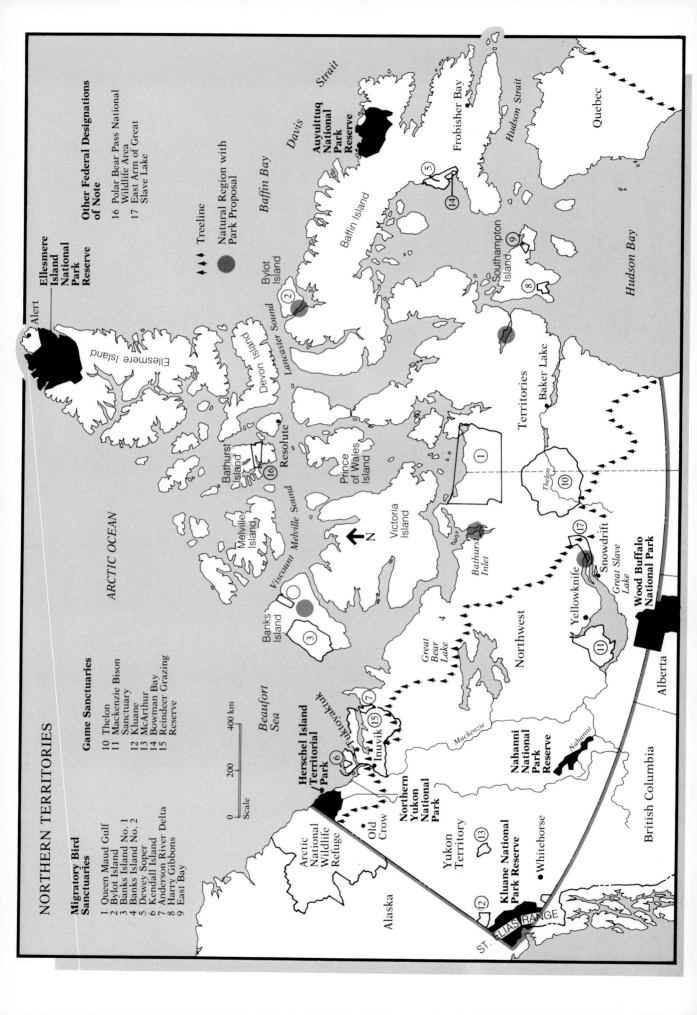

NORTHERN TERRITORIES

Migratory Bird Sanctuaries

1 Queen Maud Gulf
2 Bylot Island
3 Banks Island No. 1
4 Banks Island No. 2
5 Dewey Soper
6 Kendall Island
7 Anderson River Delta
8 Harry Gibbons
9 East Bay

Game Sanctuaries

10 Thelon
11 Mackenzie Bison Sanctuary
12 Kluane
13 McArthur
14 Bowman Bay
15 Reindeer Grazing Reserve

Other Federal Designations of Note

16 Polar Bear Pass National Wildlife Area
17 East Arm of Great Slave Lake

◄◄ ◄ Treeline

● Natural Region with Park Proposal

Ellesmere Island National Park Reserve

Auyuittuq National Park Reserve

ARCTIC OCEAN

Beaufort Sea

Davis Strait

Baffin Bay

Hudson Strait

Hudson Bay

Lancaster Sound

Viscount Melville Sound

Ellesmere Island

Devon Island

Melville Island

Bathurst Island

Prince of Wales Island

Victoria Island

Banks Island

Baffin Island

Bylot Island

Southampton Island

Alert

Resolute

Frobisher Bay

Baker Lake

Bathurst Inlet

Thelon

Great Bear Lake

Great Slave Lake

Yellowknife

Snowdrift

Wood Buffalo National Park

Mackenzie

Nahanni

Nahanni National Park Reserve

Northern Yukon National Park

Herschel Island Territorial Park

Tuktoyaktuk

Inuvik

Arctic National Wildlife Refuge

Old Crow

Yukon Territory

Whitehorse

Kluane National Park Reserve

ST. ELIAS RANGE

Alaska

British Columbia

Alberta

Northwest Territories

Quebec

N

Scale

0   200   400 km

Ellesmere), land-claim settlements (Northern Yukon), and a combination of the above. The land-use planning process and the territorial governments' development of northern conservation strategies represent two new processes that may supersede the existing ones. Although their freshness makes them fashionable, they remain unproven at this time.

While the existence of several avenues of implementation might appear at first as an advantage because of the flexibility provided, it has mostly bred confusion. The consequences of overlapping processes were shown in 1986 when the Inuit declared their opposition (since withdrawn) to the creation of three new migratory-bird sanctuaries in the eastern Arctic. The Inuit were not opposed to the sanctuaries per se, but to their establishment under a memorandum of understanding between Environment Canada and the government of the NWT that did not explicitly acknowledge the Inuit's land claim.

The conclusion to be drawn is that any establishment process that excludes legitimate stakeholders is likely to fail.

A general agreement among stakeholders (with the exception of the mining industry) about the importance of northern conservation has sometimes masked real differences in objectives. National parks are a case in point. By law, they are instruments of preservation. The NWT government and most native organizations, on the other hand, would like them to be instruments of conservation, i.e., they want controlled renewable-resource activities within park boundaries. Although Environment Canada has been willing to accommodate traditional forms of native harvesting, native organizations are continuing to insist on the possibility of commercial activities as well.

The fact that accommodating the various stakeholders in northern conservation has in the past proven difficult makes the consensus achieved in the 1984 report of the Task Force on Northern Conservation all the more remarkable. Composed of members representing government, conservation, aboriginal, and development interests, the task force was appointed by the Minister of Indian and Northern Affairs in consultation with his counterparts "to develop a framework for the creation of a comprehensive conservation policy for the Yukon Territory and the Northwest Territories (NWT) and a strategy for its implementation."

After noting that past conservation initiatives had enjoyed little success because they had engendered confrontation by focusing almost exclusively on attempts to protect specific areas, the task force recommended the adoption of a strategy consisting of two mutually supportive components: the establishment of an integrated resource management process and the designation of a comprehensive protected area network.

The detailed implementation plan to achieve these two objectives contained some innovative ideas, such as the negotiation of "conservation contracts" between government and industry. Unfortunately, the 1984 federal election, the decline in northern oil and gas activity following the drop in world oil prices, and the federal government's emphasis on deficit reduction all conspired against rapid action. As a result, the momentum behind the task force's recommendations was dissipated, and little concrete action resulted. Its report, however, still provides a sound basis for territorial and federal conservation initiatives.

THE STEPS AHEAD

The completion of a northern protected-areas network needs clarity of purpose, a consensus-building mechanism, and efficient means of implementation. Let us start with clarity of purpose.

The chief northern conservation priority today is not the preservation of endangered natural areas from industrial encroachment but rather the protection of the renewable resources, primarily wildlife, upon which the aboriginal economy depends. The aboriginal economy is under siege from the "anti-fur" movement, growing population pressures, and the rising costs of hunting, fishing, and trapping. If it does not contribute to resolving these problems, the creation of special enclaves with their own management regimes will be perceived by most northerners as an insensitive exercise whose chief purpose is the fulfillment of a national systems plan that doesn't relate to their interests.

Planning for protected areas must therefore proceed within the broader context of northern conservation strategies. Two deficiencies in the current network, in particular, will need to be remedied. First, methods to identify community-based conservation priorities, such as the protection of traditional harvesting areas and areas of aesthetic or spiritual significance, should be developed. Second, environmental values that are poorly represented in the conservation objectives of government agencies, such as concentration areas for marine mammals, birds, and fish, should be incorporated in a comprehensive protected-area network.

For its part, Environment Canada must answer the question: Should northern parks be established for different reasons and be managed differently than southern parks? If it answers yes, Environment Canada will gain local support for park establishment, but perhaps at the cost of sacrificing control over the criteria for park selection and management. If it says no, it will retain the high national standard it has established over the last century but will continue to face an uphill battle in winning the support it needs from the territorial governments and local communities to create additional national parks in the North. (It is worth noting that northern national parks are already managed differently from southern parks inasmuch as they allow the continuation of traditional harvesting activities and make explicit provisions for native economic benefits.)

As was argued above, one of the main obstacles to the development of a northern network of protected areas has been the absence of a consensus-building mechanism allowing all stakeholders to resolve their differences concerning the purpose of protected areas and the methods for their establishment. Such a mechanism could usefully be provided by the development of conservation strategies. Both territorial governments have made such strategies their priority and are already well advanced in their development. In Yukon, the highly successful "Yukon 2000" exercise, which defined the territory's economic, social, and environmental objectives for the future through extensive community consultations, provides

Above: The granitic peaks of the Ragged Range tower over Hole-in-the-Wall Lake,
N.W.T. CREDIT: PAT AND ROSEMARIE KEOUGH.
Below: River valleys, especially willow flats such as these along the Klondike River,
serve to concentrate northern wildlife. CREDIT: PETER VAN RHIJN.

one recent example of the consensus-building potential of a conservation strategy. The Department of Fisheries and Oceans and the Inuit Circumpolar Conference (an international organization of Inuit from Alaska, Canada, and Greenland) are complementing this work through the development of marine-oriented conservation strategies.

The third element needed to complete the protected-area network is the choice of a means of implementation. In the North today, two avenues show particular promise: the settlement of aboriginal land claims and land-use planning.

All of the territories, with the exception of the Mackenzie Delta/Beaufort Sea region, where the Inuvialuit claim was settled in 1984, are subject to aboriginal claims. Land-claims negotiations are obviously relevant to any strategy for the creation of protected areas. The fact that native organizations have been using land-claim negotiations to advance their conservation interests has meant that much of the North's future conservation regime will be set by the claim settlements. Agreements in principle with the Dene-Metis of the Mackenzie Valley and the Council for Yukon Indians, covering all of the Yukon and most of the NWT mainland, were reached in the summer of 1988. Negotiations with the Inuit of the central and eastern Arctic are continuing. Each of these agreements contains detailed provision for establishing protected areas, institutions, and processes to manage wildlife, land, and water and to assess environmental impacts.

The importance of the land-claim process to the establishment of protected areas was first demonstrated in 1984 when the Northern Yukon National Park and the Herschel Island Territorial Park were established as part of the Inuvialuit settlement. The pattern of protected-area designation through claim settlements is likely to be repeated. The Inuit have already negotiated the creation of at least three national parks in the central and eastern Arctic "within a reasonable period" after the settlement of its claim. The Dene-Metis are considering the establishment of the East Arm National Park in their claim settlement, as is the Council for Yukon Indians in the case of the extension of North Yukon National Park into the Old Crow Flats.

The establishment of protected areas through the land-claims process seems to be an efficient way of conserving land while meeting the needs of native people in the North. This strategy, however, has its limitations — limitations which have become increasingly apparent. Secretive in nature, land-claim negotiations exclude third parties such as industry and conservation organizations who have a direct stake in the outcome of much of what is being negotiated. Provisions are now being made to lift some of this secrecy. Second, some government departments have objected to Environment Canada's funding of new protected areas from moneys set aside for the implementation of the claims rather than its own budget.

It is worth noting in passing that land-claim settlements will make aboriginal organizations very large landowners. Together, the lands remaining in aboriginal hands after the settlement of northern claims could amount to over 16 per cent of both territories' surface. As many of these lands will be retained because of their biological productivity and their contribution to the native harvesting economy, native organizations may become the managers of a de facto protected-area network that will rival those anywhere else in Canada, and the world.

If final claim settlements are delayed — and the negotiating road has been rocky over the years — government should consider implementing those provisions of a final settlement already negotiated. "Pre-implementation" now runs against government policy because it is feared it would reduce the pressure for settlement. Negotiated provisions dealing with wildlife management and land management, however, are essential to northern conservation and in some cases have been in existence for many years. Pre-implementation would become particularly important in the event that resource development became a threat to important wildlife habitat.

The second avenue through which the establishment of protected areas will be advanced is land-use planning. The federal and NWT governments and the major aboriginal organizations of the NWT have agreed to a land-use planning process encompassing the conservation, development, management, and use of lands and resources, including inland and offshore. Its primary purpose is to advise on preferred land uses, minimize conflicts, and identify both opportunities and constraints for land uses. As a majority of the residents of the NWT are of aboriginal ancestry and have a special interest in conservation, this focus has become the foundation for land-use planning in the territories.

A land use plan has already been prepared for the Lancaster Sound region (which, in fact, includes most of the High Arctic), a second is being completed for the Mackenzie Delta, while a third is being started for the Mackenzie Valley. Each of these plans will include strategies for the conservation of renewable resources and the establishment of protected areas. Although formally the plans are advisory in nature, they are expected to guide government decision-making as they represent the result of a grass-roots consultation exercise.

A latecomer to the process, the Yukon government is now preparing a land use plan for the southwest corner of the territory (Kluane) and expects to undertake one for the North Yukon soon.

The completion of a protected-area network is not a burning issue in the North, at least not for northerners. They are preoccupied with far more fundamental problems, such as the transfer of federal programs to the territorial governments, the settlement of land claims, and economic development. Progress in establishing new protected areas has fallen far short of expectations, but in the absence of major threats to the northern environment stemming from large-scale development, this is understandable. Inasmuch as the ability of northerners to implement conservation strategies, including the establishment of protected areas, is inextricably intertwined with the devolution of greater decision-making power to the North, conservation remains at the core of the North's political agenda.

PART FOUR

STRATEGIES FOR THE FUTURE

J. STAN ROWE

The Importance of Conserving Systems

In a classic paper published in 1935, the British ecologist Arthur Tansley discussed ecology's realities:

Though the organisms may claim our primary interest, when we are trying to think fundamentally we cannot separate them from their spatial environment with which they form one physical system. It is the systems so formed which from the point of view of the ecologist are the basic units of nature on the face of the earth.

Tansley coined the term "ecosystem" for these fundamental earth-surface units whose reality he suggested but made no attempt to describe. The idea, though simple, is elusive. We have not yet learned to visualize the earth spaces in which we live as living spaces, as vital surrounding systems that sustain us. Yet when these living spaces are endangered, so are we.

A primary challenge for everyone is to think fundamentally, to get to the roots of our relationship with the planet, to dig below everyday language and concepts. Tansley's invitation to question the organic parts, to see beyond the bits and pieces that are taken to be wholes, to understand more comprehensive surrounding realities, has become an essential task today. The environmental ills smiting the world, as well as those that wait threateningly in the wings, are not acts of God sent like Job's boils to plague us. Rather, they are the result of ignorance, reflecting incomplete and fragmentary concepts about the world and the place of people in it. When conventional knowledge is wrong, wrong ideas and misdirected activities flow from it.

Tansley's summons to identify and sympathetically understand the "basic units of nature on the face of the earth"—the forests, the grasslands, the lakes and streams, the mountain wilderness—has yet to be heeded. So far we have failed to comprehend and appreciate the living world as a large global ecological system made up of smaller ecosystems.

What is important today is to change our understanding of the world, to focus on ecosystems rather than on the individual species and organisms that are parts of them. Such changed understanding of the realities around us will affect fundamentally how we live on our planet home.

ECOLOGICALLY MISCONCEIVED

In many ways, ecology has missed its calling. The word *ecology* is derived from the Greek word *oikos*, which means "home." Therefore, ecology literally means "the knowledge of home," or "home-wisdom." As such, it invites an understanding of the world's living space and all that is contained therein. Unfortunately, this insight has been blinkered by our focus on organisms. The scope of ecology has been limited to a preoccupation with protoplasmic bits and pieces set against some vague background.

From ecology's beginning, those professing to be ecologists have been concerned with one small lively component dissected out of ecosystems by biologists who, following their anatomical bent, have looked *into* the world rather than *at it*. Communities, populations, and species have drawn attention away from the larger realities of which they are a part and where much of their meaning resides. We haven't seen the hive for the bees, the forest ecosystem for the trees.

An unfortunate result is the widespread opinion that the entities of prime importance on Earth are people, other animals, and plants, rather than the globe's miraculous life-filled skin. Species attract far more attention than the earth-surface spaces that envelop them, even though over the long haul the species were born from the earth-circling fertile space that continues to provide for their support, sustenance, and renewal. Endangered species elicit torrents of public concern; endangered spaces are routinely desecrated and destroyed with scarcely a murmur of public disapproval. The priority is wrong, and from this profound error the whole world suffers.

Like a whooping-crane chick hatched by sandhill cranes, ecology has not yet discovered its singularity nor declared its independence. It has not outgrown its lowly initial status as the "fourth field" of biology, the last to arrive after morphology, physiology, and taxonomy.

Consider a recent statement: "Population biology, the discipline that deals with groups of organisms and the relationship of organisms to their environments, includes the subdisciplines of ecology," an assertion unchallenged in the reputable journal that published it. According to this widely accepted dogma, ecology takes its marching orders from biology. As a result, ecology has been thought of as a discipline that plays around the edges of biology, rather than as a more comprehensive discipline that integrates biology with all the other earth sciences.

Ecology's task is not peripheral. It is central and holistic, grappling with the overarching reality that is the ecosphere. The aim is in the name: to develop an inclusive science of the earth-home and its ecosystem parts, a concept more important by far than that of the limited field of biology.

Biology needs this wider framework, for by itself it is incomplete. Organisms do not stand on their own; they evolve and exist in the context of ecological systems that confer those properties called life. The panda is a part of the mountain bamboo-forest ecosystem and can only be preserved as such. The polar bear is a vital part of the arctic marine ecosystem and will not survive without it. Ducks are creatures born of marshes. Biology without its ecological context is dead.

Science breaks down reality, reducing it to smaller and smaller fields of knowledge. Geology, for example, that begins as study of the planet, spawns petrology, lithology, volcanology — each a subdivision and element of the original subject. In the same way, biochemistry treats a lower level of biology's subject matter, chemistry carries the division even farther, while atomic physics deals with a simplified version of chemistry's universe. In this sense, physics is a degenerative form of chemistry, chemistry a degenerative form of biology.

By the same logic, the study of organisms and species in biology represents a lower-level focus on subdivisions of the world, on fragmentary parts of larger home-systems or ecosystems. But home is more than the creatures in it, important though they are. And the study of home involves more than the study of its inhabitants. Therefore biology, rightly understood, is a subdiscipline of ecology.

The time is right to rethink ecology. Ecology is, or should be, the study of ecological systems that are home to organisms at the surface of the earth. From this larger-than-life perspective, ecology's concerns are with volumes of earth-space, each consisting of an atmospheric layer lying on an earth/water layer with organisms sandwiched at the solar-energized interfaces. These three-dimensional air/organisms/earth-water systems are real ecosystems — the true subjects of ecology. Furthermore, earth-surface ecosystems are more beautiful, more complex, more important, more deserving of attention and ethical concern, than the organisms contained as parts in them.

ECOSPHERE AS VITAL UNIT

The life-filled skin of the planet — the ecosphere — is the largest and most complete ecosystem, comprising all lesser systems such as seas and continents. In 4.5 billion years of evolution, the ecosphere with its subsystems has brought forth humans along with a host of companion organisms whose interactions with the other parts — atmosphere, earth, and water — have made the world what it is: marvellous, creative, unique, and unfortunately polluted.

Though blind to our maternal parent, the perspective from the moon shows us that we are indeed earthlings: children of the ecosphere, inhabitants of a wondrous cloud-swathed blue bubble, sharing with several million other life forms the planet's sun-warmed, gas-liquid-solid interfaces. Even without such sight evidence, events of our own making have conspired to remind us that we are deep-air animals. Cues are acid rain, a warming climate, asthma and watering eyes, strange industrial smells, and Geiger counters clicking in basements.

Few dispute today's dangerous human-caused changes in the chemistry of the ecosphere matrix: the increases in atmospheric methane, oxides of nitrogen and sulfur, carbon dioxide as well as the unknown-to-nature chlorofluorocarbons produced by the genius of chemistry. Submerged in the air layer, moving around in the murk industriously stirred up at the bottom of it, watching the canaries die, humanity is nudged into awareness of its total dependence on the health of the ecosphere, not just for well-being but for survival.

In no realistic sense can organisms — people, animals, plants — be separated

Ocean mists nourish wildflowers on Canada's east coast.   CREDIT: O. MAASS.

from the enveloping matrix of the ecosphere, which is as animated, as spirited, as they are. To think of water, soil, air, and received solar radiation as inanimate is to perpetuate a dangerous falsehood. For without these constituents, no things would merit the labels animate, organic, biotic, and alive. Life is as much a property of the planet or ecosphere as it is a property of species or organisms.

"The world is your body," said Alan Watts, and he was right. Organisms, the quintessence of stardust, water, and air, cannot survive without continually internalizing and externalizing the energy and materials beneficently provided at the planet's surface. Therefore the three-dimensional earth-surface ecosystem must become the focus of humanity's affection and concern.

ECOSYSTEMS UNSENSED

Martians examining the planet Earth from outer space would immediately perceive an ecological system of interacting and renewing parts — atmosphere, lithosphere, hydrosphere, and biosphere. If privy to human conversations and actions, they would be baffled that the most intelligent member of the fauna, though inextricably enmeshed in the air-water-soil-organisms matrix, was so careless of its milieu, so oblivious to its dependent status. Why, they would ask, are these humans — obviously equipped to be the conscience of their planet — blind to their source?

For centuries people have been unaware of the ecological systems that surround them. Marshall McLuhan thought it natural that environment should be invisible to those enveloped in it. "We don't know who discovered water," he said by way of a parable, "but we're pretty sure it wasn't a fish." Nevertheless, total immersion can hardly be the sole reason for the widespread insensitivity to larger-than-human realities. That excuse vanished with the NASA photos, showing from outer space the unique and only world, the home of all homes. With those pictures, proof of humanity's ecological status became ours.

Consider, too, what language tells about deeply ingrained attitudes to the enveloping ecological system. No adequate word for it exists; only vague, nebulous terms such as *nature* and *environment*. The latter is its own put-down, because at face value *environment* means "that which surrounds other things of greater importance." In other words, something else is the real centre of interest. Environment excuses itself and defers to less substantial things that make demands on it, things that falsely declare themselves more important. Such things today include the social system and the economic system: people and jobs.

What the world needs now are words expressing the authentic, tangible reality of the surrounding ecosystems in which organisms play their appropriate role. But words have failed us, and the reasons run deep.

Before the modern era, belief was widespread in the existence of universal orders of organization, surpassing in importance organisms in their populations and communities.[1] To the Greeks, for example, all nature was an organized whole informed by reason. This idea was also implicit in the counterculture thinking of the nineteenth-century Romantics, both in Europe and North America, contributing to the basic philosophical framework from which concerns for conservation developed. Influential in subtle ways over the last four hundred years, it has none the less been viewed as out on the radical edge rather than within mainstream thought.

The change in thinking that disintegrated organic nature and brought God's Chosen Species sharply to the fore is a legacy of the Renaissance and the Age of Enlightenment. Back then a mechanical view of the world developed, along with the medieval technology of machinery, providing the practical materialistic axioms to which Western culture has enthusiastically subscribed and from which modern science was launched. The enchanted world receded; the arts and sciences of Man took centre-stage.

God was accommodated and dismissed as the Prime Mover, the clock-maker who wound up the mainspring of the universe, set it ticking, and then, satisfied with a job well done, withdrew. In the seventeenth century, Descartes gave explicit form to the universe-as-mechanism idea, providing the key to manipulation and control. Since then, the West has practised Cartesian science, studying to discover what makes the material world tick, searching within matter for accessible levers of power. The purpose of science, said Francis Bacon, is to control Nature and force her to do humanity's bidding.

A clock-maker fabricates a mechanism from extant gears and springs that apparently explain its workings. Even when the clock is put together, the understanding of "how it works" is a function of its parts and their movements. Reduction is the key to comprehension. Applied to the world of nature, everything is understood to be composed of discrete modular components, like assemble-at-home furniture. Such a mind-set creates a world of separate things, parts and wholes, subjects and objects, internals and externals, causes and effects. Further, it insinuates into our minds the mischievous idea that parts are somehow more real and more important than wholes.[2]

This world-view delivers great power. Cartesian science has proved successful in providing knowledge-for-control in such fields as physics, molecular biology, and medicine. The procedure has the appearance of being totally effective because it follows the path of least resistance, pursuing problems that yield to it while bypassing those with which it cannot cope. Disciplines where it fails — psychology, anthropology, sociology, evolution, neurobiology, embryology, and ecology — are written off as non-science, as stamp-collecting. "Successful scientists," said Sir Peter Medawar, "tackle only problems that successfully yield to their methodology."

Just because reductionism has delivered power in certain fields, such as physics and medicine, does not mean, however, that it opens the window on reality, that Truth resides in atomic and subatomic particles. The frequently asked question "Can the whole be greater than the sum of its parts?" gives the game away, for implicit is a prior commitment to the parts. In effect the question says we *know* that the parts exist, now what about their sum? Thus, the rightness of reduction is *assumed* by questioning whether anything other than the parts can really exist.

Carried over into society, mechanistic reductionism tracks the cause of tuberculosis to a bacillus rather than to slum housing, the cause of cancer to oncogenes rather than to industrial pollution, the cause of evolution to genic mutations rather than to co-development with larger surrounding systems. The possibility that reality might be distorted by giving priority to parts over wholes is not an article of science's faith.

Books and tracts abound explaining that the individual is more important than the social group, the person more important than the world that encapsulates him or her, the foetus more important than the woman that encapsulates it. Any organism, we are told, can be computed from the complete sequence of its DNA. The brain is a holograph, the body a machine. How else do we explain the success of bio-engineers in replacing the grit, glue, jelly, and soup of the human body with neater and more efficient metals, plastics, ceramics, and semi-conductors?

In short, the Cartesian heritage is a fragmented perspective, focused downward rather than upward. The search for meaning at lower and lower levels of organization blunts the higher-level search for more exclusive realities. One-way vision threatens the future of the human race by blinding it to the surpassing importance of supra-organismic realities — the earth's sustaining ecosystems, the planet's skin, the ecosphere.

ETHICS AND THE ECOSPHERE

Perhaps the greatest mischief of scientific materialism and explanation-by-reduction lies in what is done to ethical concern. By conceiving all things mechanistically and shifting meaning to their parts, modern science strips away all sense of intrinsic value; that is, the intuition that things can have importance for their own sake, independent of their parts. What real empathy can be felt for a machine-dead universe whose explanations reside in its atoms?

A meaningless universe leaves nothing in our conscience but people feeling their own diminishing sense of importance. The only possible religion is a slowly evaporating humanism that leaves people isolated from the world of nature, alone and clinging to each other in a prison of their own making, bravely repeating that only they are important, only they have souls, only they will reap rewards in the Great Hereafter. Nothing else in the universe has value.

From the foolish precept that only humans matter it follows that the world is for exploiting; parks are for people, animals are for shooting, forests are for logging, soils are for mining. The sole basis for ethical action is the greatest good for the greatest number of people. The values of all things lie only in their ability to serve us.

Contemporary morality — the sense of right and wrong — is completely in-turned, completely focused on humankind. That focus makes it difficult, if not impossible, to be sensitively concerned about the world in the face of escalating human demands. Sustainable development, we are told, must include forceful economic growth, for how else can the needs of all the world's people be met?

Lacking an ethic that attaches importance to *all* surrounding creation, people continue to do the wrong things for the apparent "good of humanity." The irony is that five billion people — soon ten billion — all believing in people first, increasing their wants without limit, are a sure recipe for species suicide.

If what is wrong is to see the world in pieces, with people alone important, then what is right is to reperceive the world as one, a whole, organically complex, beautiful beyond compare, and to reorient to it in a way that confers first importance on it. That way, the intrinsic values of the home-sphere and its living realm will be recognized, as will the rights of things other than human to exist in and for themselves. Such a reorientation will constitute a cultural revolution, a radical change in the motivating values of Western society.

Deterioration of the ecosphere, of its ecosystems, its air-water-land-organism parts, proclaims the failure of the people-centred religions and philosophies. Global pollution shows the failure of ideologies that place "mere" before Nature and treat her as nothing more than raw material for exploitation. Wasting soils, forests, and fisheries proclaim the failure of a species-serving science bent on control, power, and exploitation rather than on compliance, compassion, and symbiosis. All environmental problems are symptomatic of failures in thought: misconceived reality, emphasizing parts at the expense of the greater whole, blindness to ecological integrity.

Fortunately, a cultural revolution that shifts the locus of values from the homocentric to the ecocentric need not be irrational. It can draw from the deeper intuitions of ecology, biology, and evolutionary history, in support of the new image: people at home on the planet. This new way of thinking will mean burying puffed-up phrases such as "made in God's image" and "a little lower than the angels," along with all the other unrealistic ideas that have motivated immoral actions towards this world we share together for awhile, actions that have brought it to its present sorry state.

Once values are straight, everything else falls into place. An ecocentric world-view elevates in importance the ecosystems that humans call land. Love of the land, love of place, love of our endangered living spaces, is the grass-roots cure for the sin of species narcissism.

The endangered spaces that must be loved and protected are the irreplaceable landscapes and waterscapes whose mosaics contribute to the health, beauty, permanency, and productivity of the globe. To perceive native landscapes and waterscapes, parks and wildernesses, as beyond price, as sacrosanct, is the saving goal that humanity must pursue.

To preserve native-landscape ecosystems is important, above all else, for its symbolism. Such preservation signals a sympathetic and compassionate attitude to the ecosphere. It affirms the following Truth:

The world was not created for people only, but for purposes that far transcend the human race with its limited foresight and imagination; and therefore it behooves all conscious inhabitants of this superb planet to nurture it as a garden, maintaining it in health, beauty, and diversity for whatever glorious future its denizens may together share.

JOHN A. LIVINGSTON

Nature for the Sake of Nature

Any attempt to make a case for a sake other than the human one is difficult. Such a notion is not easily translatable into terms that we can handle, and we are not good at thinking about things that cannot be addressed in familiar ways. But there is nothing to stop us from trying. The first part of this chapter will attempt to outline some of the important social and cultural obstacles to the protection of wild places for themselves alone. The second part will offer an alternative approach — certainly not a solution, not a guarantee, but at least an approach.

FIRST OBSTACLE — THE CONCEPT OF NATURE

We must acknowledge from the beginning that we cannot mount a case for "nature's sake" if we try to do it within the ground rules of everyday debate. We cannot prove it out by cold logic or numbers. We are doomed to defeat if we choose to accept the burden of arguing by the usual means and within the usual ideological arena. For example, any suggestion of *interests* residing in things that are non-human is generally seen as zany at best, subversive at worst. As the animal-welfare advocates well know, such a suggestion defies all our accumulated philosophical and legal traditions. Animal-"rights" proponents know what a whirlwind can be stirred up by the mention of any non-human claim upon human interest. Moral, ethical, and legal codes were invented to serve the needs of people, as was logical, rational argument.

But as every naturalist knows, nature is not rational or logical. Non-human beings have their own ways of seeing and knowing. We cannot have abstract social discourse with beings that are not human beings. The failing is not theirs, of course, but ours. For one thing, we cannot comprehend their reasoning. For another, we cannot comprehend their indifference to human purpose and destiny. Nor do they understand their appointed roles in achieving our purpose and destiny. It is as though they cannot fully understand why *they* are there! And even when they do appear to accept — or at least not to reject — their subordinate function, they do not always behave as predictably as we would like.

Every naturalist also knows that when we study nature, we like to *pretend* that we are observing adherence to universal scientific "laws." But we often forget that those laws sprang from our own foreheads in the first place. Animals and plants, to say nothing of chemical and meteorological processes, seem to be forever bending, stretching, and even breaking our laws. Nature never seems to fully accommodate itself to the scientific or philosophical "acetate overlays" by which we colour it for viewing. When it comes to the acceptance of human ways of seeing and knowing, nature is stubbornly elusive.

Nature is also elusive when it comes to definitions. We sometimes forget that "nature" itself is not an absolute, but a concept, contrived for human purposes. We needed a concept for things "other" than ourselves, so we created one. It turns out in practice that "nature" is whatever we choose, at any given moment, to say it is — no more, no less. Interpretations abound; scholars have listed literally scores of different uses of the term.

Now all this might seem harmless enough. After all, we have to label things in order to be able to speak about them, and if our usage is not always consistent, that is simply a fact of everyday life. Even if there are multiple meanings and understandings of "nature," all of them have at least some utility at some time.

But there are more serious implications in this. For us to suggest and believe in an *external* "reality" called nature is to unwittingly forge a formidable barrier between the human species and all other species. The radical separation we express as "human/non-human" or as "human/nature" is a kind of social, cultural, ideological (and indeed ecological) apartheid.

If this contrived separateness were actual, of course, then it would necessarily follow that there are as many natures as there are species on Earth — millions upon millions of natures. There would be non-moose nature, non-mudpuppy nature, non-sitka-spruce nature, and so forth. Nature would be everything, and nothing. This, you might properly say, is absurd. Perhaps so, but *if* so, then equally indefensible and bizarre would be our own belief in human/non-human nature. Logically there is no difference. We have simply taken ourselves as the defining point, rather than the moose, mudpuppy, or sitka spruce.

In everyday conversation, however, there most certainly is an assembly of ideas we express as "nature." What it is, is forever unclear. You could say that, like an ecosystem, nature is a theory. Or, like an environment, nature is an inference. Or, like Paradise, an ideal. Or perhaps a mirror reflection. Maybe a hologram. Or, an intellectual wastebasket.

In this chapter, the term "nature" is used mostly to refer to that which is *wild*, as opposed to tamed or domesticated, as in humans and their works.

However we define it, it seems clear that the "reality" we call nature is the manufactured product of our science and metaphysics, our folklore and assumptions, and other varieties of received wisdom. And it should not come as news to anyone that we play fast and loose with our "realities."

WHEN IS A SPECIES NOT A SPECIES?

Once upon a time there was a plain-looking, greyish little bird called the Ipswich sparrow. It was named for Ipswich, Massachusetts, but it nested on Sable Island, off the coast of Nova Scotia. It was always scarce; there never were many individuals, and they bred so locally that the Ipswich sparrow was high on every birdwatcher's "want" list. We had to take special pains to see one, and once we had done so, we richly treasured the experience. This state of affairs persisted for many years.

Then suddenly and without warning, the Ipswich sparrow was gone. It vanished, however, not because some storm tide or even some bulldozer levelled its nesting habitat, but because a committee of human scientists decreed that it did not exist — worse, that it had *never* existed!

Now this did not exactly jibe with the memories or the records of the many birders who had seen and enjoyed and duly noted that interesting species. After all, its name was right there on our life lists.

As it turned out, the fact that the name of the Ipswich sparrow was on all our scorecards did not make the species real. The reality, it was determined, is that the bird is actually one of several *sub*species or races of the abundant and continually widespread savannah sparrow. This was bad news for those of us who cherish numbers of species recorded, but it was good news for those who had become weary of the apparently unending creationist/evolutionist debate. It was now clear that neither God nor Darwinian selection produces and extinguishes species. Committees do.

Above: The ferruginous hawk is now a threatened prairie species as a result of human activities.   CREDIT: TIM FITZHARRIS.

Opposite: Dall's sheep eat their way along a mountain ridge.   CREDIT: KARL SOMMERER.

Pages 242 and 243: These hoodoos in Alberta's Dinosaur Provincial Park were formed 65 million years ago.   CREDIT: DUANE SEPT.

The further good news is that there are at least some of those plain little birds still around (now classified as a rare subspecies). What we choose to call them is up to us. Presumably that doesn't matter to the sparrows. But if we wish to be technical about it, the Ipswich sparrow as a species was not real, and therefore its scientific rank had to be downgraded. Indeed the ranking and grading of all of nature depend ultimately on what human beings decide is real.

PLAYING GOD

Human decisions regarding reality often seem strangely arbitrary. Take, for example, the exploring toddler who encounters a small snake, picks it up, and plays with it. The child, rapt in a joyful personal universe, is entranced. At the same time there may be a glorious sunset building in the background, to which the little innocent is sublimely oblivious. Not yet having been inculcated with the *truth* — that snakes are hideous, repellant, and low-ranking, and that sunsets are majestic, inspirational, and high-ranking — the toddler is acting on its own uneducated impulse. But that will change. Soon enough the lesson will be learned: that snakes are *really* not fit company for human beings, and that sunsets are *really* exalted. Our species conditions its young to perceive and accept certain agreed-upon realities: to see, understand, and participate in the world in narrow, predetermined ways.

None of our received truths is more pervasive and fundamental than the concept of human/non-human separateness — the ideology of apartness that, in all its implications, Peter Singer called "speciesism." Speciesism, like all forms of apartheid, rests on radical assumptions of superiority and inferiority. Qualities of superiority and inferiority dictate appropriate ranks, privileges, and interests. Our doctrine of apartness from nature allows us to assume an unchallengeable right of access to non-human beings for whatever purposes we wish. The use of non-human animals in sport, recreation, and entertainment, in experimental laboratories and in the fashion industry, are familiar instances. These are more visible than many of our other activities because their dramatic ugliness attracts public attention and controversy. Beyond that, they illustrate the problem of human cultural perception of beings who are not human as occupying lesser roles and having lesser status than ourselves in the Earth community. From this, it is a short step to regarding *all* of (non-human) nature to be at human service.

When all is said and done, whoever happens to hold physical power also holds the right to play God, to dictate rights and obligations, to define what has value, and even what is real.

WHERE ON EARTH DO WE GET THESE IDEAS?

The ideology of human "special status" in the world is ancient. We are only beginning to identify the cultural circuitry that created it. Although it dates at least as far back as the agricultural revolution, it reaches its pinnacle in contemporary industrial society — the society of science and high technology.

The advancement of the industrial-growth society and the advancement of what Thomas Kuhn calls "normal" science rest on a single vision of the world. That vision is necessarily *objective* (I/it, us/those, human/nature), and it is necessarily *instrumental* (what is it good for?). Our attitude towards the world is built on the description of that neutral non-human material out there ("resources"), and the identification of means to use that material for our advantage.

The goal of "normal" science is the understanding of the world in the interest of human enterprise. The success of human enterprise depends, at bottom, on the prediction and control of nature. That is what such contemporary ideas as "environmental impact assessment" (an impossibility) and "sustainable development"(an oxymoron) are all about. These are among its most current expressions, but they are pure descendants of the resource ethos of the late nineteenth century when the notion of resource *management* was conceived. Management, after all, suggests *control*.

Modern resource management was the brainchild of the forest industry. Gifford Pinchot, the earliest professional forester in the New World, was its most illustrious proponent: "The first great fact about conservation is that it stands for development." Pinchot thus framed the utilitarian resource imperative for North America and the world. Eighty-odd years later, the idea is still alive and kicking. It is as contemporary as the *World Conservation Strategy* and *Our Common Future* (the "Brundtland Report"), both of which suggest that "resource development" is the imperative, while "conservation" and "management" are its means.

Here we must note the power of language. The word "resource" implies human benefit, for example. But it also implies dedication to the human purpose of something that is non-human. Further, it insists on the human right, and even the human duty, to exploit it. This is why the use of the term "resource conservation" is so sadly inappropriate when applied to wild species, communities, and spaces. The expression itself indicates that we regard as property and utilities those very beings and places we would protect. It projects a tame or domesticated status upon all of wild nature. It effectively dilutes any "higher" purposes and suggestions we might bring to the task, such as arguing that something has a right to be protected for its own sake.

The word "development" is even more interesting. In its proper sense it means the gradual unfolding or realization of an organism, towards a finer, richer, fuller, higher state of being. The metamorphosis of a butterfly is a good example. In contemporary culture, however, "development" is used to describe the work of the wrecker's ball, massive construction, land speculation, and subdivision in the city core. "Developers" preside over the obliteration of forests, the destruction of waterways, the breaking of sod cover — in general, the advancement of the human enterprise and the subjugation of those *external* phenomena we call (non-human) nature. "Development" therefore insists that the human state of being is an improvement over other states of being, and that the purpose and destiny of Earth and its non-human inhabitants is to be remade in the human image.

It is for all of these reasons, and more, that advocacy of preserving wild beings and wild places is so problematic in our society. It is why the case for nature protection is virtually incomprehensible in so many civilized quarters. First, we have the general fuzziness and downright contradictions surrounding our perceptions of what nature "really is." Then, we have the institutionalized ideology of human/non-human separation — the conceptual apartheid that allows us to see the human interest as the universal purpose. These are formidable obstacles to making an argument for "nature's sake."

TO THE POINT

Now, if there is anything new about all of the above, it is that those of us who would perpetuate wildlife and wild places may be spending a little more time nowadays examining where our society is "coming from." The "practical" value of this task may be that it will indicate alternative ways of seeing and knowing.

When the "environmental movement" was born in the early 1970s, it seemed that the case for wild things and spaces might begin to rise above a people-centred view. But, with one or two exceptions, today's most prominent environmental groups continue to advocate a position still firmly cemented in the human good. Most "environmentalists" continue to express their case in terms of threats to "our" water; "our" soils, forests, and crops; "our" fisheries; "our" wildlife; and so on. Even wilderness groups dwell on "our natural heritage." Most political observers would say that, like it or not, human self-interest is still the only game in town.

Over the long haul, however, arguments presented in this way can do little to change the ancient "reality" that sees phenomena that are not human as human property and utilities. Down the road, when some species, community, or wild area happens to find itself in the path of orderly human "development," the outcome is inevitable. The result may be seen as regrettable, but rational reflection dictates that the human purpose is the higher purpose, and the higher purpose *must* be served. In short, nothing has really changed.

This is why some people have been devoting considerable effort to sorting out whether the usual "set-piece" arguments for nature protection might not be recast in a more constructive way. Those attempts have turned out to be more difficult than might have been expected. Every time we would make a modest advance, we would find ourselves backsliding. Whenever we would try to express the beauties and values of wilderness, for example, we too would often fall back on those values as "experiential amenities" or some such. We seemed to be stuck in the same human "possessive" we were trying to escape.

YOU MESS WITH NATURE, YOU MESS WITH ME

It then occurred to us that if we cannot fight the human possessive problem, why not join it? Why not *extend* the human interest beyond the human individual to *include* the non-human? This was an extremely attractive idea. Nature as one's "extended self" might serve to bridge the gap between the self–and–other, between the human–and–non-human. If, for example, I am able to see and identify the coyote or the red-tailed hawk as an extension of myself, perhaps I will act somewhat differently in view of that perception.

A few years ago I expressed it this way: "when I say that the fate of the sea turtle or the tiger . . . is mine, I mean it. All that is in my universe is not merely mine; it is *me*. And I shall defend myself."

All this meant was that if we are able to incorporate our nature experiences (not mere observations, but gut *feelings*) sufficiently deeply into ourselves, then we might expect to perceive nature in quite different ways. This building of experience into oneself would result in our behaving not as detached spectators but as participants. As a full participant, one's self-defence becomes quite reasonable — even rational. Certainly it becomes quite "natural."

There is really nothing mysterious about self-defence. Neither is there anything mysterious about a broadening from literal, skin-encapsulated self to extended self. Surely when the she-bear moves to protect her cub, that cub is more than mere property or her ward. It is her*self* — and an especially vulnerable part of herself. When the singing male songbird proclaims his spring presence to the surrounding world, he is not asserting mean-spirited proprietorship over "turf." He is announcing, identifying, and celebrating his extended self. The bear *is* the cub; the songbird *is* his chosen area.

Ownership, proprietorship, and even benign stewardship appear to be human concepts, unknown to wild species. That is why, in nature, there is, on balance, peaceful co-existence. It is why, on the human "property" where this is written, there is an ermine under the shed, a family of foxes at the edge of the meadow, a great horned owl in the hemlocks, a deer yard in the cedars, and a nest of green-backed herons by the beaver pond. None of these beings knows anything about property "rights" or real estate. But they all appear to know everything there is to know about belonging.

Belonging is about community participation. And participation is always in the present. Whatever it is that prompts the wood thrush to sing, it is not the past, which is over, and it is not the future, which never comes. The thrush sings at this moment, here, in this place. His reality is vividly and irrepressibly here and now. The thrush celebrates because he is home. Not "at" home; he *is* home. Home, for him, is also beeches and sugar maples, yellow jackets, micro-organisms, ferns, chipmunks, salamanders, and even other wood thrushes. Home is not a cold assembly of individual entities ("components"): home is a much greater reality made of the "at-one-ship" of all who constitute that place at that time. Home is the feeling and the knowledge of belonging, participated in by the whole of the community. Home is the sense of *being a place*.

Obviously, to *be* a place is an experience that is deeply personal. But that does not mean that it is narrowly ego-centred. On the contrary, the sense of being a place depends on what Morris Berman calls "participating consciousness." By this he means a feeling of personal identification with whatever is being perceived. It is a state of awareness of one's being in something that is physically external to oneself, like the she-bear's perception of her cub, like the singing wood thrush's identifying with his immediate surround.

This is why the concept of "non-thrush nature" is so downright silly, and why the concept of "non-human nature" is so twisted, addled, and dangerous. It was the institutionalization of human apartness that got us into our present pickle. It was intellectual dominance that allowed us to see nature as our estate, and to treat it as we have. This is why many now agree that the survival of nature depends not on intensified human management, but on a dramatic and fundamental shift in the way human beings and human institutions are able to perceive and receive the world around them.

Above: Quebec still contains major representations of the Canadian Shield boreal forest habitat.
CREDIT: BRUCE LITTELJOHN.

Below: The long-tailed weasel, actually a wetlands species, is now regarded as threatened on the prairies.
CREDIT: MILDRED McPHEE.

Watch a great blue heron sometime. Try not to *interpret* what it does; just try to *see* what it does. Here, it would seem, is the very model of patience, deliberation, and unhurried total participation. Poised immobile at the edge of shallow water, staring fixedly, it remains still for so long that you might wonder whether it would be able to galvanize itself into action quickly enough were the occasion to suddenly arise. But glance away for a moment, then look back. Magically, it seems, the bird has changed its posture. Now, the legs are slightly flexed, the shoulders tilted subtly downward, the long neck newly angled towards the surface. But again without motion. Frozen. At once the neck flashes straight, the slender dagger bill darts downward, and the bird is standing upright, a small fish flashing in its grasp. A quick series of gulping swallows. A slow elegant step of one stick-like leg, then another. The long dusky wings carefully and deliberately unfold, and the great slender being is airborne, swinging away from you towards altitude.

Depending on your predilection, there are alternative ways of perceiving all this. Rather than experiencing it, you might prefer to "record" it thus:

An individual great blue heron (*Ardea herodias*) was observed to exhibit feeding behaviour. The bird demonstrated utilization of the resources of its habitat, in the process providing an example of energy transformation. One ecosystem component exploited another component lower in the trophic structure. An avian predator attacked, killed and consumed an individual of a lesser taxon. Two machine parts interacted. At the conclusion of the observed activity, the bird was seen to leave.

The above observation is made possible by what Berman calls "*non*-participating consciousness." Berman describes it as a mind-set in which "the knower, or subject 'in here' sees himself as radically disparate from the object he confronts, which he sees as being 'out there.' In this view . . . knowledge is acquired by recognizing a distance between ourselves and nature."

Put somewhat more crudely, this is what I customarily refer to as "tame" ecology. Others call it "shallow," sometimes "cost/benefit," "economistic," or "resourcist" ecology. Tame ecology, of which most wildlife management is made, consists of conscious and deliberate distancing of the observer from wild nature, and the attempt to systematically explain wild nature through mechanistic rules of reduction and quantification — nature as neutral "stuff," as some have described it. Tame ecology is, of course, an artifact of Western wisdom about how to know the world through not experiencing it.

However, blows are being struck for freedom these days, even in the refereed journals, thanks to the inspiration provided by such knuckle-ball artists as the late Ed Ricketts, Joel Hedgpeth, Paul Shepard, David Ehrenfeld, and Neil Evernden, who in their liberated thinking have already made certain that the "dominant paradigm" will never be quite the same again. Theirs is a growing company of revolutionaries for whom nature is not an object, but a subject. That subject can be known, but it can only be known by the conquest of distance and objectivity, and by the authentic individual human experience of being a place, by the at-one-ship that transcends all rights and duties, all rationality, and most certainly all conventional logic.

Evernden has gone so far as to suggest, quite unblushingly, that once we have gotten over the nature-as-object hurdle, and have experienced nature-as-self, it is time to consider nature-as-miracle. Seeing nature as miraculous "does not prompt questions of control or even questions of kinship. The stance toward the world as miraculous, as awesome, or even as beautiful, could only prompt one to ask 'what *is* it?' — a metaphysical question rather than an economic or political one."

This kind of thinking is reminiscent of that of Charles Darwin, who said that nature, however defined, consists of "endless forms most beautiful and most wonderful." Now, that is not the statement of a tame ecologist. It is the visceral experience of a wild ecologist — a naturalist.

What would happen if we perceived and respected endangered spaces as miracles? Perhaps this approach can help us to protect such spaces for their own sake. But the new approach requires jettisoning all that cultural baggage having to do with nature as "things" — objects, resources, materials, etc. Over the side with that ideological burden goes human/non-human apartheid. A tall order, to be sure. But many people have done it, so more can do it.

As it turns out, getting rid of the old view is the easy part. The next step is to fill the void with an alternative world-view, an alternative appreciation and apprehension of nature. What, one wonders, would we put in place of that which we have eliminated? We have to substitute *something*. The terrible temptation is always to chuck out one ideology and stick another in its place.

But suppose, just for the sake of argument, that ideology is itself a problem. Suppose that belief systems, manifestos, revealed truths, and approved wisdom turn out to be themselves the root of our difficulties. Suppose that our servitude to inherited visions of the world is itself the most serious obstacle to the achievement of participating consciousness.

Perhaps that leaves us in an even bigger pickle than before. Perhaps not. The mere fact that all of us do not subscribe to a shared formal world-view does not mean that we do not have some shared *sensibilities*. When as individuals we receive the experience of wild nature in our livers, hearts, and bone marrow as well as our minds, we share an elemental knowledge of whole being. That knowledge may not be transferable in formal language or other convenient symbols, but a common experience of the quality of wildness is what already binds and bonds us together as defenders of wild spaces. Endangered spaces are not merely ours, not merely *us*, but things beautiful, wonderful, and miraculous. The "sake" is not ours, and perhaps not even theirs, but that of whatever brought them forth in the first place, breathed life into them, and — if we allow it — will renew them without end.

Room at the Top?

When the first wave of human families crossed from Asia to enter North America, they came as summit predators, resourceful, skilled hunters of an intelligence unmatched on the new continent. They entered ecosystems more complicated than today's, with giants among both plant and flesh eaters — superbison, mammoths, sabretoothed cats, dire wolves.

The recent epoch in North America arrived with a more simplified mix of large prey and predators. Among the latter was certainly man. In ecosystems such as the tundra and the great plains, where the climax vegetation was edible and the herbivores flourished at times in very large numbers, it is doubtful that early man had a significant impact on their populations. Elsewhere this may not have been true. In any case, it is very probable that man the predator was tied to the availability of his prey. When herds collapsed as a result of weather or predation, man starved along with the wolves.

The aboriginal people, as they proliferated and diversified in the forests and plains of what is now Canada, did so alongside the grizzly, gray wolf, and mountain lion. The grizzly, especially, posed a physical threat to the hunter, challenged his prowess and earned respect as a competitor. The Inuit knew the great white bear as a threat and competitor as well, but perhaps also as a fellow creature that left meat behind for man, in addition to foxes and wolverines. Inevitably, all the large predatory mammals became intimately interwoven into the mythology and culture of the people who lived beside them.

It was the Inuit and Dene that introduced Europeans to this continent. They guided the early exploring parties and taught them the vital arts of survival as independent adventurers in a new land. No doubt the attitudes of the first Americans to the great predators must have been part of the transfers between us, and something of the mystique has survived even into urbanized twentieth-century Canada.

There is no evidence that the native people had any concept of numbers applied to their food animals. They took what they could without concern for replacement rate or overkill. Our forebears were no better, but were equipped with muskets and money, forces that in two centuries devastated the wildlife of much of the continent.

As early agriculturists, we used the deer and elk as an essential resource and hated the wolves, bears, and mountain lions that preyed on them, threatening us and our livestock. They were poisoned, shot, and trapped in the vicinity of advancing farmsteads and beyond.

Across the entire sweep of the great plains, the ecosystem was totally destroyed. The seemingly endless herds of buffalo were displaced or slaughtered, and with them went the wolf and the plains grizzly that once followed the herds and lived off them.

West of the great plains, wildlife was much less abundant. The habitats for grazers and browsers were dispersed in a blanket of spruce and pine forests dependent largely upon fire for renewal. Here also the vagaries of weather in mountainous areas kept populations small, dispersed, and subject to periodic decimation. A delicate balance existed between the bighorn, mule deer, elk, and caribou and those that preyed on them — the mountain lion, wolf, bear, and man — a balance in which famine played a frequent part. Here, too, musket, steel trap, and poison introduced by the newcomers upset the balance.

It is erroneous to conceive of western Canada a century or two ago as a land teeming with large animals. Two hundred years ago Alexander Mackenzie made his epic journey from the Peace River plains to the Pacific coast and back. In the entire journey his party encountered but two deer and not one animal of any other "game" species.

It is a matter of record also that very severe winters about a century ago extirpated the small buffalo herds that remained in the Rocky Mountain foothills and left the elk herds, from the Rockies to the Pacific Ocean, decimated to the point that no more than four or five small herds remained.

Where the large mammals were numerous, uncontrolled hunting for food and for commerce quickly reduced them to dispersed remnants. The low point was reached as the twentieth century arrived. In New York, in Ottawa, and in provincial capitals, the fate of the large wildlife of North America aroused defendants. The names of W.T. Hornaday, Theodore Roosevelt, and Canada's C. Gordon Hewitt are prominent among those who turned the tide of ideas and successfully promoted the concept of conservation. Even then, conservation was seen as, at best, delaying the eventual elimination of the large mammals, rather than as a process for ensuring their survival indefinitely in the wild places of Canada.

In his book *Conservation of the Wildlife of Canada*, Hewitt writes:

Under the peculiar conditions that exist on the North American continent, where the opening up of enormous areas of land by agricultural development, the penetration of virgin forests by railroads, lumberman and prospectors, and the reclamation of wilderness have led to the destruction of the haunts of our wildlife, with the consequent disappearance of the greater portion of it, other measures than the promulgation of game laws, which at best are difficult to enforce completely, are necessary to insure the preservation of what wildlife remains. Of such protective measures by far the most important is the establishment of wildlife reserves, refuges or sanctuaries in which native mammals and birds are protected. Such wildlife reserves should include a sufficient area to provide ample natural summer and winter ranges for the wildlife they are intended to protect.

These sentences, though exhausting to read, contain the first statement of the concept of land for wildlife. But his paragraph continues with an interesting bit of advice to those selecting land for wildlife refuges: "They should be, and as a rule are, unsuitable for agricultural development. Nor should they include mining or other commercial properties that are likely to interfere with their purpose."

Did this really reflect his vision of the priority position of wildlife — that it must be relegated to land for which we can find no other use — or was he merely expressing the commercial pragmatism of the day? Whichever, the idea has been slow to die. Only in the past ten years have wildlife conservators been able to assert some higher priority and back it with the money to buy land upon which wildlife is the first consideration.

Across the great plains, as on the fertile lands of Southern Ontario, Quebec, the Atlantic seaboard, and in some of the valleys and estuaries of British Columbia, there was no longer a place for the large ungulates nor for the predators that depended on them. Elsewhere the burgeoning new sensitivity to the plight of wildlife eliminated market hunting and established and enforced protective legislation. Slowly the creatures began to refill the spaces left to them.

Hewitt had clearly identified the importance of habitat for wildlife, and during his time a surge of national-park designations was beginning to meet the need.

The prickly pear cactus means "prairie" to those who have seen it in the dry southern regions.
CREDIT: MILDRED McPHEE.

All five of the Canadian Rocky Mountain Parks were in place by 1920, and six of the provinces had established systems of parks or reserves within which wildlife was protected.

But while these steps towards wildlife conservation were in progress, we were also becoming a nation of experts in the alteration of landscapes. In so doing, we displaced wild species that lived there. If ever a thought was given to them, it was to assume that they had moved elsewhere into what was seen as endless Canadian wilderness. The fact that there are no wildlife refugees escaped observation. Where wildlife habitats are destroyed, the individuals that occupied them are no more. There *is* no elsewhere!

In relentless pursuit of timber, minerals, and water sources for hydro-electric–power development, we have laced the hinterland with roads, clearcut thousands of hectares of forest land, overused the grasslands, and usurped wildlife land, frequently for uneconomic agriculture. At the same time, we have denied conservation agencies the funds and people to meet the problems laid on them by these actions.

Wildlife numbers, which had been high, at least in the west of Canada during the 1940s and 1950s, began to decline in the 1960s. This did not happen everywhere. In the Yukon and Northwest Territories, the muskox and barren-ground caribou have continued to prosper.

In the area I know best (B.C.), it is revealing to compare estimates of the status of some of the large mammals in 1965 and 1988. Black-tailed deer, mule deer, and caribou are only about one-third as numerous today, white-tailed deer three-fifths, mountain goat, moose, and Rocky Mountain bighorn sheep about one-half, while numbers of elk, California bighorn, and Stone's sheep are unchanged. Any alteration in status of the large predators is unknown, as there were no estimates of the numbers of grizzly bears, wolves, wolverines, or mountain lions in British Columbia in the 1960s. Approximate numbers today are: 3000 mountain lions, 5000 wolverine, 6000 wolves, 6000 to 7000 grizzlies, and 120,000 black bears.

An important element in the declines has been alteration of habitat. Temporary and local instances of overkill have generally been reversed, and positive steps have seen some previously extirpated populations re-established by transplant.

The 1940s saw the introduction of the knowledge and approach of biological science to the conservation of wildlife across Canada. Research techniques have resulted in an enormous increase in the understanding of the biology of species, as well as insight into the working of population biology. We are now able to monitor the impact of management practices and habitat change on all species, but inadequate funding limited progress.

The biologists introduced to public thinking the design and process of conservation, and the concept of the ecosystem. The dedicated naturalists who were the source and support of the conservation movement could recognize hundreds and even thousands of species. To them a marsh or a forest was inhabited by "friends" that could be identified, watched, and enjoyed. The ecologist, while frequently no less a naturalist, sees the world as associations of organisms functioning as systems in intimate relationship with the physical environment. Thus the soil, water, plants, and animals compose an interactive solar-energy–processing system. A bit unromantic, perhaps, but a reasonably accurate picture of the living world.

In each ecosystem, organisms participate in food chains. Presiding over each is a top or summit predator. Therefore, in each of the ecosystems in Canada, one or more carnivorous species occupies this summit role and focuses the energy of the system into their lifestyles. The killer whale in the near-shore marine ecosystem or the polar bear in the Arctic ice ecosystem are examples.

Some of these paramount predators owe their success to their versatility. The grizzly bear and gray wolf together occupied the summit position in the western mountains, as they did also in the great plains ecosystem and the subtundra-taiga ecosystem — testimony to their extraordinary adaptability.

However, the apex position has its problems. Each of the predatory species is tied to the well-being of its prey. Anything that brings catastrophe to its normal prey is sooner or later damaging to the predator. The impact may be as final as death by starvation. But more frequently the individual predator responds by slower growth, later sexual maturity, reduced litter size, longer intervals between breeding, the loss of a higher than usual proportion of its young, or higher mortality in all ages. The predator's reproductive process goes into slow gear until the prey sources recover.

It has been suggested that the summit predators might provide a sensitive indicator of the well-being of the ecosystem over which they preside. The information they can yield will depend on the level to which their biology is monitored. Research that provides a classified inventory, including sex and age ratios and the rate of loss of known individuals, will provide a useful indication as to whether or not food is adequate in amount and by season and how the system is meeting the needs of the predator. If data are obtained on growth rates, age at first reproduction, litter size, death of the newborn young, and interval between litters, still more can be inferred.

It must be remembered, however, that most large predators, while they may have their preferred prey, are concerned only with a supply of meat either killable or carrion. Thus a thriving wolf population in Jasper National Park may tell you nothing about the status of the mountain caribou or bighorn there, because the moose and elk may provide for the wolf's needs even though the caribou and bighorn are gone.

For those of us who believe passionately in the importance of maintaining at least representatives of each of the remaining ecosystems intact, it is disquieting to ask what will be the consequence to the ecosystem if one or more species of the summit predators is lost. To be specific, what would be the changes in the Yellowstone ecosystem if the grizzly bear is no longer part of it? This question, perhaps more than any other, points to the deficiency of our research on all of

Above: Woodland caribou are classified as "rare" in Canada, which means they are also scarce as food for natural predators.   CREDIT: DENNIS W. SCHMIDT.

Left: The polar bear is a conservation success story, but it is still vulnerable to overhunting and arctic oil spills. CREDIT: FRED BRUEMMER.

the summit predators. There has been so little research done on multiple-predator systems, or on the role, in detail, of each of the major predators in the system, that precise prescriptions of the consequences cannot be provided. Certainly the consequences will differ for each species and system.

It can be predicted, for instance, that one consequence of the extirpation of the polar bear from some parts of its range would be a decline in arctic foxes, which scavenge the remains of seals killed by the bears. But it may be that the impact on the ecosystem of the removal of its summit predators is more subtle.

Is the overpopulation of elk in parts of the Yellowstone ecosystem a consequence of the vanished wolf? Was the Kaibab explosion of mule deer really a consequence of predator control? We do not know. Would there be detectable changes if the wolverine vanished from the Rocky Mountain Parks? Probably not. But to many of us Canada would be greatly diminished by the loss. Increasing numbers of people are determined that these powerful carnivores shall survive. But these creatures will only do so if we resolve that they shall, and are prepared to alter our behaviour in ways that will leave them the habitat and resources they must have.

Sentiment in Canada is against the extermination of any species of our native fauna and flora. In general, we like to believe that we are clever enough to extract a high standard of living for ourselves without inflicting the final violence on any of the creatures that preceded us on the continent.

We have studied the birds and mammals until we know their distribution and identity in detail. We have some appreciation of the numbers of a few of them and of the lives of even fewer. The creatures that have been most grievously damaged by our modification of the landscape and our propensity for slaughtering its inhabitants have engaged our concern. Their plight is acknowledged publicly and they are on the docket of both federal and provincial governments for special attention with public funding.

Political concern for wildlife and wildlands fluctuates with the preoccupations of our political parties, but none can long ignore the public concern for a healthy environment in which all life flourishes. Many of the wildlife objectives on this broader environmental agenda can best be achieved if we proceed, with urgency, to identify the habitat needs in terms of space and resources of the most demanding of the wild species, the summit predators.

SINGLE SPECIES OR SYSTEM CONSERVATION?

Our response to the decline in numbers of many species of plants and animals is generally single-species oriented. When a high profile bird or mammal approaches endangerment, a response is triggered — task forces are established, meetings are held, and talented people are given the resources to nurture the troubled species back to health.

At the same time those that must guard our *ecosystems* and their wealth of species are too often understaffed and underfunded. There is a growing realization that while single-species salvage operations are urgent, a blanket of protection can be given to a host of creatures through the conservation of large samples of ecosystems. Canada lacks the many large wildlife refuges that have proven so successful in the United States. In Canada, national parks are the only protected areas large enough to answer the need. They are of the utmost importance and yet insufficient of themselves, and saddled with problems that diminish their effectiveness in ecosystem conservation.

The experience in Europe and in the United States is clear. The large carnivores will only survive in the wild when they can be protected from overkill in a habitat that provides the resources and space they need. Only this strategy will maintain populations large enough to overcome the hazard of genetic accident and the weather-induced vagaries of food supply. In the coterminous United States, this means survival based on national parks and contiguous protected areas.

It is difficult to avoid the conclusion that in Canada south of the Yukon and Northwest Territories, large predators will survive almost exclusively in protected areas — national and provincial parks, wilderness areas, and wildlife refuges. The time is urgent to seek out the areas necessary and to arrange for the perpetuation of these endangered spaces. To achieve this we must know for each species:

- How large a population we must have in order to be confident that it can survive indefinitely.

- The land area required to support such a minimum viable population.

- The special facilities and prey resources required to support such populations.

- How *many* such areas we need to adequately protect the species or subspecies of concern.

A MATTER OF NUMBERS
It is an article of faith among biologists that the minimum population of a species that is likely to survive for a thousand years is one that will preserve its full genetic diversity. One criterion for such a population is that the rate of inbreeding be less than 1 per cent.

Biologists have struggled for years with this concept and have developed several ingenious formulas for calculating the so-called minimum viable population (MVP) for a number of species. Each of these rests on known mating characteristics plus a number of assumptions, of varying accuracy, for any population of creatures. For example, the MVP for an elk population has been calculated to be 214 animals, at 7 adult males per 100 females; for the northern goshawk, 46 adults, at 50:50 sex ratio.

Similar calculations have recently been applied to the grizzly population of Interior B.C. In this species a relatively small number of dominant males service most of the females. It is also characteristic of the species to have a period of

Above: Fall poplars glow in the foothills of the Rocky Mountains.   CREDIT: PETER VAN RHIJN.

Centre: The bobcat, nocturnal and seldom seen, probably earned its reputation as a fierce "wildcat" when trapped or cornered by dogs.
CREDIT: ESTHER SCHMIDT.

Below: Moose are hunted by both wolves and man; the result has been a competition seldom won by the wolf.   CREDIT: MILDRED McPHEE.

Left: The Canadian lynx is still abundant, though numbers fluctuate dramatically with prey populations. In Europe it has become an endangered species.   CREDIT: TOM W. HALL.

five to eight years from birth before the females begin to produce cubs. Under these circumstances, the required number of breeding males is estimated as eighty-eight, and breeding females as ninety. These conditions could be met in a population of 393 bears of all ages. This is a large population and its support necessitates provision of a very large area of suitable habitat.

There are many examples of species which have been reduced to small numbers and have subsequently recovered. The sea otter, elephant seal, and Gualalupe fur seal are examples that come easily to mind. Then, too, the sixty to eighty brown bears that have survived for many years in the Abbraza National Park, Italy, and the famous wolves of Lake Superior's Isle Royale are illustrations of populations that persist despite small numbers. True, they have not stood the test of 1000 years.

Other natural experiments that will provide clues to the matter of MVPs for grizzly bears and wolves include the brown bears and wolves that have persisted for as long as recorded history on several islands in southeastern Alaska. The wolves of Riding Mountain National Park, Manitoba, have persisted, surrounded by man-altered landscape, as have the wolves of Algonquin Park in Ontario.

FOCUS ON DIVERSITY

The grizzly, gray wolf, and mountain lion have occupied an extent of the continent that involved great diversity of climate and habitat. It is unlikely that the white wolves that hunt Peary's caribou and muskox on the Arctic Islands are genetically the same as the fuscous wolves that catch salmon and hunt sitka deer in the estuaries of the British Columbia coast.

The massive brown bears of Kodiak, Baranof, Chichagof, and Admiralty islands in Alaska occur in Canada along the Alsek River of northwest British Columbia. But, they are surely different and distinct in important ways from the silver-tips of the central interior of B.C., Alberta, and the Yukon, and uniquely different from the barren-ground grizzly, of the tundra east of the Mackenzie Valley.

What then should be our objective as trustees of this diverse genetic endowment? Are we to be satisfied with just one or two populations of each of these fascinating and varied creatures, surviving where by chance we have left them some room?

To me, it is extremely important, wherever the interplay of environmental extremes and biological response have led to a creature uniquely adapted to a distinctive ecosystem, that we provide for its survival. We are not so resource-poor and lacking in skills that we cannot provide for continuing populations of each of the distinctively adapted forms of the great carnivores of Canada.

All five of the summit predators — the polar bear, grizzly, wolf, wolverine, and mountain lion — are relatively scarce, by nature elusive, and by force of man largely confined to remote areas. This combination of characteristics has made them difficult and very expensive to study. Even so, a handful of energetic, ingenious, and dedicated researchers have, over the past twenty-five years, provided a broad basis of understanding of the biology of each of them.

The Polar Bear

This great bear, the largest living carnivore, is in Canada confined to the Arctic Islands, the coast of the Arctic Ocean, Hudson Bay, and northern Labrador. It is primarily a predator upon seals, especially the ringed seal, so much so that I venture there would be few polar bears in Arctic Canada if a calamity befell the ringed seal.

The species has been the subject of an intensive international study, beginning twenty years ago when its numbers appeared to be declining rapidly. An important finding of the study was that the circumpolar population is not nomadic but organized into subpopulations. These are centred on regions that provide special areas for winter denning by the females, and the ice conditions that provide access to seals. Each subpopulation uses a very large area; for example, Hudson Bay is occupied by several hundred polar bears. Another population of between 700 and 900 uses the vast expanse of southeastern Baffin Island.

The Canadian population appears to be maintaining relative stability with an annual carefully regulated kill by Inuit hunters of 386 bears. No present threat to the population is seen, and there seems little reason to contemplate establishing refuges in which the bears would be totally protected, with the possible exception of key denning areas.

Undisturbed maternity dens are essential for the birth and survival of polar-bear cubs. Denning areas require conditions of snow and exposure that are confined to somewhat limited areas. Next to denning sites, in order of importance to bear conservation, is access to huntable populations of ringed seals.

If the eventuality arose, denning areas on the seaward tips of Cumberland, Hall, and Meta Incognita peninsulas of southeastern Baffin Island, and adjacent seal habitat are among areas that could provide the basis for effective refuges. But the need for a wildlife refuge is an acknowledgement of failure to properly conserve the larger area.

The unthinkable eventuality of warfare in our Arctic regions, a major oil spill, and the unpredictable consequences of climatic warming that could alter the distribution of ice and the ringed seal could eliminate the polar bear from some of its present range.

The Grizzly and Brown Bears

The grizzly is an accomplished generalist. It once ranged from the Arctic coast to the mountains of northern Mexico. Early men fished for salmon alongside the giant brown bears on the rivers of the Pacific coast, and human hunters waited with grizzlies at the prairie fords to ambush the bison herds.

This bear is a competent predator upon mammals as large as moose, elk, and bison. It is a consummate fish catcher, an effective scavenger, and as need requires, can survive largely as a herbivore. But it must have space.

Above: Mother and cub eye a human observer in a west coast estuary, a sensitive grizzly habitat.
CREDIT: LARRY AUMILLER.

Below: Abundant bison once meant abundant wolves and grizzlies in prairie Canada.   CREDIT: GREG STOTT.

Right: Though not foreseen when they were originally established, Yoho and other Rocky Mountain parks now constitute a large carnivore conservation area in Canada.
CREDIT: J.A. KRAULIS.

How much space? The starting point in this calculation lies in the question, how many bears constitute a minimum viable population? In addition to the MVP calculation of 393 bears, we have clues from field situations.

The grizzlies of the greater Yellowstone ecosystem were estimated in 1974 to number about 230. By 1987 they had declined to 200, including only fifty breeding females. The region that supports the bears totals some 20,000 square kilometres, much of it on national forest lands outside the protection of Yellowstone Park. The slow decline of the population in recent years is the consequence of a legal harvest, illegal hunting, and removal of problem bears. The total of these losses to the population exceeds replacement rates. These are controllable losses and do not indicate an inadequate population or insufficient space and resources.

A relatively simple approach to the space question is to use carrying-capacity experience of different ecosystems. Several estimates are available from very large areas. They range from 42 square kilometres per bear in the northeastern Brooks Range of Alaska, through 26 square kilometres per grizzly in the central interior from south Yukon along the Rockies to northern Montana, and only 1 square kilometre on the rich habitat of Admiralty Island, Alaska.

Clearly with the question of how much space is required to assure long-term survival of 400 grizzlies, the essential information is what is the proposed area's capacity to provide for the bears.

The Gray Wolf

The wolf is the most controversial of all North American wildlife species. Since the early days of European settlement, those who raise livestock have demanded their elimination. Indeed, it has been pursued until, in the entire area of the forty-eight United States, only a few dozen individuals remain. In Canada, it is still abundant over large parts of the West and North.

Many sportsmen and wildlife managers join in insisting that wolf numbers on big-game ranges be regulated as part of wildlife management. Few, however, urge extirpation. For other naturalists, environmentalists, and some hunters and conservation professionals, however, the wolf is a symbol of vanishing wilderness. They espouse gentle management or outright protection.

Given the money and the will, it is possible to remove large parts of a wolf population, even to eliminate them from some areas. And although they match this vulnerability with the capacity to restore their numbers very rapidly, it is worth reviewing the basic requirements of the space needed for a viable population of this species. By theoretical calculation, a minimum of fifty freely inter-breeding adults is the core of a viable population.

Isle Royale, Michigan, an island of 544 square kilometres, has maintained a population of from seventeen to fifty wolves for some forty years and at no time did the breeding adults exceed ten. Riding Mountain National Park, Manitoba, has an area of about 3000 square kilometres and has for years supported a wolf population fluctuating between 50 and 125 individual animals based primarily on the rich food resource of elk, moose, and deer. In general, then, each wolf needs an area of about 25 to 50 square kilometres.

Since the essential resource for a wolf population is an abundance of large mammals for prey, it is useful to turn the question "How big an area?" into how much prey is required to support the MVP. This has been calculated as 3600 to 11,000 kilograms of potential prey per wolf per year, a figure that can vary depending on the reproductive success of the prey and the other carnivores present. This means an area that will support 30 moose or 150 deer for each wolf of the MVP population of 250. This number of wolves will consume a minimum of 153 tonnes of meat per year!

Any way you look at it, if we want self-regulating wild populations of wolves to be part of the wilderness heritage, large areas will have to be protected.

The Wolverine

There is little published research on this species and no estimates of the size of a viable population. The species has smaller litters than the wolf and appears to have lower rearing success. Pending the completion of calculations, one can only guess that a population of between fifty and one hundred may be viable.

I know of no studies of unharvested populations and natural densities are unknown. Studies of a harvested population in the Yukon yielded a density of one wolverine per 93 square kilometres. Other studies in northern B.C. yielded a density of one per 207 square kilometres. The point is that the wolverine is obviously another animal with a need for large areas over which to seek its food.

Despite heavy trapping pressure over many years, this animal has persisted. A thorough study of unhunted populations within a national park is urgently needed to provide data required to plan conservation strategies. Wolverines occur in parts of Banff, Jasper, and Yoho national parks and have persisted for at least fifty years, thus providing a direct clue as to a satisfactory area. Their major demand is for an abundance of carrion, which in turn means a rich prey base.

The Mountain Lion or Cougar

As with the wolverine, there are no published references providing data on cougar populations in protected areas. Nor have I found calculations of a potentially viable population. It follows that one can only guess at the number of animals that should be designed for in the planning of a refuge for this species.

In general, the mountain lion is a resourceful creature and has shown an ability to exist quite close to areas of human population despite persistent killing. With intelligent regulation of the kill by hunters, it should remain indefinitely in the mountains and forests of western Canada without provision for refuge protection. Density figures for habitats similar to those of western Alberta and central and eastern British Columbia are from 29 to 58 square kilometres per lion.

The mountain lion is probably more habitat-specific in its requirements than other "senior" predators. Although it can maintain small populations over terrain of little relief, it thrives best in broken country where ungulate prey is abundant. It is a stealth predator and must approach close to its prey before launching an attack. Unlike the other summit predators of Canada, it cannot excavate a den and is dependent upon the shelter of caverns and tangles of wind-thrown timber for denning.

SPACE FOR THE TOP

Our estimates of minimum viable populations of these creatures are not large in terms of all Canada — 300 to 400 grizzlies, 150 or so wolves, and as many mountain lions in each of three or four ecosystems. A team for World Wildlife Fund Canada is translating these numbers into actual geographic locations with growing excitement. Certainly the areas will be large, but they *are* identifiable and more important, they *are* still available. For now.

In these new areas it will not be enough that the bears, wolves, wolverines, and mountain lions can live without threat from man. Here, their well-being will be *first* in all decisions. Road construction, timber harvest, hydro-electric impoundments, forest-fire control, the hunting of large mammals by man — all will be examined and regulated for their impact on the priority species and their prey base.

These will be fascinating places, which will draw people from all parts of the world. There will be a need for ingenuity if people are to be planned into these places in ways that are not harmful to the visitors and to the creatures that are their primary focus. The concept is that two or more of the predator species will be present in each special carnivore area, along with a reasonably intact assortment of other flesh eaters and their prey. We are sadly ignorant of the workings of multi-predator systems and will have to move slowly as research provides more insight.

We urgently need to devise such new strategies to conserve the summit preddators, and one particular area offers attractive immediate opportunities. The Rocky Mountain National Parks, together with the adjacent provincial parks of British Columbia and the wilderness areas of western Alberta embrace some 50,000 square kilometres already dedicated to wildlands and wildlife protection. Recognition of this magnificent example of the Rocky Mountain forest ecosystem as a special carnivore wilderness would be a world first and would provide a focus and stimulus to a new kind of management. The new venture would capture imaginations world-wide and put Canada in the forefront. We would be embarking upon a new relationship between Canadians of the twenty-first century and the impressive species that have been intimately associated with the history and the vision of our land.

The Rocky Mountain carnivore wilderness would be the first step in the new adventure of identifying and establishing the additional areas required to give similar opportunity to the summit predators of other ecosystems. The research required to devise and manage these areas effectively for the carnivores, while keeping them open to people who find fascination and inspiration in them, will advance our understanding in many fields, from political science to population biology.

The task is urgent. The potential that still exists is being lost as endangered spaces are being swallowed by our thoughtless devotion to development at any cost.

MONTE HUMMEL

The Upshot

> In Canada . . . a representative series of wilderness areas can and should be kept. . . . It will be contended, of course, that no deliberate planning to this end is necessary; that adequate areas will survive anyhow. All recent history belies so comforting an assumption. . . . To what extent Canadians . . . will be able to see and grasp their opportunities is anybody's guess.
> Aldo Leopold, *A Sand County Almanac*, 1949

This quotation, from one of the most influential conservation works ever written, demonstrates something appreciated by very few people — that Aldo Leopold often turned his thoughts to Canada, urging us to recognize the wilderness opportunities still within our grasp. Although *A Sand County Almanac* continues to be a wellspring for conservation thought, as Leopold's own children have remarked, it is "widely read and quoted, but the basic tenets have been all but forgotten." Leopold himself wrote, "Despite nearly a century of propaganda, conservation still proceeds at a snail's pace; progress still consists largely of letterhead pieties and convention rhetoric. On the back forty we still slip two steps backward for each forward stride."

When you pare away all the "letterhead pieties and conservation rhetoric," the job ahead for Canadians can be quite succinctly stated:

• Presently the national park system is only 54 per cent completed, with twenty-one of thirty-nine natural regions represented, leaving us with eighteen regions still to be represented by a minimum of eighteen parks.

• We have forty-five national wildlife areas, and ninety-nine areas identified as candidates but still unprotected.

• Of the twenty-nine natural regions identified for national marine parks, only two are currently represented by such protected areas.

• Eight of the twelve provinces and territories have park systems plans; i.e., clearly stated "finishable wilderness agendas." New Brunswick, Prince Edward Island, Newfoundland, and Northwest Territories have yet to map their natural regions and set representation targets.

- Of the eight provincial and territorial jurisdictions that *do* have such plans, only four are more than halfway down the road to completion.

- If we accept the Brundtland Report recommendation of aiming for 12 per cent of the landscape in legally protected areas, Canada is well short, at 6.3 per cent (only 2.6 per cent if we exclude areas where logging, mining, or hunting are permitted). In terms of area, federal, provincial, and territorial jurisdictions have presently reserved approximately 63 million square kilometres, and protected about 23 million square kilometres, versus a minimum goal of 120 million square kilometres.

These numbers, of course, can be juggled and variously interpreted. But they have a way of focusing the mind and putting substance to Leopold's challenge as to whether Canadians "will be able to see and grasp their opportunities."

In the end, whether we move on this "unfinished agenda" will reflect what we as Canadians value. Do we, or do we not, want wilderness to make up at least 12 per cent of our future? In answering this question, we have three fundamental options:

1. Consciously decide that wilderness is not important, and plan our future accordingly.
The consequences of this option would be substantial loss of what we have already protected, coupled with protection of virtually no more — a landscape totally dominated by the activities of people and a statement to the rest of the world that Canadian society wishes to live "without wild things."

2. Muddle along in our present state, having made no conscious decision, and let whatever shakes out constitute all that we've got.
The consequence of this option would likely be retention of some of what has already been protected, coupled with some additional areas, but falling drastically short of reasonable goals and targets established by governments themselves. In the long term, there would be erosion of already protected areas, and no option to protect more because the opportunity had been forgone in the last decade of the twentieth century.

3. Consciously decide that wilderness is important and plan our future accordingly.
The consequences of this option would be to hang on to what has already been protected in addition to completing a network of wilderness areas representing the natural diversity of Canada. It would be a clear statement to ourselves, and to the rest of the world, that Canadians *do* want at least 12 per cent of their environment to remain in a truly natural state.

In considering these choices, two very important points should be kept in mind. First, we don't have forever to make such choices. There comes a point when it's too late; i.e., too much of the land and waterscape has been "developed" to allow for the option of protection. Already, it's too late in some areas. For example, we will never have wilderness parks (minimum 50,000 hectares) in at least two of the natural regions of Southern Ontario because there simply isn't that much contiguous land left in a natural state. The same is true for the tall-grass prairie in Manitoba, and old-growth forests in the Maritimes. On a national scale, the time horizon left for Canadians to choose whether or not we want to set aside an adequate network of wilderness areas is likely the next ten years. Beyond that, our choices will be severely limited or non-existent.

Second, we make these choices not just for ourselves, but for others. As Doug Pimlott put it, "Areas preserved from exploitation provide future generations the opportunity to make choices which should be *their* right to make, as well as *ours*." In effect, if we don't move on a wilderness agenda for Canada, we are not only robbing our children of their natural heritage, we deprive them of their very choice to protect it.

A MAP FOR GETTING THERE

If we *do* choose to plan a future for wilderness, how would we go about it?

Presumably, the first step would be to obtain a clear mandate in the form of public opinion. But it appears we have that already. For example, in a 1987 national Gallup poll, over 95 per cent of Canadians voiced their approval of government spending to preserve our wilderness areas. This high level of support extended across all regions of Canada, and among all socio-economic groups. Not surprisingly, 96 per cent of those who had visited a national or provincial park within the past two or three years favoured such spending, but even among those who had not made such a visit the approval level was high, at 91 per cent. These kind of data are further buttressed by powerful Canadian opinion in favour of protecting the environment in general. For example, 93 per cent of us say we shouldn't relax environmental laws to achieve economic growth, 88 per cent say protecting the environment is more important than keeping prices down, 87 per cent are upset about the lack of action taken to protect the environment, 84 per cent participate in wildlife-related activities, 82 per cent express concern about saving endangered species, 70 per cent say we should do more to protect the environment even if it means jobs must be lost in the process, and 70 per cent believe that major spending on the environment would in fact have a *positive* effect on the economy.

In light of such overwhelming support, it is downright deceitful for decision-makers to be cautious about providing conservation leadership, using the excuse that "public opinion hasn't caught up yet." And those of us already active in the environmental field might give second thought to extensive (and expensive) "public education programs." The fact is the Canadian public is miles ahead of decision-makers in the field of conservation. There's no need to wait; if anything, we might well fear public impatience.

So, having obtained clear public backing, the next step in tackling Canada's wilderness agenda will be to make sure that each jurisdiction in Canada (provincial, territorial, and federal) has a clear parks and wilderness system plan. This simply means publicly stating a cabinet-approved set of goals for the number and size of areas that must be legally established to adequately represent the natural regions and hence the biological diversity encompassed by each political jurisdiction. System plans are like maps. Without such a map, our chances of successfully negotiating new territory aren't great. With a map, we have a good idea of where we're going and when we've arrived. Such maps, or plans, present

Opposite: Prairie sloughs, targeted for protection under the $1.5 billion North American Waterfowl Management Plan, have already been 40 per cent drained.
CREDIT: TIM FITZHARRIS.

Above: The endangered piping plover, a delicate symbol of vanishing wetlands in Canada.
CREDIT: DUANE SEPT.

Centre: The white pelican became a symbol of hope in 1987 when it was the first species to be removed from the Canadian endangered species list.
CREDIT: WILF SCHURIG.

Below: The black-footed ferret, once an abundant Canadian prairie species, is now confined to a handful of captive animals in the U.S. Midwest.
CREDIT: EDGAR T. JONES.

a "finishable agenda" — something that is greeted with relief by both the proponents and opponents of wilderness.

Third, once we have public support and a clear definition of the job to be done as reflected in system plans, we must vigilantly monitor how well the provincial, territorial, and federal governments are doing in implementing them. For example, are they only 10 per cent down the road to completion, or 90 per cent? Is there a clear time limit for when each system must be completed, or are they more or less drifting along, happy with whatever they get, on the assumption that 100 per cent is strictly an ideal, not practically possible? Unfortunately, this unambitious tendency to regard goals as measuring sticks only, not as achievable ends, is tragically Canadian, and it calls into question the purpose of establishing such plans in the first place. In order to avoid this trap, wilderness advocates must ensure that when park-system plans are announced, they are coupled with clear deadlines and unequivocal commitment of financial resources for completion. This, in turn, requires a network of well-informed individuals and groups who are prepared to ride herd on progress, not just in the negative sense, but in a constructive, co-operative manner as well. After all, there is no inherent reason why protecting wilderness is purely a government responsibility. On the contrary, there are many indications that non-government and private interests are crucial to getting the job done.

Now let's pull things together. The underlying assumption of this book is that we have ten years or less left to protect at least 12 per cent of Canada in a wild state. According to the strategy outlined above, that means we have ten years to (a) establish system plans in each jurisdiction in Canada and (b) commit the lands and waters necessary to meet these plans. Therefore, a reasonable goal would be to have system plans in place in every jurisdiction by 1990, to have each 75 per cent completed by 1995, and 100 per cent completed by the year 2000. Specifically, that would mean a finished system of parks and wilderness areas, ecological reserves, and wildlife areas in each province and territory, plus completion of the national marine and terrestrial park systems and national wildlife areas by the turn of the century.

This is going to take considerably more political vision than currently experienced in this country. However, it is not a vision unsupported by public opinion; rather it is a vision demanded by Canadians. We must persuade our elected officials to be less concerned about the political consequences of protecting wilderness, and much more concerned about the political and ecological consequences of not doing so.

OBSTACLES WORTH OVERCOMING

What is outlined above is nothing less than a national challenge for Canada. As such, it must capture the national imagination, ironically in much the same way that "developing" the country has in the past; for example, building the national railway. In tackling this one, however, we should be mindful of the obstacles that will inevitably present themselves.

Principal among these obstacles, is what currently exists under the banner of the "wise-use movement," also variously referred to as "multiple-use" or "integrated resource management." This point of view is honestly held by its advocates. Indeed, its greatest danger is that on the surface it seems so fair. It argues quite simply that there is room for everyone, that there is no real need to polarize the debate about wilderness into strict protectionist/preservationists versus industrialist/despoilers, because we can have our cake and eat it too.

For example, the wise-use advocates argue there is no reason why we can't have logging or mining in a wilderness area. Logging, after all, is a "renewable resource" activity. If done properly, the trees will grow back, providing younger, more vigorous stands for both loggers and hikers to enjoy. Mining, though not based on a renewable resource, nevertheless can be a self-contained activity (assuming it isn't a large surface strip mine), especially with state-of-the-art recycling of waste and effluent controls.

In the wise-use view, it is a waste of resources *not* to conduct activities such as logging and mining wherever they are possible, wilderness or not. In fact, it is *irresponsible* not to do so. It is a betrayal of a deeply held ethic that mankind must husband or manage resources wisely. It is our sacred mission to responsibly cultivate, nourish, and use the good earth so beneficently given to us for this purpose. We must protect the earth *for*, not *from* people.

The problem with this view, of course, is that it recognizes virtually no place that should be left alone. It is an entirely admirable philosophy applied to that portion of our land and waters that will be developed, but it fails to appreciate the value of leaving at least 12 per cent in as "unmanaged" a state as possible. At its best, the wise-use philosophy provides us with responsible tools for managing natural resources based on sound conservation principles. At its worst, it serves as an argument for developing every square centimetre of the planet. In 1965, William O. Douglas, a U.S. Supreme Court Justice, addressed this point.

> Multiple use has meant many things to many people and it has been often stretched and distorted to fit special needs . . . Special interests have used it to exclude or include according to their selfish desires. It has not always been used to mean that land should be dedicated to those uses which measured by the public interest, represent highest or best use . . . Multiple use must not be allowed to become a free-wheeling concept that allows every section of the public domain to be put to all possible uses.

Often, it is wilderness advocates who are accused by the wise-use proponents of being the special interest group. We're told we want to "lock up" wild country against the public interest for the purpose of a single use enjoyed only by an elite few. But Justice Douglas powerfully addresses this accusation as well:

> Wilderness use is never a "single" use, though it does of course exclude some uses, e.g., logging, road construction, parking lots, motels and the like. But it embraces a wide variety of uses . . . and activities which many consider to be devotional. I speak of spiritual values akin to those experiences when the sunset

is riot with colour — the sense of wonder at snowcapped peaks, the restfulness which comes from being in an alcove in the woodland, the roar of wind in a high wild ridge and its soft music in a pine forest in the valley, the immense solitude of a trackless forest, the ripple of water in an alpine lake far removed from the noise of traffic, the feel of rapids against a canoe, the roar of cascades at the mouth of a canyon transformed into a cathedral by walls hundreds of feet high.

It is these uses, so eloquently sketched by Justice Douglas, that the wise-use advocates have difficulty with. And herein lies their great weakness, because Canadians value such uses, and have an abiding suspicion about whether or not industrial uses are so easily harmonized with them. For example, a 1987 Decima poll indicated 78 per cent of Canadians felt logging does either permanent or temporary harm to wilderness areas, 78 per cent felt this way about mining development, 78 per cent felt this way about oil and gas development, and 71 per cent felt this way about hydro-electric development. Therefore, as fair and tempting as the wise-use philosophy may sound at times, if we accept it, we must never lose sight of what we might lose.

It's going to be an interesting struggle. Just as the environmental movement has become more sophisticated in its goal-setting and operating style, so has the opposition. Therefore, the next ten years in Canada may not be characterized so much by a win/lose, extremist, fight-to-the-death over wilderness, but by a more professional competition as to who can sound the most reasonable. Nevertheless, what is at stake will be either saved or not. There will be times when a clear line must be drawn, a point beyond which we simply cannot go without sacrificing the natural values of what we cherish.

All of this leaves us in desperate need of an unashamed wilderness ethic in the best traditions of people like Leopold, Douglas, and Pimlott. In his essay "The Land Ethic," Leopold advises,

> Quit thinking about decent land use as solely an economic problem. Examine each question in terms of what is ethically and aesthetically right, as well as what is economically expedient. A thing is right when it tends to preserve the integrity, stability and beauty of the biotic community. It is wrong when it tends otherwise.

When Leopold was pressed on how we are to judge, measure, weigh, and trade off such abstractions as beauty, stability, and integrity, he said simply, "I shall not debate it. Either you know it in your bones, or you are very, very old."

The authors of this book, along with thousands of Canadians, feel wilderness "in their bones" and know exactly what Leopold is talking about. It's something personal and fundamental. But can we rest tonight, knowing that people without this feeling in their bones are deciding the future of wilderness in Canada? Leopold never rested — he went down fighting a fire. Pimlott never rested — he died fighting cancer, still urging that this book be written. None of us can rest. We must not become very, very old.

Canadian Wilderness Charter

1. Whereas humankind is but one of millions of species sharing planet Earth and whereas the future of the Earth is severely threatened by the activities of this single species,

2. Whereas our planet has already lost much of its former wilderness character, thereby endangering many species and ecosystems,

3. Whereas Canadians still have the opportunity to complete a network of protected areas representing the biological diversity of our country,

4. Whereas Canada's remaining wild places, be they land or water, merit protection for their inherent value,

5. Whereas the protection of wilderness also meets an intrinsic human need for spiritual rekindling and artistic inspiration,

6. Whereas Canada's once vast wilderness has deeply shaped the national identity and continues to profoundly influence how we view ourselves as Canadians,

7. Whereas Canada's aboriginal peoples hold deep and direct ties to wilderness areas throughout Canada and seek to maintain options for traditional wilderness use,

8. Whereas protected areas can serve a variety of purposes including:

a) preserving a genetic reservoir of wild plants and animals for future use and appreciation by citizens of Canada and the world,

b) producing economic benefits from environmentally sensitive tourism,

c) offering opportunities for research and environmental education,

9. Whereas the opportunity to complete a national network of protected areas must be grasped and acted upon during the next ten years, or be lost,

We the undersigned agree and urge:

1. That governments, industries, environmental groups and individual Canadians commit themselves to a national effort to establish at least one representative protected area in each of the natural regions of Canada by the year 2000,

2. That the total area thereby protected comprise at least 12 per cent of the lands and waters of Canada as recommended in the World Commission on Environment and Development's report *Our Common Future*,

3. That public and private agencies at international, national, provincial, territorial and local levels rigorously monitor progress toward meeting these goals in Canada and ensure that they are fully achieved, and

4. That federal, provincial and territorial government conservation agencies on behalf of all Canadians develop action plans by 1990 for achieving these goals by the year 2000.

How You Can Help

The authors of *Endangered Spaces* want it to be more than a book. Its real purpose is to kick off a ten-year campaign to complete a wilderness network in Canada. To accomplish this, we urgently need a network of people who share our concern.

Please join us. Having read our book, add your name to ours as a supporter of the Canadian Wilderness Charter. If you wish, I'll send you a parchment copy suitable for framing or display, to symbolize your support. Thousands of other Canadians are doing the same thing, indicating their concern and willingness to lend a hand. I'll also keep you posted on annual progress as we press for our goal by the turn of the century. Just fill in the card enclosed in your book, and drop it in the mail.

If you're not already aboard, please consider joining the local organization which is working to protect wilderness in your region of Canada. A list of such groups follows. They will welcome your help, and by working together we *will* make a difference.

Monte Hummel
President
WORLD WILDLIFE FUND CANADA
60 St. Clair Avenue East   Suite 201
Toronto, Ontario
M4T 1N5
Telephone: 416-923-8173

Conservation Organizations

NATIONAL ORGANIZATIONS
Assembly of First Nations
Suite 300
47 Clarence Street
Ottawa, Ontario
K1N 9K1
Phone: 613-236-0673

Canadian Council on Ecological Areas
  Secretariat
Place Vincent Massey
351 St. Joseph Boulevard
Hull, Quebec
K1A 0H3
Phone: 819-997-4991

Canadian Environmental Law Association
243 Queen Street West
Toronto, Ontario
M5V 1Z4
Phone: 416-977-2410

Canadian Nature Federation
453 Sussex Drive
Ottawa, Ontario
K1N 6Z4
Phone: 613-238-6154

Canadian Parks and Wilderness Society
Suite 1150
160 Bloor Street East,
Toronto, Ontario
M4W 1B9
Phone: 416-972-0868

Canadian Wildlife Federation
1673 Carling Avenue
Ottawa, Ontario
K2A 3Z1
Phone: 613-725-2191

Nature Conservancy of Canada
794A Broadview Avenue

Toronto, Ontario
M4K 2P7
Phone: 416-469-1701

Probe International
225 Brunswick Avenue
Toronto, Ontario
M5S 2M6
Phone: 416-978-7014

Wildlife Habitat Canada
Suite 301
1704 Carling Avenue
Ottawa, Ontario
K2A 1C7
Phone: 613-722-2090

World Wildlife Fund
Suite 201
60 St. Clair Avenue East
Toronto, Ontario
M4T 1N5
Phone: 416-923-8173

NEWFOUNDLAND
Newfoundland Wilderness Society
P.O. Box 5132
St. John's, Newfoundland
A1C 5V3

Tuckamore Wilderness Society
11 Carty Place
Corner Brook, Newfoundland
A2H 6B5

Wilderness and Ecological Areas Advisory
   Council Secretariat
P.O. Box 4750
St. John's, Newfoundland
A1C 5T7
Phone: 709-576-2420

PRINCE EDWARD ISLAND
Island Nature Trust
P.O. Box 265
Charlottetown, PEI
Phone: 902-892-7513

NOVA SCOTIA
Ecology Action Centre

Suite 520
1657 Barrington Street
Halifax, Nova Scotia
B3J 2A1
Phone: 902-422-4311

NEW BRUNSWICK
Conservation Council of New Brunswick
180 St. John Street
Fredericton, New Brunswick
E3B 4A9
Phone: 506-458-8747

QUEBEC
Fondation pour la sauvegarde des espèces
   menacées (FOSEM)
8191 Avenue du Zoo
Charlesbourg, Quebec
G1G 4G4
Phone: 418-622-0313

Union québécoise pour la conservation de
   la nature
160 76th Street East
Charlesbourg, Quebec
G1W 2G5
Phone: 418-628-9600

ONTARIO
Federation of Ontario Naturalists
355 Lesmill Road
Don Mills, Ontario
M3B 2W8
Phone: 416-444-8419

Sierra Club of Ontario
Suite 303
229 College Street
Toronto, Ontario
M5T 1R4
Phone: 416-596-7778

Temagami Wilderness Society
Suite 307
19 Mercer Street
Toronto, Ontario
M5V 1H2
Phone: 416-599-0152

Wildlands League
Suite 206

229 College Street
Toronto, Ontario
M5T 1R4
Phone: 416-595-0443

MANITOBA
Manitoba Naturalists Society
302 – 128 James Avenue
Winnipeg, Manitoba
R3B 0N8

SASKATCHEWAN
Saskatchewan Natural History Society
1860 Lorne Street
Regina, Saskatchewan
S4P 2L7
Phone: 306-780-9273

Saskatchewan Wildlife Federation
Box 788
Moose Jaw, Saskatchewan
S6H 4P5

ALBERTA
Alberta Wilderness Association
Box 6398, Station D
Calgary, Alberta
T2P 2E1
Phone: 403-283-2025

Bow Valley Naturalists
Box 1693
Banff, Alberta
T0L 0C0
Phone: 403-762-4160

Canadian Parks and Wilderness Society
  (Alberta office)
11759 Groat Road
Edmonton, Alberta
T5M 3K6
Phone: 403-458-8658

BRITISH COLUMBIA
Friends of Ecological Reserves
Box 1721, Station E
Victoria, B.C.
V8W 2Y1
Phone: 604-731-6716

Northwest Wildlife Preservation Society
Box 34129, Station D

Vancouver, B.C.
V6J 4N3
Phone: 604-736-8750

Outdoor Recreation Council of B.C.
334 – 1367 West Broadway
Vancouver, B.C.
V6H 4A9
Phone: 604-737-3000

Sierra Club of Western Canada
314 – 626 View Street
Victoria, B.C.
V8W 1J4
Phone: 604-386-5255

Valhalla Wilderness Society
Box 224
New Denver, B.C.
V0G 1S0
Phone: 604-358-2449

Western Canada Wilderness Committee
1520 West 6th Avenue
Vancouver, B.C.
V6J 1R2
Phone: 604-731-6716

NORTHERN CANADA
Canadian Arctic Resources Committee
111 Sparks Street
Ottawa, Ontario
K1P 5B5
Phone: 613-236-7379

Ecology North
Box 2888
Yellowknife, NWT
X1A 2R2

Inuit Circumpolar Conference
Suite 510
170 Laurier Street West
Ottawa, Ontario
K1P 5V5
Phone: 613-563-2642

Yukon Conservation Society
Box 4163
Whitehorse, Yukon
Y1A 3T3
Phone: 403-668-5678

Conservation Lands and Waters in Canada: Area and Number of Reserves[1]

TOTAL AREA IN SQ. KM.
NUMBER OF RESERVES

	NATIONAL PARKS	NATIONAL WILDLIFE AREAS, MIGRATORY BIRD SANCTUARIES	PROVINCIAL/TERRITORIAL PARKS	PROVINCIAL/TERRITORIAL WILDLIFE AREAS	PROVINCIAL/TERRITORIAL WILDERNESS AREAS	PROVINCIAL/TERRITORIAL ECOLOGICAL RESERVES	OTHER PROVINCIAL/ TERRITORIAL RESERVES	AREA OF PROVINCE/TERRITORY	% OF PROVINCE/TERRITORY RESERVED	TOTAL AREA OF RESERVES WITH NO LOGGING, MINING OR SPORT HUNTING.[2]	% OF PROVINCE/TERRITORY RESERVED WITH NO LOGGING, MINING OR SPORT HUNTING
BC	6302 / 6	54 / 15	52,337 / 387	177 / 6	1315 / 1	1558 / 120		948,596	6.5	22,685	2.4
ALTA	54,085 / 4.8	145 / 7	1365 / 106	680 / 8	5607 / 4	185 / 10	309 / 114	661,185	9.4	56,420	8.5[3]
SASK	4781 / 2	827 / 23	9081 / 31	18,848 / 1662	—	8 / 1	769 / 298	651,900	5.1	6289	1.0
MAN	2976 / 1	1 / 2	14,314 / 60	30,658 / 74	—	178 / 9	15,666 / 5	650,087	9.8	3189	.5
ONT	2171 / 5	443 / 23	56,273 / 217	9240 / 45	618 / 37	—	539 / 323	1,068,582	6.5	24,249	2.2
QUE	935 / 3	661 / 42	4000 / 16	67,000 / 16	—	484 / 21	537 / 1	1,540,680	4.8	5956	.4
NB	445 / 2	62 / 7	217 / 49	3219 / 19	—	—	1 / 3	73,436	5.4	663	.9
NS	1332 / 2	66 / 15	131 / 107	1396 / 25	—	1 / 2	3 / 4	55,49i	5.3	1387	2.5
PEI	26 / 1	1 / 1	42 / 67	29 / 5	—	—	—	5657	1.7	97	1.7
NFLD	2338 / 2	9 / 1	235 / 75	—	1070 / 1	23 / 6	—	404,517	.9	2597	.6
YT	32,183 / 2		114 / 1	5918 / 2	—	—	—	482,515	7.9	32,273	6.7
NWT	74,698 / 3.2	113,405 / 15	130 / 44	26,464 / 3	—	—	—	3,379,684	6.4	98,658	2.9
CANADA	182,272 / 34	115,674 / 151	138,239 / 1160	163,629 / 1865	8680 / 43	2437 / 169	17,824 / 748	9,922,330	6.3	254,463	2.6

1. This table is based on data compiled in *Heritage Conservation—The Natural Environment* (November 1987) by E. Neville Ward and Beth Kilham, as updated to December 1988 through correspondence with each jurisdiction.
2. Not including hunting by aboriginal people under treaty or land claim settlements.
3. Two-thirds of this area is accounted for by the Alberta portion of Wood Buffalo National Park.

Notes and Selected Bibliography

WILDERNESS AND THE CANADIAN PSYCHE

1. Northrop Frye, cited in John Wadland, "Wilderness and Culture," *Park News*, Summer 1982, p. 12.
2. Neil Evernden, *The Natural Alien, Humankind and Environment* (Toronto: University of Toronto Press, 1985), p. 32.
3. Evernden, *The Natural Alien*, p. 123.
4. George Woodcock, "Terror and Regeneration: The Wilderness in Art and Literature," *Park News*, Summer 1982, p. 3.
5. William Francis Butler, *The Great Lone Land*, cited in Bruce Litteljohn and Jon Pearce, eds., *Marked by the Wild* (Toronto: McClelland and Stewart, 1984), p. 19.
6. Pierre Elliot Trudeau, "Exhaustion and Fulfilment: The Ascetic in a Canoe," in Borden Spears, ed., *Wilderness Canada* (Toronto: Clarke, Irwin & Company Ltd., 1970), p. 5.
7. W.L. Morton, *The Canadian Identity* (Toronto: University of Toronto Press, 1972), p. 5.
8. Arthur R.M. Lower, *My First Seventy-five Years* (Toronto: Macmillan, 1967), p. 291.
9. Arthur R.M. Lower, *Canadians in the Making* (Toronto: Longmans, Green, 1958), p. 443.
10. Archibald Lampman, "Temagami," cited in *Marked by the Wild*, p. 72.
11. Alfred DesRochers, "I Am the Dwindled Son," cited in Littlejohn and Pearce, *Marked by the Wild*, p. 224.
12. A.J.M. Smith, "The Lonely Land," cited in Littlejohn and Pearce, *Marked by the Wild*, p. 61.
13. Wayland Drew, *The Gaian Expedient* (New York: Del Rey/Ballantine Books, 1985).
14. Drew, *The Gaian Expedient*.
15. Walter Bauer, "Canada," cited in Littlejohn and Pearce, *Marked by the Wild*, p. 221.

WILDERNESS PARKS: A CONCEPT WITH CONFLICTS

Darling, F., and Eichhorn, N. 1967. *Man and Nature in the National Parks*. Washington: The Conservation Institute.
Foster, J. 1978. *Working for Wildlife*. Toronto: University of Toronto Press.
Moodie, S. 1852. *Roughing It in the Bush*. 1962 ed. Toronto: McClelland and Stewart.
Nelson, J.G., ed. 1970. *Canadian Parks in Perspective*. Montreal: Harvest House.
Whiteford, H.N., and Craig, R.D. 1918. *Forests of British Columbia*. Ottawa: Commission of Conservation.

CANADA IN A GLOBAL CONTEXT

Burhenne, Wolfgang E., and Irwin, Will A. 1983. *World Charter for Nature*. Berlin: Erich Schmidt Verlag GmbH.
Chipeniuk, Raymond. *Changes in the Extent of Wilderness in Canada, ca. 1980 to 1988*. Unpublished manuscript.
Flamm, Barry R. 1982. *The Future Wilderness System*. Washington: Wilderness Society.
IUCN. 1985. *1985 United Nations List of National Parks and Protected Areas*. Gland, Switzerland and Cambridge, U.K.: IUCN.
Martin, Vance, ed. 1988. *For the Conservation of Earth*. Golden, Colorado: Fulcrum Inc.
McNeely, Jeffrey A., and Miller, Kenton R. 1984. *National Parks, Conservation, and Development — The Role of Protected Areas in Sustaining Society*. IUCN Commission on National Parks and Protected Areas, Proceedings of the World Congress on National Parks, Bali, Indonesia, 11–12 October 1982. Washington: Smithsonian Institution Press.
Minister of Environment's Task Force on Park Establishment. *Parks 2000 — Vision*

for the 21st Century. Toronto: Nature Conservancy of Canada.

Nash, Roderick. 1982. Wilderness and the American Mind. New Haven: Yale University Press.

Nelson et al., eds. International Experience with National Parks and Related Reserves, Series 12, Waterloo: Department of Geography, University of Waterloo.

PRIVATE STEWARDSHIP

Alberta Fish and Wildlife Division. 1987. The Landowner Habitat Project. Edmonton: Alberta Forestry, Lands and Wildlife.

Hilts, S., and Moull, T. 1989. Natural Heritage Stewardship Program 1988 Annual Report. Guelph: Dept. of Land Resource Science, Univ. of Guelph.

Hoose, P.M. 1981. Building an Ark. Covel, Ca.: Island Press.

Ministry of Natural Resources. 1982. Land Acquisition Alternatives — Executive Report. Toronto: M.N.R.

Reid, R. 1988. Bringing Trust to Ontario. Report to the Federation of Ontario Naturalists, Toronto.

Russell, R.D., and Howland, R.M. 1988. Prairie Pothole Project 1987 Annual Report. Regina: Saskatchewan Parks, Recreation and Culture.

Van Patter, M. 1986. Landowner Incentive Mechanisms to Promote Wetland Protection in Ontario. Toronto: Federation of Ontario Naturalists.

Wake, D. 1981. Nature Reserves, A History of Commitment. Seasons 21 (4) :46–49.

Wildlife Habitat Canada. 1988. Wildlife Conservation on Private Land. Ottawa: W.H.C.

EAU CANADA! A NEW MARINE-PARK SYSTEM

Borgese, Elizabeth Mann. 1987. The Future of Oceans: A Report of the Club of Rome. Montreal: Harvest House.

Graham, Robert, ed. 1988. Marine Lake and Coastal Heritage: Proceedings of a Conference. Waterloo, Ontario: Heritage Resources Centre, University of Waterloo.

Henwood, Bill, and Coates, Brent, eds. 1988. Proceedings of the Workshop on National Marine Park Planning. Ottawa: Canadian Parks Service. In Press.

Lien, Jon, and Graham, Robert. 1985. Marine Parks and Conservation: Challenge and Promise. 2 vols. Toronto: Canadian Parks and Wilderness Society.

NEWFOUNDLAND AND LABRADOR: A SPECIAL PLACE

Cormack, W.E., and Bruton, F.A., ed. 1928. A Journey Across the Island of Newfoundland in 1822. London: Longman's Green and Co.

Fowler, A., and Pittman, A. 1979. 31 Newfoundland Poets. St. John's: Breakwater Books.

Government of Newfoundland. 1980. Managing All Our Resources — A Development Plan for Newfoundland and Labrador. St. John's: Newfoundland Information Services.

Horwood, H. 1987. Dancing on the Shore. Toronto: McClelland and Stewart.

Macpherson, A.G., and Macpherson, J.B. 1981. The Natural Environment of Newfoundland, Past and Present. St. John's: Memorial University Printing Services.

Montevecchi, W.A., and Tuck, L.M. 1987. Newfoundland Birds — Exploitation, Study, Conservation. Cambridge: Nuttall Ornithological Club, Harvard University.

Northcott, T.H. 1974. The Land Mammals of Insular Newfoundland. St. John's: Wildlife Division, Government of Newfoundland.

Rowe, F.W. 1977. Extinction — The Beothuks of Newfoundland. Toronto: McGraw-Hill Ryerson.

South, G.R. 1983. Biogeography and Ecology of the Island of Newfoundland. The Hague-Boston/London: Dr. W. Junk Publishers.

THE FOREST AND THE SEA: MARITIME PRIORITIES

Beardmore, R.M. 1985. *Atlantic Canada's Natural Heritage Areas*. Ottawa: Canadian Government Publishing Centre, Supply and Services.

Denys, Nicolas. 1908. *The Description and Natural History of the Coasts of North America (Acadia)*. Translated and edited, with a memoir of the author, collateral documents, and a reprint of the (1672) original by William F. Ganong. The Champlain Society.

Erskine, D.S. 1985. *The Plants of Prince Edward Island*. Reprinted with new records, nomenclatural changes, and corrections and deletions by Catling, P.M., Erskine, D.S. and MacLaren, R.B. Ottawa: Agriculture Canada, Research Branch Publication.

Hinds, H.R. 1986. *Flora of New Brunswick*. Fredericton: Primrose Press.

Isnor, W. 1981. *Provisional Notes on the Rare and Endangered Plants and Animals of Nova Scotia*. Halifax: Nova Scotia Museum Curatorial Report No. 46.

Keddy, P.A. 1985. Lakeshores in the Tusket River Valley, Nova Scotia: Distribution and Status of Some Rare Species, including *Coreopsis rosea* Nutt. and *Sabatia Kennedyana* Fern. *Rhodora* 87 (851): 309-320.

Nichols, G.E. 1935. The Hemlock-White Pine-Northern Hardwood Region of Eastern North America. *Ecology* 16(3): 403-422.

Roland, A.E., and Smith, E.C. 1969. *The Flora of Nova Scotia*. Halifax: Nova Scotia Museum.

Taschereau, P.M., ed. 1974. *Ecological Reserves in the Maritimes*. Terminal report of the scientific advisory panel Region 7 (Maritimes). Canadian Committee for the International Biological Programme, Conservation of Terrestrial Communities Subcommittee.

Taschereau, P.M. 1985. *The Status of Ecological Reserves in Canada*. Ottawa: Canadian Council on Ecological Areas, and School for Resource and Environmental Studies, Dalhousie University.

ONTARIO'S PARK SYSTEM COMES OF AGE

Addison, W.D., and Bates, J.D. 1974. Wilderness in Ontario. *Ontario Naturalist*, March, June, and September.

Algonquin Wildlands League. 1980. *Wilderness Now*. Toronto: Algonquin Wildlands League.

Beechey, T.J. 1988. Protecting Ontario's Ecological Diversity. Presentation to the 15th Annual Natural Areas Conference, Suny College of Environmental Science and Forestry. Syracuse, N.Y.: June 6–9.

Cook, Heather. 1983. Report to the Wildlands League on Parks Achievement in the District Land Use Guidelines. Toronto.

Ontario Ministry of Natural Resources. 1978. *Ontario Provincial Parks Planning and Management Policies*. Toronto: M.N.R.

Ontario Ministry of Natural Resources. 1982. *Report of the Task Force on Parks System Planning*. 2 vols. Toronto.

Pimlott, Douglas. 1966. Should We Support Ontario Parks? Presentation to the 1966 annual meeting of the Ontario Federation of Anglers and Hunters. Mimeographed.

Rickwood, Peter. 1983. Battle Lines Drawn for Our Northlands. *Toronto Star*: March 21.

University of Waterloo. 1982. Ontario Provincial Parks: Issues in the 80's. *Environments*, 14(1).

MISUNDERSTANDING THE PRAIRIES

Arthur, George. 1984. The North American Plains Bison: A Brief History. In G.J. Mitchell, ed. Man: User and Modifier of

Canadian Plains Resources. *Prairie Forum* 9, no. 2. Regina: Canadian Plains Research Centre, University of Regina.

Brundtland, Gro Harlem. 1987. *Our Common Future.* Oxford: Oxford University Press.

Burpee, L.J., ed. 1927. *Journals and Letters of Pierre Saultier de Varennes de la Veredrye and His Sons, with Correspondence between the Governors of Canada and the French Court, Touching the Search for the Western Sea.*

Butler, William Francis. 1872. *The Great Lone Land.* London: Sampson Low, Marston, Low and Searle.

Carson, Rachel. 1962. *Silent Spring.* Boston: Houghton Mifflin.

Doughty, A.G., and Chester, Martin, eds. 1929. *The Kelsey Papers.* Ottawa: Public Archives of Canada and Public Record Office of Northern Ireland.

Forsyth, Adrian. 1983. The End of Emptiness. *Equinox* 11: 66–78.

Lynch, Wayne. 1984. *Married to the Wind.* Vancouver: Whitecap Books.

Mitchell, George J. 1984. The Importance, Utilization, Management and Future of Wild Game Animals on the Canadian Plains. In G.J. Mitchell, ed. Man: User and Modifier of Canadian Plains' Resources. *Prairie Forum* 9, no. 2. Regina: Canadian Plains Research Centre, University of Regina.

Mowat, Farley. 1984. *Sea of Slaughter.* Toronto: McClelland and Stewart.

Nelson, Samuel J. 1984. Geological History of the Interior Plains. In G.J. Mitchell, ed. Man: User and Modifier of Canadian Plains' Resources. *Prairie Forum* 9, no. 2. Regina: Canadian Plains Research Centre, University of Regina.

Ray, Arthur J. 1984. The Northern Great Plains: Pantry of the Northwestern Fur Trade, 1774–1885. In G.J. Mitchell, ed. Man: User and Modifier of Canadian Plains' Resources. *Prairie Forum* 9, no. 2. Regina: Canadian Plains Research Centre,

University of Regina.

Rowe, J. Stan and Coupland, Robert T. 1984. Vegetation of the Canadian Plains. In G.J. Mitchell, ed. Man: User and Modifier of Canadian Plains' Resources. *Prairie Forum* 9, no. 2. Regina: Canadian Plains Research Centre, University of Regina.

Umfreville, Edward. 1790. *The Present State of Hudson's Bay Containing a Full Description of that Settlement and the Adjacent Country; and Likewise of the Fur Trade.* London: C. Stalber.

Warkentin, John. 1964. *The Western Interior of Canada, A Record of Geographical Discovery, 1612–1917.* Toronto: McClelland and Stewart.

CONSERVATION IN THE YUKON AND THE NORTHWEST TERRITORIES

Canadian Parks and Wilderness Society. 1987. *Park News* 23, no. 1, special northern edition.

Environment Canada. 1982. *Canada's Special Places in the North: An Environment Canada Perspective for the '80's.* Ottawa: Supply and Services Canada.

_____. 1983. *Environment Canada and the North: A Discussion Paper.* Ottawa: Supply and Services Canada.

Fisheries and Oceans Canada. 1987. *Canadian Arctic Marine Conservation Strategy.* Ottawa: Supply and Services Canada.

Indian and Northern Affairs Canada. 1986. *Northern Mineral Policy.* Ottawa: Supply and Services Canada.

Jull, Peter. 1986. *Politics, Development and Conservation in the International North.* Ottawa: Canadian Arctic Resources Committee.

Kovacs, Tom. 1987. National Overview for Canada on National Parks and Protected Areas in the Arctic. In Nelson, J.G., and Needham, Roger, eds. *Arctic Heritage: the Proceedings of a Symposium.* Ottawa: Association of Canadian Universities for

Northern Studies.

Task Force on Northern Conservation. 1984. *Report*. Ottawa: Department of Indian Affairs and Northern Development.

Task Force on Park Establishment. 1987. *Parks 2000 — Vision for the 21st Century*. Toronto: Nature Conservancy of Canada.

THE IMPORTANCE OF CONSERVING SYSTEMS

1. Merchant, Carolyn. 1980. *The Death of Nature*. San Francisco: Harper & Row.

2. Levins, Richard, and Richard Lewontin. 1985. *The Dialectical Biologist*. Cambridge Mass.: Harvard University Press.

Ehrlich, Paul R. 1987. Population biology, conservation biology, and the future of humanity. *BioScience* 37(10): 757–763.

Lenihan, John. 1979. Is Man a Machine? In Lenihan, John and Fletcher, William W., eds. *The Environment and Man*, vol. 9: *The Biological Environment*. New York: Academic Press.

Rifkin, Jeremy. 1985. *Declaration of a Heretic*. Boston: Routledge & Kegan Paul.

NATURE FOR THE SAKE OF NATURE

Darwin, Charles. 1964. *The Origin of Species*. Cambridge, Mass.: Harvard University Press.

Ehrenfeld, David. 1978. *The Arrogance of Humanism*. New York: Oxford University Press.

Evernden, Neil. 1988. Nature in Industrial Society. In Jhally, Sut, and Angus, Ian, eds. *Cultural Politics in Contemporary America*. New York: Routledge, Chapman and Hall.

———. 1985. *The Natural Alien*. Toronto: University of Toronto Press.

Kuhn, Thomas. 1970. *The Structure of Scientific Revolutions*. 2nd ed. Chicago: University of Chicago Press.

Livingston, John A. 1986. Ethics as Prosthetics. In Hanson, Philip P., ed. *Environmental Ethics: Philosophical and Policy Perspectives*. Burnaby, B.C.: Simon Fraser University.

———. 1981. *The Fallacy of Wildlife Conservation*. Toronto: McClelland and Stewart.

———. 1973. *One Cosmic Instant: a natural history of human arrogance*. Toronto: McClelland and Stewart.

Pinchot, G. 1947. *Breaking New Ground*. New York: Harcourt, Brace.

Shepard, Paul. 1982. *Nature and Madness*. San Francisco: Sierra Club Books.

ROOM AT THE TOP?

Bath, A.J., Dueck, H., and Herrero, S. 1988. Carnivore Conservation Areas (Draft) W.W.F.

Curatolo, J.A., and Moore, G.D. 1975. Home Range and Population Dynamics of Grizzly Bear (Ursus arctos L.) in the eastern Brooks Range, Alaska. Biol. Report Ser. Canad. Arctic Gas Study Ltd. and Alaska Arctic Gas Co., vol. 32: 1–79.

Hewitt, C. Gordon. 1921. *The Conservation of the Wildlife of Canada*. New York: Chas. Scribners.

Hornocker, M.G., and Nash, H.S. 1981. Ecology of the Wolverine in Northwestern Montana. *Canadian Journal of Zoology* 59: 1286–1301.

Knight, R.R., and Eberhardt, L.L. 1984. Projected Future Abundance of the Yellowstone Grizzly Bear. *Journal of Wildlife Management* 48: 1434–1438.

Lacava, J., and Hughes, J. 1984. Determining Viable Population Levels. Wildlife Society Bulletin 12: 370–376.

Martinka, C.J. 1974. Population Characteristics of Grizzly Bears in Glacier National Park, Montana. *Journal Mammal* 55: 21–29.

McCrory, W., and Herrero, S. 1987. *Preservation and Management of the Grizzly Bear in B.C. Provincial Parks: The Urgent Challenge*. Victoria, B.C.: McCrory Wildlife Services for B.C. Parks and Recreation Division.

Pall, Orval, Jalkotzy, M., and Ross, I. 1988. *The Cougar in Alberta*. Calgary: Arc Associated Resource Consultants Ltd.

Peek, J.M., et al. 1987. Grizzly Bear Conservation and Management: A Review. *Wildlife Society Bulletin* 15: 160–169.

Peterson, Rolf O., and Page, R.E. 1988. *The Rise and Fall of Isle Royale Wolves, 1975–1980*.

Seidensticker, J.C., et al. 1973. Mountain Lion Social Organization in the Idaho Primitive Area. Wildl. Monogr. 35.

Shields, W.M. 1983. Genetic Considerations in the Management of the Wolf and Other Large Vertebrates: An Alternative View. Canad. Wildl. Serv. Rept. Ser. 45: 90–92.

Stirling, I. 1988. *Polar Bears*. Ann Arbor: University of Michigan Press.

Theberge, J.B. 1983. Considerations in Wolf Management Related Genetic Variability and Adaptive Change. In Wolves in Canada and Alaska. Canad. Wildl. Serv. Rept. Ser. 45: 86–89.

THE UPSHOT

Douglas, William O. 1965. *A Wilderness Bill of Rights*. Toronto: Little, Brown and Company Canada Ltd.

Leopold, Aldo. 1949. *A Sand County Almanac*. New York: Oxford University Press.

Author Biographies

François Bregha is a resource policy consultant currently working with the Rawson Academy of Aquatic Science in Ottawa. Bregha has worked on issues related to energy and environmental policy and northern development. As Director of Northern Affairs for Environment Canada in the mid-1980s, he was involved in land claim negotiations and the Department's review of its northern conservation objectives.

John Broadhead lives on the Queen Charlotte Islands, where he works as an artist, author, carpenter, and commercial fisherman. As a founding director of the Islands Protection Society and the Earthlife Canada Foundation, he was a key participant in the effort to preserve South Moresby. For this contribution, he was awarded the Douglas Pimlott Award in 1987 and the Governor General's Conservation Award in 1988.

Yorke Edwards spent the earlier part of his career developing parks and wildlife interpretation programs. From 1974 to 1984, he was Director of the B.C. Provincial Museum. Currently, he is a freelance consultant and writer. Edwards has served on the boards of the Canadian Nature Federation, the Canadian National Sportsmen's Shows, the Nature Conservancy, and the Canadian Council on Ecological Areas.

Harold Eidsvik, a native of British Columbia, is a forestry graduate of both the University of British Columbia and the University of Michigan. As Senior Policy Adviser at The Canadian Parks Service Eidsvik is also responsible for international conservation affairs. Currently, he is Chairman of IUCN's Commission on National Parks and Protected Areas. In this capacity, he has visited and worked with park officials and non-government organizations in more than sixty countries.

Georges Erasmus is a Dene Indian from Fort Rae, Northwest Territories. Since 1985, he has held the elected position of National Chief of the Assembly of First Nations. Previous posts include Regional Staff Director for the Company of Young Canadians, Chairman of University Canada North, and President of the Indian Brotherhood of the Northwest Territories. Erasmus is a director of World Wildlife Fund Canada and a member of the Board of the Canadian Tribute to Human Rights. In 1987, he was appointed to the Order of Canada.

Bristol Foster is a naturalist whose vocation has taken him to many parts of the globe, including Kenya where he set up a graduate student program in wildlife ecology at the University of Nairobi. He returned to British Columbia to become Assistant Director and then Director of the B.C. Museum in Victoria. He was then appointed Director of Ecological Reserves for the province. In 1984, he left government service to become an independent ecological consultant.

David A. Gauthier is an assistant professor of resource management in the Department of Geography at the University of Regina. He has conducted research on caribou, moose, wolves, and bears in the southern Yukon, golden eagles in Kluane National Park, and small mammals in Algonquin Provincial Park. He is a past director of the Alberta Wilderness Association and an active participant in the coalition of conservationists that has worked for the establishment of Grasslands National Park.

Arlin Hackman was raised in rural Alberta, where hunting and regular visits to mountain parks gave him an early interest in conservation. He has worked as an environmental researcher and advocate for a variety of government and private agencies. From 1978 to 1983, he was Executive Director of the Wildlands League, where he led the successful campaign for 155 new provincial parks in Ontario. Since 1987, he has served as Co-ordinator of the Wildlands, Wildwaters Program at World Wildlife Fund Canada.

J. David Henry is Associate Professor at the Saskatchewan Indian Federated College and the Department of Biology at the University of Regina. He has been a key player in efforts to revise the National Parks Act of Canada and to establish Grasslands National Park. His recently published book *Red Fox: The Catlike Canine* is a popular account of his field research on foxes extending over fourteen years.

Stewart Hilts is Associate Professor in the Department of Land Resource Science and in the School of Rural Planning and Development at the University of Guelph. He is Research Director of the Natural Heritage Stewardship Program, a research project that has led to the introduction of Ontario's Natural Heritage Stewardship Award. Hilts is one of the authors of *Islands of Green: Natural Heritage Protection in Ontario* and is a past president of the Guelph Field Naturalists.

Monte Hummel is President of World Wildlife Fund Canada. A well-known Canadian environmentalist, Hummel was chairman and co-founder of Pollution Probe and currently holds a number of positions in the environmental community. These include membership on the boards of the Canadian Coalition on Acid Rain and the Canadian National Sportsmen's Shows.

Jon Lien is a professor of animal behaviour in the Department of Ocean Studies and the Department of Psychology at Memorial University of Newfoundland. He is the leader of the university's Whale Research Group and for the past decade has worked with Newfoundland's inshore fishermen to save large whales entangled in fishing gear.

Bruce Litteljohn joined the faculty of Upper Canada College in 1965. As well as teaching, he has served as Director of the College's Outdoor School and as Head of History and Geography at the Preparatory School. Litteljohn has a long history of active involvement in conservation, particularly with the Wildlands League in Ontario. Both a photographer and a writer, his books include *Marked by the Wild, A Sea Within: The Gulf of St. Lawrence,* and *Superior: The Haunted Shore.*

John A. Livingston teaches in the graduate Faculty of Environmental Studies at York University. Prior to this appointment, he was the first executive producer of CBC's "The Nature of Things." Livingston has been president of the Federation of Ontario Naturalists and the Canadian Audubon Society. He is also a founding partner in LGL Ltd., environmental research associates. He has written nine books, including *CANADA: A Natural History, The Fallacy of Wildlife Conservation, Arctic Oil,* and *One Cosmic Instant.*

Barry May is a medical doctor practising in Corner Brook, Newfoundland. He has worked extensively on protecting wilderness areas in that province as a member and past chairman of the Newfoundland and Labrador Wilderness and Ecological Reserves Advisory Council. He is founder of the Tuckamore Wilderness Club and has also served as a trustee of the Canadian Parks and Wilderness Society.

Elizabeth May is an environmental activist and lawyer living in Ottawa. She has been actively involved in environmental issues for twenty years. She led the successful opposition to aerial spraying of spruce budworm in Nova Scotia and was a central figure in the opposition to the spraying of phenoxy herbicide. From 1986 to 1988, May served as Senior Policy Adviser to the federal Minister of the Environment.

Kevin A. McNamee was born in Montreal and attended both McGill University and the University of Waterloo. He is former Conservation Director of the Canadian Parks and Wilderness Society. McNamee played a major role in the creation of Ellesmere Island, South Moresby, and Grasslands national parks. He has visited many of Canada's wilderness regions.

Ian McTaggart-Cowan has devoted his career to university teaching and to the study of systematics, biology, and the conservation of birds and mammals. He has a prestigious record of public service, which has included membership on the Fisheries Research Board of Canada and the National Research Council, the vice-presidency of the International Union for the Conservation of Nature and Natural Resources, chairmanship of the Arctic Institute of North America, and the chancellorship of the University of Victoria.

Harvey Mead teaches philosophy at the St. Lawrence Campus of Champlain Regional College. He is a founding member of the Union québécoise pour la conservation de la nature and has co-ordinated that organization's efforts to develop a Quebec conservation strategy. A former national director of the Canadian Nature Federation, Mead's current commitments include membership on the Board of Directors of Great Lakes United and the Quebec Government's Round Table on Environment and Economy.